HALLIBURTON

Halliburton

By Jonathan Root

HALLIBURTON

THE BETRAYERS

ONE NIGHT IN JULY

THE MAGNIFICENT MYTH

A Biography by JONATHAN ROOT

Coward-McCann, Inc.   New York

Acknowledgment is gratefully made for permission to reprint extracts from the following works:

The Bobbs-Merrill Company: *The Royal Road to Romance* by Richard Halliburton, copyright, 1925 by The Bobbs-Merrill Company; *New Worlds to Conquer* by Richard Halliburton, copyright, 1929 by The Bobbs-Merrill Company; *The Flying Carpet* by Richard Halliburton, copyright, 1932 by The Bobbs-Merrill Company; *Richard Halliburton: His Story of His Life's Adventures,* copyright, 1940 by The Bobbs-Merrill Company.

The Condé Nast Publications Inc.: "New Ladies' Clubs to Conquer" by John Riddell from *Vanity Fair,* September, 1928, copyright 1928 by The Condé Nast Publications Inc.

Time magazine: "Playboy," May 30, 1927; "Innocent Abroad," July 8, 1940.

The New Yorker: "Talk of the Town," December 14, 1929. Reprinted by permission.

Library of Congress Catalog
Card Number: 65-20408

Second Impression

MANUFACTURED IN THE UNITED STATES OF AMERICA

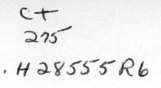

TO

Jeanne Anne

Acknowledgments

IN reconstructing Richard Halliburton's phenomenal career, and the frantic private life which sustained it, I traveled more thousands of miles than I ever intended or can now accurately calculate; I talked to hundreds of persons who knew him, however slightly, or encountered him, however briefly, and whose attitudes ranged from rapturous admiration to unrelieved contempt. I would like to thank several of these people by name, not only for the value of their contributions, but also for their great courtesy and generosity of time and effort:

Richard's father, Wesley Halliburton, of Memphis, Tenn., who allowed me to inspect all of his son's personal correspondence and private documents; Moye W. Stephens of Pasadena, Calif., who piloted "The Flying Carpet"; William Alexander of Hollywood, Calif., who designed and built "Hangover House"; Captain Charles Jokstad of San Mateo, Calif.; publicist Walter Gaines Swanson of San Francisco; Mrs. John (Zola Halliburton) Rex of Los Angeles; Thomas Wheeler of American President Lines; my colleagues, James Benet and Barney Peterson of the San Francisco *Chronicle;*

Novelist Kathleen Norris, for her gracious reminiscences; Malcolm Stuart Boylan of Los Angeles, author and raconteur; poet Eric Barker of Big Sur, Calif.; Professor Celeste Wright of the University of California at Davis; Mrs. Jeanne C. Tucker of Sacramento, Calif.; Mr. and Mrs. Wallace T. Scott of Laguna Beach, Calif.; Neil Gregory, Malcolm Adams and James Cortese of the Memphis *Commercial-Appeal;* Gordon Torrey of New York City; Alexander P. Clark, manuscript librarian at Princeton University Library; Edmund S. DeLong, public information director at Princeton;

Richard's Princeton roommates, Irvine S. Hockaday of Kan-

7

sas City and John Henry Leh of Allentown, Pa.; Roderic B.
Crane of the Municipal University of Omaha, Neb.; William
Stoneman of the London bureau of the Chicago *Daily News;*
Robin Kinkead of Pan American Airways; Miss Lois Stewart
and William Finneran of The Bobbs-Merrill Company, who
made their files available to me and who gave me permission to
quote from Richard's published books and to reproduce photographs from them.

Much of the material in the book was also derived from newspapers and periodicals, especially *The New York Times,* the
Los Angeles *Times, Newsweek, Time,* the *Ladies' Home Journal, Esquire, Architectural Record, Travel, American* magazine, and the February 1, 1960, issue of *Vogue,* an article
"Halliburton's Banana Peel," by R. C. Phedan.

Once again, I am indebted to Abe Mellinkoff, city editor of
the San Francisco *Chronicle,* for giving me time to write the
book; to my friends Niven Busch, Jan and Kim Stussy, Luther
Nichols, Dick Berg, Stuart James, William Kilpatrick and Peter
Breinig, for many kindnesses; to Mary Ann Anderson for typing
the manuscript; and to Ellis Amburn and John J. Geoghegan
for indispensable counsel.

I am especially grateful to the Huntington Hartford Founda-
tion of Pacific Palisades, Calif., for awarding me a fellowship
in residence, thus enabling me to complete the book sooner
than I had hoped.

—JONATHAN ROOT

New York City
March, 1965

Sweet are the uses of adversity;
Which, like the toad, ugly and venomous,
wears yet a precious jewel in his head;
And this our life, exempt from public haunt,
finds tongues in trees, books in the running brooks,
sermons in stones, and good in everything.

—WILLIAM SHAKESPEARE
(*As You Like It*, Act 2, Scene 1)

Contents

I
The Sea Dragon, 15
II
The Memphis Boy, 39
III
The Royal Road, 63
IV
The Making of a Celebrity, 97
V
A Vagrant Conquest, 141
VI
The Flying Carpet, 169
VII
Siberian Exclusive, 209
VIII
The End of the Road, 245
Index, 281
Photographs follow page 144

I

The Sea Dragon

The brave man carves out his fortune, and
every man is the son of his own works.

—MIGUEL DE CERVANTES
(*Don Quixote*)

✥ I ✥

IT was an unseasonably mild and sunny December afternoon
in the year 1938 and Richard Halliburton lounged lan-
guorously in a deep wicker chair on the veranda of the Hong
Kong Foreign Correspondents Club, listening in mock dismay
to a group of journalists merrily predicting his death.

"You're stretching your luck this time . . ." said one.

". . . Far beyond the intervention of Providence," added
another.

"You are, in fact," said a third, "going to the well once too
often."

Halliburton had heard it all before and it was always accompanied by a great deal of laughter. You'll never make it, they
said, what are you trying to do? Kill yourself?

Halliburton turned his head from time to time and looked
down the slopes of Victoria Peak to the jeweled city below him
as though it were an estate he had just purchased. Not that he
coveted it, but he was convinced that his uncounted fans regarded him as a man who, by virtue of extravagant daring,
owned the world; his private oyster from which he harvested
for everybody great pearls of romance. He believed, too, that
appearances might not be everything, but men are often held to
be what they appear at a distance. He was also aware that his
audience of the moment was responsible for much of the giddy
publicity that was leisurely enlisting the renewed attention of
the world, so he was careful of his poses.

He held a glass of iced ginger beer in one hand and fondled
the leaf of a drooping potted palm with the other. He wore a
dark grey double-breasted suit, a pale grey shirt and a black
knit tie. An immense white handkerchief overflowed from his

15

breast pocket. His dark blonde hair was long and thick and combed back and his eyes were intensely blue. He was thirty-eight years old, almost thirty-nine, but he looked much younger; sometimes he looked like a little boy. He regarded his amiable detractors respectfully but he tried not to hear what they were saying. Finally, the insouciance which was among his trademarks overcame him.

"You gentlemen depress me," he said, with his boyishly ingratiating smile. "You sound exactly like the timid folk of Kansas City or Chicago whose drab and unimaginative lives I have spent years trying vainly to inspire."

The gentlemen all groaned derisively, in a chorus.

"You haven't failed," said a man from United Press, in feigned solemnity. "I was in Singapore only a month ago and the American consulate there was full of stranded young men who said they were only following your advice—to see the world without spending any money."

Halliburton winced. A slippered Chinese houseboy scuffled past, scooped up the empty ash tray from the table at Halliburton's elbow and made the motion of emptying it into a brass bowl he carried. Then he slid the ash tray back and flicked an alarmed glance at Halliburton who rewarded him with a smile.

"You forget," said Halliburton, draining his glass and setting it on the table, "that adversity is a necessary ingredient of adventure; no adversity, no adventure. If adversity doesn't come my way, I go out and find it."

He rose from the chair, straightened his lapels, bloused out his handkerchief and pushed back an errant lock of hair from his forehead. He grinned as he turned to leave.

"Don't worry about me," he said, half over his shoulder, "I never do."

Halliburton went into the club, through the bar and lobby and out to the street, silently debating whether to take a taxi or the tram. He couldn't afford a taxi, he told himself, but if he rode the tram someone would recognize him and he would have to talk to them. There were several taxis in the rank in front of the club and he climbed into one, directed it to the

Kowloon ferry slip and sat back brooding. He was worried sick.

Hong Kong might have paid less attention to Halliburton had not its inhabitants been so anxiously concerned with the imminence of war. There were parties everywhere night after night and people celebrated with an intensity that suggested each party might be the last. Halliburton had arrived in the British Crown Colony in the closing months of 1938, when war was plainly visible on almost any horizon, and he may have seemed like an omen of reassurance. He was a self-appointed symbol of an age of romance and wonder and, more importantly, one of the few bright frivolous happenings in a world tense with the iron perversities of nations.

Halliburton had come to Hong Kong to build a junk of large proportions in which to sail nine thousand miles across the Pacific to the San Francisco World's Fair, opening in the spring of 1939. By his own account, and that which appeared endlessly in the press, he was to undertake this voyage with a crew consisting of one professional seaman, two amateur yachtsmen from Maine and several young American collegians who had, in effect, paid him for the privilege of being aboard. It was heartening that he could calmly embark on such an adventure oblivious of all harbingers of international disaster.

He was confronted daily, for instance, with the fact that the Japanese conquest of Manchuria had spread south through all the eastern provinces of China and was moving inexorably on, shoving before it a torrent of ragged refugees who were, even now, dying by the thousands in the streets of Hong Kong of beriberi, cholera and starvation. His reaction to them was less shock and horror than revulsion and resentment, for tragedy was not of his world. He had less trouble shutting out the drums of Hitler who had invaded Austria and compelled Britain, France and Bavaria to consent to the dismemberment of Czechoslovakia, the first major stride in the grand Nazi plan.

It would have been difficult to ignore Halliburton altogether in any event, for he still rode the tide of an enormous popularity which had the weight of fifteen highly-publicized years behind it.

He was still the dashing vagabond idol of the world; a messianic sort of figure to legions of worshipful adolescents, a dauntless hero whom women of various eligible ages longed to marry, the flaming handsome youth all American matronhood appeared to wish for a son. The matrons' husbands gave him a certain grudging admiration for his fame, which, fed on itself, was apparently invincible.

While he captured the fancies and affections of millions of people, he never earned the respect of the powerful critics who mocked him as Richard-the-Literary-Lion-Hearted and appraised him, at best, as a desperate man driven by a relentless compulsion to prove his manhood and by a staggering need for money. He had great literary ambitions, but few pretensions, yet he set off festering literary controversies. While he smarted under critical scorn, his popularity never wavered in good times or bad; he streaked and bounced and sputtered around the universe of his time like a wayward comet; he was irresistible.

He was, in fact, the author of seven runaway best sellers in fifteen languages and the toast of the lecture platform in every American city whose population was sufficient to rate a post office. He was the recipient of more praise, adulation, contempt and ridicule than any other public figure of his time. He was the man who had made a rich career out of a light-hearted defiance of death in all the strange and wonderful places on earth. His millions of ardent fans could recount, with the accuracy of a baseball zealot reciting batting averages, the escapades by which he had captivated them. Like Lindbergh or Admiral Byrd, he was a legend in his own time. His historic swim across the Hellespont, from Asia to Europe, became a standard for daring and endurance although it was less than five miles and scores of better swimmers made it effortlessly.

Halliburton was not the first man to swim the length of the shark- and alligator-infested Panama Canal, but the first to persuade Canal authorities to permit him through the locks. He lived as Robinson Crusoe on a desert island and as a convict on Devil's Island. He stowed away on luxury liners, bought and sold slaves in Timbuctoo and marched with the French Foreign

Legion. In the image of Hannibal, he crossed the Alps on an elephant, and he traversed the Malay Peninsula on foot in a monsoon, thrashing cobras with his cane. He re-traveled Homer's Odyssey, pursued the ghost of Cortez through Mexico, and dived into a Mayan "well of death." He took an open-cock-pit biplane across the hostile and uncharted Sahara, surviving a forced landing; he set out in the same plane up the south face of Mount Everest and narrowly escaped crashing to his death on a frozen granite ridge. He climbed the Matterhorn for no reason, or so he said, other than to enable a companion to spit a mile, and he was jailed in Gibraltar as a spy.

He had fallen in love, in plaintive, ethereal fashion, with Kashmiri maidens, Parisian ballerinas, Castillian countesses, Persian princesses, and an otherwise exotic assortment of ripe, innocent and undefilable virginity, from Madagascar to Mindanao.

If there was anything he had not done, neither he nor his fans could think of what it might be. Yet if his proposed trans-Pacific voyage seemed a cut below all the rest, no one could say why.

Halliburton was doing it, he said, in a sort of emulation of an outraged Chinese war lord who in 1875 sent a flotilla of armed junks to California with the notion of obtaining redress for the abuse of coolie labor in the building of American railroads. The junks made land by mistake at Monterey, instead of San Francisco, and their crews were acclaimed as heroes. This so disarmed them that they scuttled their ships and became Monterey's Chinese community, ultimately prospering beyond their most extreme expectations in the operation of grocery stores, restaurants, laundries and fish packing sheds.

Halliburton, however, would commit no such navigational error. He would sail directly and triumphantly through the Golden Gate and dock at the fairgrounds on Treasure Island where he had leased berthing space for the sole purpose of taking fairgoers cruising on San Francisco Bay at one dollar per head.

One not only read about Halliburton in the papers, but one

heard about him everywhere, from the tough waterfront bars of Kowloon where he was the butt of endless jokes, to the austere fastness of Government House where he was regarded with an official, cynical, incredulous detachment. By Christmas of 1938, there were only two abiding topics of conversation at virtually all cocktail parties—the looming war and Halliburton. Along his own erratic social orbit, Halliburton left a wake of mostly charmed admirers; elsewhere, there was considerable conviction that he would never get to San Francisco alive.

Among the colony's maritime population, principally among the British Naval officers who went dining and dancing every night at the Hong Kong Hotel, the voyage Halliburton contemplated was foolhardy.

"The Japs will blow that ruddy junk galley west the moment she sticks her prow into the Formosa straits," was the way they put it. And it was true that the Japanese Navy had what amounted to an impenetrable blockade of the China Coast and its ships were indeed sinking junks by the dozens.

"If she ever gets out of the harbor," someone was bound to add. "There are more pirate boats than fishing scows between the Kowloon docks and the channel."

This was also true. There was an unprecedented abundance of pirates in the harbor, driven south by the Japanese. Mirs Bay and Bias Bay, two seamy shacktown coastal settlements within handy reach of Hong Kong, were crowded to capacity and beyond and the audacity of the pirates was seemingly boundless. One band had even sacked the Hong Kong-Kowloon ferry one moonless night, escaping the swarm of police launches which had responded in minutes to the ferry's radio call for help. Hong Kong was also seriously infested with informers who alerted the pirates to prospective victims, and with fences who disposed of the loot through the Portuguese colony of Macao to the south. Within days after the keel for Halliburton's junk was laid in Fat Kau's Kowloon shipyard, the pirate tipsters came to gaze upon it much as a panther would regard a suckling pig in a flimsy corral. Pirates were tried daily in the Hong Kong courts but the law was no deterrent to them.

If the Japs or the pirates did not get Halliburton, it was said, the weather would. He had announced that he planned to sail north from Hong Kong through the Formosa Straits (where exposure to the Japanese fleet and pirates was probably at its maximum), then northeast along the coast of Japan to the 32nd parallel and due east to Midway Island. Since he was sailing in the midst of the winter monsoons, such a route meant that for much of her long haul across the Pacific the junk would have perverse and frequently relentless wind and seas clawing at her from behind.

Halliburton heard all this and to some extent dismissed it. He intended to equip the junk with two-pounder brass cannon and an arsenal of shotguns and if he could not thus repel pirates, he could at least outrun them for the junk also would have a 100-horsepower diesel engine. As far as the Japanese were concerned, Halliburton regretted his anti-Japanese tirades from the lecture platform over the years, but there was no help for it now. The Japanese Government had given him a guarantee of safe conduct for the voyage but he knew it was no guarantee of anything. All he could do was paint U.S. flags on both sides of the ship, fly an immense flag from the masthead and hope for the best.

His dominant anxiety was money. For a man who had made a fortune writing and talking, he was remarkably broke and he had exhausted every imaginable resource including his new home in Laguna Beach, California, which he had mortgaged to the limit.

He thought about his rapidly dwindling funds as he strode off the ferry and started along the waterfront to the shipyard. It was taking much longer than necessary to build the junk and the cost was increasing out of all proportion to the delays. He had expected to be able to build it for $2,500. Fat Kau had quoted him a price of $5,000 but at the rate things were going the cost would hit $10,000 or more, not including the salaries of the captain and the chief engineer and living expenses for the crew members who were housed in the Kowloon Hotel.

Halliburton had financed the voyage by forming a corpora-

tion in California—the Halliburton Trans-Pacific Chinese
Junk Expedition, Inc.—and selling shares in it. The principal
shareholders, besides Halliburton, were four young men from
well-to-do New England families who were also sailing as crew
members. Two of them were from Maine and had considerable
Atlantic Coast sailing experience, Gordon Torrey, twenty-
three, from Bar Harbor, and John R. Potter, twenty-four, of
Southeast Harbor. The other two, George Barstow III, of
Sharon, Connecticut, and Robert Chase of Milton, Massachusetts, were novices at sea. Barstow, who was twenty-one, was a
student at the Julliard School of Music in New York. Chase was
twenty-two and a senior at Dartmouth. Halliburton's cousin,
Vida, a Los Angeles socialite, and her mother, Mrs. Erle Halliburton, wife of the oil well cementing company millionaire,
were also shareholders.

The affairs of the corporation were handled by Wilfred
Crowell, an executive with the Schwabacher paper company
and stock brokerage firm in San Francisco, and by an attorney
there, J. Richard Townsend.

Halliburton communicated his problems and worries by mail
almost daily to Crowell who could only reply that he was
unable to raise additional funds and that, worse, if the junk did
not reach San Francisco when the World's Fair opened in
February, the management of the Fair might cancel the mooring
lease. Other concessionaires wanted it.

When the junk was finally christened the *Sea Dragon*,
launched and moored at Main Wharf No. 2 in January, Halliburton was in bed in the Kowloon Hotel with a raging eczema
the doctor attributed to nerves. Seeing the junk actually in the
water cured his eczema. There was no doubt she was a beautiful ship; a standard Wenchow design, but 75 feet long, nearly
double the normal length, and bright red in color. She had a
towering poop, some 12 feet taller than most junks, and the
transom was so colorfully decorated with dragons that it suggested an advertisement for a manufacturer of Chinese lacquer.
She rode the harbor swell with the gentle rhythm of a porch
swing, but Halliburton also had to admit she looked top-heavy,

an illusion later heightened when the 90-foot mainmast was stepped. "I hope she doesn't roll over and sink before she leaves the harbor," Halliburton told acquaintances, with an uneasy laugh.

To save money, he moved his crew out of the Kowloon Hotel and into the half-finished ship, a move which emphasized a further source of worry: his captain.

❦ 2 ❧

John Wenlock Welch had been hired by Halliburton as the *Sea Dragon*'s captain—at $250 a month—shortly after the first burst of publicity about the voyage in the summer of 1938. Halliburton had received 982 unsolicited letters from young men and women all over the country begging for the chance to make the trip, and he had been sifting uselessly through them in his suite at the Chancellor Hotel in San Francisco when Welch called on him.

Welch was a native Australian who had run away to sea at the age of fourteen and made several voyages in Pacific grain clippers. He was now forty-two, held master's papers and had worked as technical advisor in Hollywood on two seafaring movies. He was a husky, handsome six-footer with a booming voice and he had been sailing out of San Francisco as a second mate aboard United Fruit Company "banana boat" freighters to Latin America.

The fact that Welch was working only as a second mate troubled Halliburton, but Welch dismissed all doubts. "There aren't enough master's berths to go around," he said, and immediately won Halliburton with a directness and an irresistible air of confidence and authority.

Some of Halliburton's initial misgivings returned as he and Welch sailed to Hong Kong aboard the *President Coolidge* and he discovered Welch was almost too aggressively gregarious, a dominating raconteur with an interminable supply of sea stories, not a few of which were breathtaking accounts of his conquests of lonely female ship passengers.

Once the junk was launched and Welch loudly assumed her command, another layer of his character came to light.

24

"He's a regular Captain Bligh," Halliburton reported in a letter of despair to Crowell in San Francisco. "He treats everybody like dirt and is always talking about putting them on bread and water. If half the crew doesn't quit me before we sail, I'm sure we'll have a mutiny at sea. The only thing that redeems him is that he knows ships better than anyone I've ever met. But he flies into an uncontrollable rage if anybody disagrees with him. It's all I can do to keep peace."

Welch was especially hated by thirty-four-year-old Paul Mooney who had been Halliburton's secretary and associate for several years, and who periodically threatened to quit and go home to Washington, D.C. Halliburton would remonstrate with Welch, who would make a brief effort to be more amiable.

"But I can't stand incompetence," Welch would say, gritting his teeth and glaring about him.

Potter and Torrey, the two Maine yachtsmen, moved back into the Kowloon Hotel at their own expense to get away from Welch. Henry Von Fehren, a former ship's engineer Halliburton had also hired in San Francisco, was the only one who did not argue with Welch. He was good-natured and somewhat phlegmatic and he busied himself with the below-decks installation of the engine whenever Welch went on a rampage.

Finally, Halliburton began to avoid Welch as often as possible, and would disappear for days, returning only to make sure the ship's outfitting was progressing. At least part of his absences were taken up writing a series of fifteen articles entitled "The Log of the Sea Dragon" for the San Francisco *News* and the Bell Syndicate which had paid him $6,000 for them.

He was seen frequently in a variety of places and he wore the furtive air of a boulevardier torn between a desire to be noticed and a fear of process servers. He spent much of his time in the company of an eighteen-year-old boy, a tall and gangly youngster with sleek black hair, an alive complexion and exceptionally slender, tapered hands. They would sit by the hour at the bar of the Hong Kong Hotel, wordlessly sipping grenadine and soda and driving the bartender to a curious distraction by their leaden silence. The boy gave the impression of enduring rather than enjoying the relationship, and Halliburton seemed preoccupied and bored. Returning to the ship late one night he told Mooney that he had been everywhere and done everything and that death was the only experience that still excited him.

The crowds which came daily to stare at the junk, and at its glamorous owner, when he was there, were growing daily, not a few of them professional seamen who began making disparaging remarks about both the design and construction of the ship. Halliburton heard their criticisms indirectly but by mid-January, when the junk was ready for a shakedown sail around the harbor, people he met at various social gatherings openly challenged the ship's seaworthiness and vague misgivings settled over Halliburton.

He pressed the matter with Welch who gave him no reassurance beyond arrogantly dismissing all criticism. But after the first trial cruise, during which some of the Chinese shipbuilders became violently seasick, Welch ordered a number of changes in the rigging and dumped 10 tons of concrete ballast in the hold. The junk's shallow draft had caused it to drift alarmingly.

Halliburton was on the verge of submitting the ship to a Lloyds of London insurance inspection when, on January 26, the liner *President Pierce* steamed into Hong Kong and docked at the pier next to the one at which the *Sea Dragon* was moored.

Halliburton stared at the *Pierce* for a long time and then remembered that its captain was a salty old sea dog named Charles Jokstad who, when master of a lesser ship seventeen years before, had caught Halliburton as a stowaway on a trip from Surabaya to Singapore. Jokstad had allowed him to work out the passage and they had parted amiably. Halliburton walked over to the *Pierce* to renew the acquaintance and Jokstad invited him to lunch.

Jokstad was a Norwegian who had gone to sea at the age of nine and had won his master's papers before he was twenty-five to become the youngest captain in the U.S. Merchant Marine. He had commanded everything from fishing boats to luxury

liners and he had a reputation as one of the toughest masters
afloat. Halliburton asked him to inspect the *Sea Dragon* and
the two of them strolled over to the junk after lunch. Welch
was on deck supervising a gang of Chinese workmen who were
caulking seams and painting, and Jokstad, who knew Welch,
greeted him coolly, further undermining Halliburton's confidence in his captain. Jokstad strode up and down the deck
in silence, peering over the sides at intervals, and he was plainly
shocked. Always a man of few words, Jokstad was at his most
terse.

"The shroud lines," he announced, "there's nothing
holding them but screws in the planking. They'll let go in the
first good breeze."

He climbed up to the poop deck and waggled the tiller.
"The stock of the rudder has at least an inch of clearance; it's
loose. A heavy sea will snap it off."

Without waiting for an answer, he strode imperiously to the
nearest hatch and dived below. Halliburton and Welch followed him, stunned. Jokstad peered into the bilge with disgust,
studied the diesel engine with an expression of incredulity and
poked gingerly at the glass ports in the main cabin with his
finger. He shook his head balefully.

"Those aren't portholes; they're windows. The sea will smash
them before you've gone 10 miles. The engine is mounted to
the ribs with leg screws and it'll shake loose. The ship rides too
high in the water; it'll blow around like a cork. You need at
least another 10 tons of ballast."

Welch and Halliburton stared at each other in mounting dismay, if not horror.

"I'm sorry," said Jokstad, "but you better get an insurance
survey to find out what else is wrong." He added, sarcastically,
"There must be something else."

Jokstad ignored Welch when he left and Halliburton walked
with the old mariner down the gangway and up the dock to the
street.

"What's your course to San Francisco?" Jokstad asked, and
Halliburton told him.

"You'll never make it," the captain replied. "It's too far north. You'll have gale winds behind you and a heavy following sea. You might stand a chance if you go south to, say, the 22nd parallel—if you can fix up that ship. But I wouldn't take her ten feet from the dock."

"I've got to," Halliburton answered, in a tone of annoyance. "I'm committed. Anyway, adventuring is my business."

"You're not an adventurer," Jokstad said, grunting, as he turned to leave, "you're a damned fool."

Halliburton had the engine remounted and steel sheeting placed over the cabin windows; the shroud lines were bolted down and workers from the shipyard fitted a wooden collar around the top of the rudder stock which seemed, for the time being, to end its wobble. Halliburton called in a Lloyd's insurance surveyor who issued the generally reassuring appraisal that the ship was "solidly constructed." But he also cautioned that the junk's high poop and vast canvas spread called for "the utmost vigilance at sea." Halliburton insured the ship for $10,000.

The *Sea Dragon* sailed from Hong Kong on February 4, 1939. Halliburton had hired a Portuguese mess boy at the last minute, and all his relatives, which must have included half the local Portuguese colony, were at the dockside, cheering. The Chinese shipfitters hoisted strings of popping firecrackers to the masthead, in the grand Chinese tradition of sailings. The liner *President Coolidge,* moored nearby, blew its whistle and hundreds of its passengers lined the rails to wave without knowing what they were waving about. At the same time, by sheer coincidence, a pair of British Navy planes roared overhead. The junk's departure seemed duly auspicious as it lurched away from the dock and chugged across the congested harbor, threading its way through a conglomerate of lesser junks and sampans and an occasional inbound freighter. The crew set the bright orange foresail once the ship was clear of the dock. Outside the harbor entrance Welch ordered the immense white ribbed mainsail raised and, soon afterward, the scarlet mizzen. The ship picked up a brisk starboard breeze and started up the coast of China at better than six knots. Much to Halliburton's alarm, the Formosa Straits were alive with other Chinese junks, each one of which he immediately suspected of being a pirate vessel, but the *Sea Dragon* continued on its way unmolested. It passed several passenger ships during the night and exchanged radio greetings. By dawn, fourteen hours out of Hong Kong, the ship had covered nearly 100 miles and Halliburton began to predict the arrival at San Francisco in about nine weeks.

At noon, however, the junk ran head-on into a storm. The brilliant sun vanished behind a gloomy cover of dense black clouds, the sea rose ominously and the wind clawed at the junk from all quarters. In less than an hour, the mizzen sail and the radio aerial had been ripped away. Half the crew became violently seasick, aggravated by fumes from the diesel which Welch was running at full throttle to give the ship steerageway. In trying to reef the mainsail, Potter suffered a hernia and was lashed into his bunk and Mooney fell down a hatchway and broke his ankle. Welch accused Potter of malingering, and he suspected Mooney as well, and threatened to refuse them both food and water.

The *Sea Dragon* struggled on another day before Halliburton ordered Welch to put about and make a run around the southern tip of Formosa and head for Keelung on the island's north coast. The weather continued to worsen. In addition to the mounting sea and wind, the rain fell in a suffocating torrent. More than half the crew was below decks, seasick or otherwise ill, choking and gasping on engine fumes, and there wasn't enough manpower to properly handle the ship since it required at least two men at the tiller to keep her on course and, more important, to keep her from broaching to in the wild sea. Then, when several seams began to leak alarmingly, Halliburton ordered Welch to beat a retreat back to Hong Kong, now only 300 miles to the west. It was midnight of February 9 when they reached the harbor entrance and Welch nearly drove the vessel onto the rocks trying to find the channel in the dark. The junk ignominiously dropped its anchor at 2 a.m. off

Dailey's shipyard at Kowloon, and Potter and Mooney were taken to the hospital. The Portuguese mess boy described the voyage as six days of terror and resigned.

The next day, Halliburton set about in search of a Chinese crew while Welch called in the shipfitters to repair the extensive damage to the junk. A week later, she was hauled into drydock for installation of an 18-inch fin keel which Welch hoped would reduce her frightening tendency to roll.

❦ 3 ❧

Halliburton was embarrassed by his return to Hong Kong but, worse, the loss of time put him in critical financial difficulty. By the time the repairs and modifications had been made to the junk, he didn't even have enough money left to pay the crew when the ship reached San Francisco and both he and his fellow shareholders were afraid the crew would be angry enough to levy an attachment on the junk. Under maritime law, a crew is entitled to half its wages due when its ship docks at any port. If the *Sea Dragon* stopped at Midway the crisis would hit that much sooner and he cabled frantic pleas for money to his publisher and his friends. He finally got $500 from his publisher and he persuaded one of the shareholders, Barstow, to put up $1,500 in addition to the $4,000 he had already invested.

Nothing, however, could compensate for the delay. The World's Fair would be open before he could get there and he had no assurance the Fair would continue to reserve berthing space. He was also apprehensive that the considerable suspense and interest in the voyage he had generated among American newspaper readers through his Bell series might dissipate before he arrived.

On top of everything else, a letter from his attorneys in San Francisco informed him that he had been named corespondent in a divorce action brought by a Los Angeles physician and bibliophile whose wife had coyly courted Halliburton for years, sending him rare volumes from her husband's library. It was as close to infidelity as she ever came.

The accusation was preposterous, he told Crowell in another long letter, but it worried him all the same.

31

Halliburton went to the hospital to visit Potter, about to undergo surgery for his hernia, and was shocked to hear him say:

"Dick, I wouldn't go back on the boat even if I could. Welch is not only a martinet, he's not a very good sailor. I don't think he knows much about navigation, either." But Potter also gave him another $500.

"I know," Halliburton answered, after a pause, "but I think we'll be all right." He did not refuse the money.

Gordon Torrey, the other New England yachtsman, came to him the next day, pleading appendicitis.

"I don't mind taking a chance now and then," he admitted finally, "but I'm not going to commit suicide."

Halliburton was too despairing to protest, but in his last letter to Crowell before sailing again, he wrote: "I hope you are praying for me to occidental gods. I have no faith in Chinese deities." Welch, he added, was totally incompetent.

James Sligh, the *Sea Dragon*'s cook, who had left a wife and two children behind in Los Angeles, became embroiled in a near-violent dispute with a Kowloon merchant and was arrested for disturbing the peace. Halliburton paid his fine, which amounted to $50. It galled him out of all proportion to the money involved and provoked him to do a curious thing. He spent several hours trying to reconstruct a financial record of his life, jotting down in the notebook he always carried every dollar he could remember having made, furiously searching in his private morass of frantic recollections. He sat cross-legged on the *Sea Dragon*'s poop as he did it, oblivious of the Chinese shipfitters still painting and caulking around him, and of Welch's loud-voiced supervision of them. When he was through, he went below to the main cabin and found Mooney seated at the wardroom table checking an inventory of supplies. Halliburton dropped the notebook onto the table and pointed to it.

"Do you realize I am a millionaire?" he said, in pained earnestness.

"What do you mean?" snapped Mooney, irritably. "You're broke."

"I mean, a millionaire is a man who has made a million dollars, isn't he?"

Mooney stared at him without answering.

"Well, I estimate that I have earned at least a million dollars; I can't even remember all the money I made. Why am I always broke?"

Mooney looked down at the sheaf of papers and began writing.

"I don't know either," he answered dully. "All you ever think about is money."

Halliburton felt his anger flooding inside him so he turned and hurried up on deck. There had been enough bickering. His final letter to Crowell was still unmailed and Halliburton took it from his jacket pocket and added a glum postscript: he was surrounded, he said, by petty and vindictive people. The encounter had scored Mooney, too, and that night he wrote to a friend in Los Angeles that all he could foresee in the voyage was futility and despair.

Halliburton had intended to take a Chinese couple with him as passengers, and he wanted the wife pregnant so the baby could be delivered in mid-Pacific. "I've plenty of experience as a midwife," he assured his newspaper readers. But he abandoned the plan in favor of a baby giant panda he hoped to obtain from a Hong Kong animal exporter. He gave up this idea, too, after discovering that pandas are apt to be sensitive to their surroundings and might be seasick the entire trip, if they lived that long. He settled finally on a more prosaic kind of mascot and took a pair of black chow puppies aboard.

The second sailing of the *Sea Dragon* was delayed almost a month by repairs, by the Chinese New Year's celebrations, and by the search for a crew. Halliburton managed to hire at last three Chinese sailors and a Chinese boatswain, and two semi-professional seamen whom he persuaded to jump ship and sail with him for $65 a month. One sailor was from the liner *President Coolidge,* the other from the *President Pierce.*

The junk was swept by a following breeze out into the South China Sea for the second time on the afternoon of March 4, 1939. Her departure was viewed with astonishment by onlookers who had never seen the garish ship before, and with new forebodings by Hong Kong's maritime colony. Some people never learn, they said.

For all the years he had spent in ships of one kind or another, Halliburton knew very little about them and less about the sea itself, and he spent the first hours of every voyage in an agony of apprehension. He was suffering thusly now, as his junk lunged eastward at six knots into the looming darkness, but he did not sacrifice the pose his public had come to expect of him. His slight body was braced upright against the mizzen mast, his long dark blond hair whipped by the wind, his jacket collar flapping against his boyish face, and his eyes on the far horizon; he was not, however, gazing at adventure; he was fighting down the undulating gorge of motion sickness, aggravated by anxiety over the fact that he was sailing almost two costly months behind schedule.

Pirates and the Japanese Navy were also on his mind in addition to the festering conflict between Welch and the members of the crew. He was worried as well about the ship's name; the Chinese didn't like it and said it was a bad omen. "A dragon is a land animal," one of them had explained to him. Another told him they had seen a rat leave the ship just before she sailed and Halliburton was horrified to learn, after two days at sea, that the Chinese sailors had brought cockroaches aboard. "As long as they thrive," the Chinese boatswain pointed out, "we are in no danger."

In time, he shut his mind to all this, as he always had, and saw only his challenge and the glory beyond it.

Halliburton radioed reports of his progress daily to Crowell in San Francisco and on March 13, nine days after leaving Hong Kong, he reported that he was 1,200 miles at sea and that all was well. The ship had passed Okinawa and the other Ryukyu Islands and was almost due south of the lower tip of Japan.

The daily radio reports of position and weather continued without event, indicating the junk was making better than 100 miles a day along a somewhat zig-zag course and probably would be in San Francisco by mid-May. Everybody aboard, including two black chow puppies, had recovered from seasickness, the days were sunny and the ship took the sea in ladylike fashion, sliding gently through moderate swells.

On March 21, an overcast closed in and the wind and sea began to rise. On March 22, the overcast darkened and the wind and sea, still gaining velocity, shifted to the south and then to the west, pushing the junk from her starboard quarter. Welch reefed the mainsail that night and put two men on the tiller as rain squalls lashed the ship. By morning, the wind had risen to gale force. On the following day, March 24, 1939, the storm reached typhoon proportions. All radio contact was lost.

His disappearance, however, did not receive universal acceptance and he remained in death—if that was where he was—as gigantic a legend as he had been in life.

II

The Memphis Boy

If you hit a pony over the nose at the outset of your acquaintance, he may not love you, but he will take a deep interest in your movements ever afterwards.

—RUDYARD KIPLING
(*Plain Tales*)

⊷§ I §⊶

THE intensity with which Richard Halliburton lived his life was rooted, someone once suggested, in the distinction that as a boy of six he was the only male student in a school otherwise attended by 350 girls. The year was 1906 and the institution was the Hutchison School for Girls in Memphis, Tennessee.

Richard was enrolled there because his mother, a former Cincinnati music teacher whose maiden name was Nelle Nance, was a member of the faculty, and because the headmistress, an engaging and scholarly spinster named Mary G. Hutchison, had long been a friend of the Halliburton family. She inserted herself, in fact, in the role of Richard's grandmother, since he had none, and Richard accepted her. He couldn't pronounce the title in his early childhood, however, so he called her "Ammudder," a name he reserved for her all her life.

Richard's father, Wesley Halliburton, was a graduate civil engineer from Vanderbilt University, a descendant of Scots who settled along the Atlantic Coast and in the Deep South in the eighteenth century, and a great nephew of the eighteenth century Nova Scotia judge, Chandler Haliburton (*sic*), who created the character "Sam Slick" and thereby became known as a founder of New World literary humor. Wesley Halliburton explained that his southern forebears had acquired, by industry and virtue, "many acres and many slaves," and that they lived by "an enlightened materialism and a healthy code of morals," an attitude he attempted to pass on to his son.

When Richard was three, his parents gave him a brother, who was named Wesley and who became separated from Richard by more than years. Wesley turned into a robust, competitive youngster, while Richard kept to himself, playing with a

39

mongrel dog named Teddy or riding a pony, Roxy, which his father had bought him, through the gently sloping and wooded countryside around Memphis. He rode the pony with a recklessness that alarmed his mother and to her pleas for caution he responded with even more daring until one day he was thrown and dragged for several hundred feet. At last his foot jolted free from the stirrup, and he was dropped, battered and bleeding, in the middle of a stubble field. The pony, startled afresh by the loss of its floundering burden, had bolted out of sight and Richard was alone in what he described years later, in recalling the incident, as a curious euphoria that seemed to be heightened by the pain and the exotic sensation that he was alone in the world. Then the shriek of a bluejay intruded reality on his consciousness and he dragged himself home to the ministrations of his mother which he found suffocating.

Richard's parents had come to Memphis shortly after his birth from Brownsville, Tennessee, and Richard spent his summers visiting family friends there or at his parents' summer cabin at Tate Springs in the mountains of eastern Tennessee. Even at the age of twelve, Richard went his way separately from Wesley who played with other youngsters, and formed instead a close relationship with his father who taught him to play golf and tennis. They often went on weekend walks of 25 miles or longer. Even after Richard grew to manhood, his father would recall "we were always good friends." The elder Halliburton had given up his engineering profession in favor of real estate and land speculation in Tennessee and Arkansas, and he prospered profoundly.

Richard had been enrolled in the meantime in the Memphis University School for Boys where he excelled scholastically and played the violin with some promise. He also attended dancing classes and by the time he was thirteen he was a skilled dancer. That summer, he and his parents spent a month in Asheville, North Carolina, and he and a little girl named Cornelia McMurry astonished the Battery Park Hotel ballroom crowd with a sparkling performance of the Hesitation Waltz.

Whenever he left Memphis, even for a weekend, Richard

wrote long and intimate letters to Miss Hutchison. She and Richard's mother apparently were the primary intellectual influences in his youth. At the age of thirteen, for example, he is reading Cicero; he doesn't like it but he suspects it is important, especially when he discovers that other boys his age never heard of Cicero.

On his fifteenth birthday in January of 1915, Richard developed what was diagnosed as a tachycardia (rapid heartbeat) of unknown cause and he was taken from school and put to bed. He remained in bed for four months, showing little or no improvement, and his mother took him to Battle Creek Sanitarium where, by August, the condition began to abate. Mrs. Halliburton remained at the Michigan sanitarium with her son until August when a wealthy industrialist, affectionately interested in Richard, took him on a camping trip into Wisconsin's north woods and then to his home in St. Paul, Minnesota. His father wrote him almost daily letters, fearful the boy would "disregard your physical affliction and put pleasure first," but Richard led a restrained life.

Between his wealthy host and the sons of affluent families he had met at Battle Creek he decided against his father's wish that he attend Vanderbilt and began to think in terms of Princeton. And at his mother's urging, he also began to think about a prep school far removed from Memphis. Most of the youths at Battle Creek had been from Culver or Lawrenceville, he reported in his letters home, and he favored Lawrenceville because it led directly into Princeton. He noted also that the two schools were only six miles apart.

Lawrenceville welcomed Richard that fall and the following year, 1916-17, he was made editor-in-chief of the school newspaper. When he was graduated in the spring of 1917, he was selected to compose the music and write the lyrics for the class ode. The United States had declared war on Germany in April and Richard, like his classmates, felt strongly about the Hun:

> Great builder of God-fearing men
> Great advocate of noble life,
> We leave thee now, true sons to be,

Throughout this time of strife;
To fight the wrong, the right to free,
Trust us 'til we come back to thee;
Lawrenceville, Lawrenceville
Trust us 'til we come back to thee.

The second stanza was more directly patriotic, containing the vow to cross the Atlantic to fight, if necessary, and the melody bore lugubrious resemblance to an anthem Carrie Jacobs Bond might have written.

He also managed to misspell Lawrenceville on the title page: it came out "Larwenceville."

It was at Lawrenceville and Princeton that Richard met several young men who turned out to be important cornerstones in his furious life and whose friendship he took great pains to retain. Among these friends were Irvine O. Hockaday, who became a wealthy Kansas City stockbroker; John Henry Leh, son of a department store owner from Allentown, Pennsylvania, and an heir to his father's business; James Penfield Seiberling, son of the founder of Seiberling Rubber Co. and later its president; Edward L. Keyes III, who became a prominent St. Louis physician.

Richard entered Princeton in the fall of 1917, coinciding with the entry of his brother, Wesley, into Lawrenceville. But in November, Wesley was stricken with what may have been rheumatic fever. He was hurried home to Memphis where he died five weeks later at the age of fourteen. Richard went home for the funeral and the Christmas holidays and apparently was stunned at the depth of his parents' grief. Returning to Princeton in January, Richard parted from his mother and father on the Memphis railroad station in an agony of reproach.

"You're very fortunate," said his mother, her voice taut and her face set to grip her emotions. "Princeton will force your mind to other thoughts. Your father and I have only our grief."

Tears were in all their eyes now, but the anguish was Richard's.

"That's not true," he cried, "you have me and I love nothing else but you and Dad."

But soon afterward, Richard's letters home reveal a sudden, semi-bitter awareness that life within the dimensions of a family can be fraught with undeserved cruelties, or that domestic happiness is a fragile, if not downright perishable, state.

He began to look forward to going to war. Princeton operated a military training camp for the summer of 1918 and Richard attended it. When the fall term opened, the university asked students to express a preference for branch of service and Richard chose the Navy because he thought it would increase his chances of getting overseas. He regretted his decision, however, because most of his friends chose the Army and in October many of them were packed off to Officer Training Camps. He also discovered that Navy officer training was closed to students under twenty, an obstacle he surmounted by lying about his age (he was only eighteen). He found the Navy classes a desultory affair and he wrote to Naval officials complaining about the inactivity and lack of discipline. He was also working four days a week as a waiter in the Naval training mess hall, rushing platters of "appalling, greasy and ill-prepared food" to ten tables jammed with hungry student-sailors.

Occasionally, the Navy students were taken to Atlantic City where they spent the day shooting the sun with sextants on the end of a pier. These outings also exposed him to the adulation the civilian population was lavishing on anybody in uniform and it so emboldened him that one night he and a companion picked up two girls on the chilly boardwalk and took them dancing until 1 o'clock in the morning. It was the same day that United Press correspondent Roy Howard had prematurely reported the Armistice and Atlantic City was wildly celebrating the Allied victory. To Richard, the war's end was frustrating.

"There seems to be something in turmoil inside me all the time," he wrote to his father. "The idea of leading a monotonous, confined, respectable life is horrible to me."

On November 11, the war in fact over, Richard went to the officers commanding the Princeton training units and argued that a celebration parade through the town of Princeton was in bad taste; prayerful gratitude for peace was more appropriate than merriment over victory, he said, and a religious service was held on the campus parade grounds. Afterward, 3,000 cadets paraded down Nassau Street.

Richard visited Lawrenceville frequently, riding the six miles on his bicycle or walking, to visit teachers there he had grown fond of and once he looked in the room that had been occupied by his brother and "it hurt almost as much as it did the first time. Thanksgiving will have little meaning hereafter. It is the anniversary of his first week of illness."

Richard complained more frequently now of a growing restlessness, a compulsive kind of physical discontent that he relieved by walking alone, especially at night or on Sunday. He often went to Trenton, 10 miles away, and one night he kept going to Philadelphia. It took him all night to cover the 40 miles and he arrived barely in time to catch a train back to his first class of the day at Princeton.

In the winter of 1919, Richard was elected to the board of the *Daily Princetonian.* It was a victory he achieved over eight other candidates and it coincided with a decision to be a writer. He had shocked his English professor with a burlesque, in doggerel, on Antony and Cleopatra, and with an erudite 4,000-word essay on the character of Napoleon III. He had also decided, he wrote his mother, "that a man's education is in proportion to his knowledge of Paris and France and French." To his father's warnings that he was in danger of becoming "too esthetic," Richard replied that he would be "very happy if I could get to the heart of the esthetic things I like without missing any of the really practical ways and means of living."

Richard also professed an interest in girls, few of whom ever took him seriously. He was a consummate dancer and a gay companion much in demand among the girls from Trenton and New York and Philadelphia who were enchanted by his frivolous high humor. He was "constantly exhilarated," recalled one brunette whom he dated several times, "and 'Smiles' was his favorite song." He pursued a socially prominent young lady from Trenton with what his friends interpreted as serious intent, and he reported to his father that he appeared to be besting a classmate in the race for her constant affection.

But the classmate won out and later married the girl. Richard, the girl recalled, "seemed quite bitter about it for a long time." In any case, it was the last serious courtship of his life, if that was what it was in the first place. The young lady appraised him as the most delightful companion she had ever dated, noting that he neither smoked nor drank, was delightfully unpredictable, charming and thoughtful. Instead of taking her home from a dance one balmy spring Friday night, for example, Richard suggested they go canoeing in the moonlight which they did until dawn. But she didn't want to marry him.

At the age of nineteen, Richard was a slender blue-eyed youth of almost fragile handsomeness. His blonde hair, worn long on top and short at the sides, was parted on the left side toward the middle and combed straight back.

As a member of the *Princetonian* editorial board, Richard felt qualified to criticize his instructors for laxness in discipline and for failing to demand more work from students. In response to this, his history professor began giving daily tests. Richard had failed on one occasion to read his assignment the night before and the subject of the test was unknown to him. He scrawled across the test paper, "I can't be expected to preach and practice both." The professor said nothing.

Richard's impertinence had been in evidence since his freshman year when he refused to wear the traditional beanie cap and persisted in walking on lawns forbidden to first year students, and he did so at the cost of his general popularity. "I am a non-conformist," he explained, and some considered it an arrogant attitude. He would have been barred from several campus activities, the Cap and Gown Society among them, had not the friends with whom he roomed in the ancient red brick fastness of Patton Hall formed a lobby to force his acceptance.

Some of his letters to his mother and father during his second year at Princeton display the insufferable condescension typical of the university sophomore.

"I find I am a perfect example of an Epicurean—or rather, would like to be. Don't decide whether that is well or not until you really understand what an Epicurean is. . . ."

The turmoil that was seething within erupted when he went home to Memphis in June of 1919. He spent a few days there, and announced he was going off to Brownsville to visit an old family friend. He never got there.

∽§ 2 §∼

Mrs. Halliburton drove her son to the Memphis railroad station on the afternoon of July 14, 1919, to catch the train for Brownsville. The train wasn't due for half an hour and Mrs. Halliburton offered to wait but Richard, with a nervousness that should have been suspicious, urged her to go back home. She and Richard's father had planned to spend the weekend at a house party in Montgomery, Alabama, and she was anxious to get ready as they were driving there the following morning, a Friday. The Brownsville train came and went and Richard was still at the station, trying to make himself inconspicuous behind some baggage carts at one end of the platform. He waited there until midnight when he climbed aboard the train to New Orleans.

Atha Thomas, the young friend he had ostensibly gone to visit, came to Memphis Friday morning and went directly to the Halliburton home, a two-story red brick house on Central Avenue. Mrs. Halliburton was near hysterics with the realization that her son had run away, but her husband knew that, wherever Richard had gone, it was only the smoldering compulsions of late adolescence and that he would eventually come home.

"He thinks we're out of town until Tuesday," he told Mrs. Halliburton, "and on Tuesday morning there will be a letter waiting at my office. He doesn't know we're still in Memphis and he thinks he hasn't been missed."

Just the same, the notion that Richard might have checked into a Memphis hotel with a woman occurred to him and he investigated it. Then he contacted the conductor on the Thursday train to Brownsville and learned Richard had not been aboard it.

"There's nothing we can do but wait," he said, after both he and Mrs. Halliburton had telephoned all Richard's friends they could think of.

The letter the elder Halliburton had anticipated did, indeed, arrive on Tuesday morning, postmarked New Orleans.

"I know it was cruel of me to slip off as I did," Richard wrote, "but I knew too well that if I mentioned my plan and you did not agree with it you would talk me out of it."

He was going to Europe, he said, and he was leaving that very Tuesday night. He had drawn all his savings—$65—from the Memphis bank and had paid the $15 spending money his father had given him for the ticket to New Orleans. He acknowledged that he was suffering from an "overpowering obsession" but there was no help for it. He had signed on as an ordinary seaman aboard the freighter *Octorara* sailing for Hull, England. He would be paid $80 a month—or $54 for the three weeks of the voyage—which would land him in Europe with about $95. He begged his parents not to attempt to stop him, and he assured them that he was not running away from home; he was running from "my old self."

The truth, he said, was that he had been planning the trip for months; it would be the first great adventure of his life but he promised to return to Princeton the following February, using extra summer session credits to make up for the fall term he would miss. But to his roommates at Princeton he declared dramatically, "I may never see you again."

His letter to his father, however, brought the following telegram:

GO TO IT AND MAY YOU HAVE A BULLY TIME. A LITTLE SURPRISED YES. DON'T FAIL TO WRITE US. FOR GODS SAKE TAKE CARE OF YOURSELF, BUT GET THIS TRIP OUT OF YOUR SYSTEM. WISHING YOU BON VOYAGE, DAD.

But his father later wrote a painful letter, citing his son's thoughtlessness and describing the anguish Richard's mother had suffered for three days, and Richard was duly ashamed.

Richard had arrived in New Orleans in the midst of a violent waterfront strike, as a witness to which he narrowly escaped injury, and it was three weeks before the *Octorara* sailed. Richard and another student-crewman, a sophomore from Rice Institute named Allen Longbridge of Houston, shared quarters at the Catholic Service Club because the boat was hot at night and swarming with mosquitoes.

Richard's first chore as one of six crewmen was to clean 38 brushes which were stiff with hardened paint. He did it in five hours, he boasted, using kerosine, hot water and soap. The work otherwise—scraping, painting and loading stores—was hard and unpleasant and he was grateful for the friendship of Allen whom he described as "quite cultivated and a very pleasant companion."

The *Octorara* sailed on August 8 but engine trouble at sea forced the ship into Norfolk for repairs. Richard was suffering from heatstroke, seasickness, abuse from other members of the crew, plus a severe case of ship's boils, and when the vessel dropped anchor at Norfolk he was ready to forget the whole trip. His parents had gone to their summer cabin at Tate Springs and Richard got permission from the captain to visit them. It was a six-hour bus ride and when Richard finally arrived, he was a shocking sight. He was covered with boils, the skin on his face and arms was sunburned and peeling, his lips were cracked and blistered and he was gaunt and weak. He threw himself into his mother's arms and announced that he was through with the sea. He had no intention of returning to the ship. Mrs. Halliburton dressed his wounds, fed him and comforted him and told him she wished he could stay but he was obliged to return to the ship.

Richard was stunned. He had expected that his family would be overjoyed at his return and insist that he remain, sparing him further torment and suffering on the *Octorara*. But his mother, sensing what was in his mind, forced him to go back. In later years, Richard termed the incident the turning point in his life.

"If my mother had let me stay home," he said, "it would

have destroyed my self-confidence for life. She recognized that it was a crisis in self-reliance and she made me meet it."

The captain of the freighter was even more surprised than Richard for he never expected to see the youth again; in addition to his own self-respect, Richard also earned the respect of the captain and after a few days he began to enjoy the voyage. The ship stopped first at the Azores, and Richard exclaimed "Oh, what a glorious sight," in the first of the thousands of long, detailed letters he wrote home to his parents all the rest his life. From Horta to Hull, the ship labored through a succession of storms and heavy seas at half speed. Richard and everybody else aboard was painfully seasick but it failed to chill his enthusiasm. The trip, he said, had made him very hard-boiled. But the ship had no sooner wound its way up the Humber River and docked in a snowstorm, than Richard realized he was ill-prepared to tour Europe.

"I know only enough now to know that I have everything to learn about Europe," he wrote his mother, vowing to study furiously when he returned to Princeton. "Europe's geography is at my fingertips, but not its history and literature."

Richard had grown a moustache on the ship, a black bleak thing that began to droop at the ends, so he shaved it off at Hull and bought himself a walking stick "as substitute proof that I am a grown man."

Britain was in the grip of a general strike when he arrived, and he walked around nearby Lichfield, open-mouthed and eager, talking to everyone who would respond. He stopped in a hotel public room, stood in front of the fireplace and chatted for several minutes with General Edmund Henry Allenby, the deliverer of Jerusalem, without knowing until later who he was.

Paid his month's wages and given a certificate of discharge by the *Octorara*'s captain, George Anderson, who rated his character and ability as "very good," Richard celebrated his freedom by going to a Charlie Chaplin movie, *Sunnyside,* and taking half a dozen Lichfield street urchins in with him. "Charlie," he observed, "was not half as funny as those kids."

The next day Richard set out for Manchester, on foot, and ended up walking over most of England. After Manchester he went to Ecclesfield, then to Leek and Ashemore where, to his amazement, he slept in a 300-year-old inn "whose feather beds were not much younger." Then he was off to Uttoxeter and along the Dove River back to Lichfield where he visited Dr. Samuel Johnson's birthplace. Stratford was next, and on the way he was completely agog at the village churches, the castles and the cathedrals. It was pouring rain when he reached Kenilworth Castle, and there were no other tourists so he had the guide to himself. "The man was an encyclopedia of Kenilworth knowledge . . . He stood where Amy Robsart stood and quoted Scott's story [of the mysterious death of the wife of the Earl of Leicester who then became the lover of Queen Elizabeth I] . . . and then he did Elizabeth with all the gestures . . . and he showed me the room which Leicester sacked all of Europe to furnish." Leicester had only invaded Belgium and Holland, and was defeated, but to Richard it seemed like he had sacked all of Europe. "I was living in 1560," he said.

In Stratford he met an Australian soldier and the two of them toured Shakespeare's birthplace and then Trinity Church where they stood on the Bard's grave and took snapshots of the inscription, "Good friend, for Jesus' sake forbeare. . . ." They saw Anne Hathaway's cottage and they rented a punt and paddled on the Avon. He went to a movie that night and wished he hadn't; "it rather ruined my mood—sort of the sublime to the ridiculous."

It took him only two days to walk to Oxford to which he again applied the adjective "glorious—such as America can never have with all her millions." He became intrigued with the idea of attending Oxford after Princeton.

In London, he went to the theater (*Cyrano*), to the ballet, the National Gallery and the Tate, to the Victoria Embankment where the German submarine *Deutschland* was docked, and to St. Paul's Cathedral which provoked the pronouncement that he did not like the architecture of its seventeenth-century designer, Sir Christopher Wren. He also complained that London restaurants, "although their menus would hide the side of a house, are out of everything except tea without sugar and toast with margarine."

He stayed in London a week and flew to Paris in the open cockpit of a 12-passenger Handley-Page airplane which circled Amiens and Richard could see the last of the trenches dug by British troops.

He saw the sights of Paris in two days, walking at a furious rate, and discovered that his college French was useless; he took a room in a French boarding house, whose guests included two American girls attending the Sorbonne, and he enrolled in language classes at the Alliance Française. He also cabled home for money because he was broke.

He walked everywhere and the gendarmes, thinking he was either mad or bewildered, sought to put him aboard buses or trams whenever he asked directions. He walked to Versailles and to Lille and through the battlefields of the Somme, and Arras, and he was shocked at the stark aftermath of war and death, and troubled by the struggles of the French farmers to reclaim their land from shell holes and barbed wire and to rebuild their demolished homes. When he saw the rubble of Lens, he said it looked like Memphis, blown to bits.

Richard had been to Paris almost six weeks, including his tour of the battlefields; he was making slow progress with his French language studies and he was restless and bored. He was surprised that he had not been accosted by Parisian prostitutes, whose ranks he had always assumed were legion, but he stayed on in Paris almost until Christmas and booked passage home on the *Adriatic,* sailing the end of January. He had determined to return to Princeton and get it over with, although he admitted he was homesick for New Jersey. His classmates were writing him regularly and "the place seems to have gone mad over parties, proms, excitement . . . you know I hate to miss a party."

His decision to come home was applauded by his father, who, worried about his son falling prey to a "designing French girl," urged him to return "to the even tenor of your way."

This angered Richard and he shot off a bristling reply that, as it turned out, was his eternal philosophy of life.

> I *hate* that expression [even tenor] and as far as I am able I intend to avoid that condition. When impulse and spontaneity fail to make my way uneven then I shall sit up nights inventing means of making life as conglomerate and vivid as possible. Those who live in the even tenor of their way simply exist until death ends their monotonous tranquility.
>
> No, there's going to be no even tenor with me. The more uneven it is, the happier I shall be. And when my time comes to die, I'll be able to die happy, for I will have done and seen and heard and experienced all the joy, pain, thrills—any emotion that any human ever had—and I'll be especially happy if I am spared a stupid, common death in bed. . . .

There was more, but it only reiterated what had gone before. His mother and father were alarmed by it, but decided not to take it seriously. However, Richard was not merely writhing against the bonds of parental authority, he was telling what he felt about all mankind, for the letter carried as much scorn as it did rebellion.

He also wrote that he had met an engineer from California, a man he identified only as Mr. Sanford, and that the two of them would spend Christmas in the south of France. But before he left, he spent $5 his father had sent him to see Anna Pavlova dance in Chopin's *Les Sylphydes* and while it was "graceful beyond words," the performance was "studied and conventional . . . devoid of any thrill." The great Russian ballerina was then almost forty and, some said, past her prime. She died eleven years later.

Richard and his friend toured Marseilles, Nice, Lyons and Monte Carlo, where Richard was refused admittance to the casino because he was only nineteen, and he returned to Paris to find the Seine flooding parts of the city and all the gas turned off. The sailing of the *Adriatic* was postponed by a waterfront strike, so Richard came home January 17 aboard the French liner *Savoie,* assuring his father he needn't worry about "bringing you a daughter."

❧ 3 ❧

Richard spent the Easter holidays of 1920 alone with his father at Harper's Ferry, the site of John Brown's last stand, and the two of them hiked compulsively along the Potomac and through the Shenandoah Valley and over the battlefield of Antietam. They walked much of the way in silence; Richard wondering how to deliver what he feared would be heartbreaking news, and his father, knowing it was coming, wondering how to meet it. The elder Halliburton was prepared to offer Richard a three-month European trip as a graduation present, but he discovered his son wasn't the least interested. Richard finally proclaimed, in a fevered way, that his only desire was to vagabond around the world. His father said nothing, for he was certain Richard disliked discomfort and noise and dirt and he attributed the longing to mere romantic restlessness of post-adolescence; it would wear off under the abrasions of reality.

They walked into Washington toward the end of the week, had lunch with their Tennessee Congressmen, and then went walking again in Rock Creek Park. Their talk this time was impersonal; what women's suffrage, just enacted by Congress, would mean to American politics, and to American men; and whether the United States should be a member of the League of Nations, even though Congress had decreed against it the year before. They also talked about Prohibition, but it was largely academic. Richard had no interest in drinking, and his father, who had a detached appreciation of fine bourbon, noted that it was unlikely there would ever be an acute shortage of it in Tennessee.

Richard had returned to Princeton in the middle of the term but instead of being behind he was, in the eyes of his class-

54

mates, who both envied and resented his adventure in Europe, a cut above the average college student. He finished the term by being voted "the most original member of the class" and by being elected editor-in-chief of the Princeton *Pictorial,* otherwise known as *Pic.* A weekly, it was the most unsuccessful of all four campus publications and was, in fact, $1,100 in debt when Richard took its helm.

Richard spent the summer with three classmates on a pack trip in the Rocky Mountains out of Browning, Montana. They shot a surfeit of grouse and squirrel and caught rainbow trout until Richard said he could never eat another one, and they complained bitterly to each other over the obstinacy of their two Indian guides whom Richard found "as irresponsible as our southern niggers."

Richard decided to write an article about the trip and send it off to *Field & Stream.* He titled it "The Happy Hunting Grounds" and, with Tennyson ringing in his head, began it— "Half a league onward into the forest primeval rode the six horsemen. Elk to the left of them, bears to the right of them, mountain sheep on top of them bellowed and thundered. . . ." The magazine bought the article, for $150, and published it eight months later.

If Richard had any doubt that he wanted to spend his life as a writer-adventurer, the check from *Field & Stream* dispelled it.

When he returned to Princeton in the fall of 1920, he selected only those courses he thought would be of direct use to him. The curriculum committee balked at what it described as his short-sighted single-mindedness but he won its members over by an admirable perseverance and was permitted to take Shakespeare, poetry, money and banking, public speaking, Oriental literature, Victorian literature, modern painters, French and something called "American Ideals." The dean thought he was overworking himself.

The *Pic* was not only broke and in debt, Richard discovered, but it had a circulation of only 400—the smallest on campus. He attacked this by making the entire staff, including himself, so-

56 ᙥ HALLIBURTON

licit subscriptions door-to-door, and by converting the magazine from a thoughtful chronicle of campus life into an irreverent, tongue-in-cheek rotogravure kind of publication choked with candid snapshots; students bought it to see if their pictures were in it. This format enraged the staffs of the other campus publications but Richard pretended not to notice. In time he drove the circulation up to 2,000 and one Saturday afternoon in November, Richard and his staff moved into the crowds attending the Yale-Princeton game and sold 5,000 copies. To maintain his success with *Pic* and to keep abreast of his classes, Richard often worked day and night, frequently running on four or five hours' sleep. He no longer had time for those solitary, introspective walks through the New Jersey countryside.

He was buoyed not only by his own achievements but by the elations of his times which prevailed over uneasy events. The First World War and the prosperous expectations which had followed it had produced a horde of new American millionaires despite the feeling in more affluent circles that the Sherman anti-trust act and the advent of the eight-hour day for industry were forerunners of socialist decay and collapse. Theodore Roosevelt had died, Russia was awash in revolution and chaos, the *Titanic* had sunk and nearly everybody was still frightened by the influenza epidemic of 1918 which had taken 20 million lives throughout the world, more than half a million in the U.S. alone.

But Richard and his contemporaries were absorbed by the idea that the world of the past had been a mistake, and everything worthwhile was rooted in today or tomorrow. Victorian morality and Puritan restraint were giving way to the Jazz Age and the dawn of sex for everybody, and Havelock Ellis became a thrilling household name. Lytton Strachey wrote his critical biography of Queen Victoria and appeared to set off a literary trend dedicated to debunking history's heroes. There was so much expectancy in the world that Richard did not mind when Princeton went solidly Republican for Warren G. Harding. "The sun will shine just as bright and we'll have just as many worries and pleasures as under Democratic rule," he wrote to his father who was still urging him to make thoughtful decisions before embarking on the "routine of life."

Richard had no use for such advice. "Oh, to live a life that is NOT routine," he replied, "and NOT in a rut so deep one can't see over the sides to the limitless horizons beyond." He was going to chase those horizons, and that was all there was to it.

His resolve became even stronger when travel writer Harry Franck, whose *Vagabond Journey Around the World* was among the season's book hits, arrived at nearby Lawrenceville to lecture. Richard hustled over and wangled a dinner invitation. Franck answered a torrent of questions from his young admirer willingly enough, but seemed taken aback by Richard's confidence. Franck had not made his success overnight.

"I can't start at the bottom like a bank clerk," Richard protested. "I can't work for anybody else. I've got to be my own boss."

Tennessee real estate had settled into a minor slump and Richard's father suffered business reverses which provoked him to remonstrate again with his son about choosing a rewarding way of life. Richard's only reply was that he hoped his father would not have to make sacrifices to put him through college and to describe himself, apologetically, as "a pretty expensive hobby."

Richard undertook some severe self-reappraisals on the occasion of his twenty-first birthday, January 9, 1921. "I feel like Conrad in quest of his youth," he wrote. "Nine more years and I'll be thirty and the last vestige of youth will be gone . . . I can look forward to no joy in life beyond thirty. I see there the end of my ability to enjoy and love and live—it's only existence for me after that. That's the disadvantage of being one of this ultra-modern generation—we are satiated before Nature intended us to be."

But he also began to think more intensely and specifically about what he was going to do after graduation; and about how he was going to make his vagabondage pay. He was so absorbed with this, with editing the *Pic* and with his studies that he had no time for anything else. He made one trip to New York in

March to the Metropolitan to hear Mary Garden in *Faust* and Amelita Galli-Curci in *Rigoletto* and sat in the uppermost balcony "along with all the other garlic-smelling wops." He had no time to think about the senior prom and when it came, later in March, he had no girl so he went alone. For a public speaking class assignment, he delivered a 15-minute harangue on the "lost academic spirit" at Princeton which he said was now turning out nothing but businessmen.

In April he began planning his itinerary for his great vagabond trip and he also outlined the book he would write about his adventures:

> It will be a great melting pot of history, literature, personal autobiography, humor, drawings, paintings, photographs, pathos, romance, adventure, comedy, tragedy, all branching off, but an integral part of the most vivid narrative of real experiences of a very live, open-eyed and sympathetic young man on an unconventional and originally-executed circumnavigation of the globe, all bound up in a large and richly-covered volume with *Wanderlust* in big gilt letters across the front. There can be no failure. I don't want a Baedeker, nor a Harry Franck, nor a Mark Twain, nor a Frederick O'Brien, but something of each plus chiefly me.

At the same time, the imminence of his departure from Princeton saddened him for he thought of the academic depth and natural beauty of the place and he vowed to return there to make his home. "It's only a town of 6,000, but half the homeowners are in *Who's Who*," he noted. Albert Einstein had just arrived for a spring lecture series. He also realized that when it came to academic honors, he had none, nor any genuine claim to them. "But perhaps the higher life, as an author of exalted unreadable literature, has not enough action and freedom for me." At the same time, he spoke again of spending a year at Oxford. "I'd only be twenty-two then; I could spare a year."

To this uncomfortable introspection his father replied, "If your ambition is to be superintellectual, living in an atmosphere of vague idealism, then you should have striven for Phi

Beta Kappa. But remember, by introspection you can prove
yourself a hopeless imbecile."

Richard was appalled that so many of his classmates were
stepping directly from college into marriage, family, and a staid
career that he pledged to remain a bachelor.

"A bachelor is a selfish egoist," replied his father, and Richard said he didn't see how marriage could prevent that. Then
he read Browning's *Paracelsus,* discovered Browning had written it at the age of twenty-two, and despaired that he would
ever succeed as a writer. "Perhaps I'd best start selling grocer-
ies," he said, still awed by the poem.

Earlier in the year, Richard talked scornfully to his friends of
the "prosaic mold" into which they were surrendering themselves, and when spring came he had an offer of a companion
on his journey around the world. Irvine (Mike) Hockaday, a
member of a wealthy Kansas City family, Richard's roommate
and perhaps his closest campus friend, wanted to go with him.
Richard was delighted and the two of them spent hours together marking the route of their journey on a map of the
world: Holland, France, Germany, Spain, Italy, Greece,
Turkey, India, Tibet, Malaya, China, Japan. . . .

On May 31, the anniversary of his brother's birth, Richard
was moved by stirrings suggestive of guilt to wonder, in a letter
to his mother, whether he had any right to go abroad and leave
his parents alone for such a long period of time. "Mrs. Hockaday has two other sons to comfort her," he wrote, "and you
have none." But morbidity, even then, did not linger long in
Richard's mind.

Spring came to Princeton that year with an almost explosive
fervor, or so it seemed to Richard. The campus corridors of oak
and elm and maple trees erupted overnight into a cloud of
summer green, and the air was a caress of the fragrances of
moist loam and apple blossoms from the orchards toward Trenton.

He spent his afternoons on a rock beside the banks of Stony
Brook reading from *Dorian Gray,* "Live, live the wonderful life

that is in you. Be afraid of nothing. There is such a little time that your youth will last . . . Youth! Youth! There is absolutely nothing in the world but youth!"

His last memory of Princeton was the Patton Hall house party, full of bright and eager young men and soft lovely girls in the new knee-length cotton dresses and short bobbed hair that smelled of innocence when you danced with them to a phonograph playing a new hit tune like "The Japanese Sandman" or "Look for the Silver Lining."

"I hope to heaven," said Richard, "that I will get abroad unencumbered by any sentimentalism and not waste perfectly good hours writing letters to some uninterested girl."

But when the morning came for him to take the train to New York, he ran all the way to the railroad station for he could not bear to leave such a richly beautiful place.

III

The Royal Road

The heart's impulse is the voice of fate.

—Friedrich von Schiller

❧ I ❧

GIVEN other motives, Richard Halliburton might have been in the vanguard of American expatriates. Ernest Hemingway was already in Paris in 1921 but he had yet to establish himself as the spokesman for the Lost Generation. Richard considered himself a Young Modern in gentle revolt against his elders, but he also felt he had to prove himself to these elders— and to his stuffy Princeton roommates and their families—and to prove himself in their terms; he was more interested in success than he was in mere personal emancipation and he was confident, supremely confident, that he would be a success. He was, of course, infected by the epidemic of youthful egotism sweeping the earth, its symptoms soon to be painfully articulated by F. Scott Fitzgerald and later harnessed by Mussolini and his budding Italian Fascists who took for their national anthem a song which began, "Youth, youth, springtime of beauty."

Richard and Mike Hockaday spent four days roaming the New York docks and hiring halls before being signed on aboard the 6500-ton freighter *Ipswich* as ordinary seamen. Hundreds of American college students were in New York then trying to work their passage to Europe for the summer and the competition for berths for novice sailors was keen. Richard acknowledged the fact that the *Ipswich* was available because an executive with the shipping firm which owned the boat was a Princeton alumnus. "I must admit," he said some years later, "that Princeton proved an 'open sesame' for me everywhere I went."

The *Ipswich* was six weeks crossing the Atlantic to Hamburg, and Richard's experience aboard the *Octorara* the year before made the voyage familiar even though the ship went north to the Grand Banks, across a stormy north Atlantic and through the North Sea. Both he and Mike were seasick for part of the journey and the decks of the freighter were so cold and soaked with spray that he could not spend romantic hours reading poetry and gazing at the setting sun or the rising moon as he had done aboard the *Octorara* on its leisurely course on the balmy southerly Gulf Stream.

Richard's attitude toward the trip, unlike that of Mike who was simply enjoying a brief adventure, was that he had gone to work and his determination to succeed compelled him to write at least 1,000 words a day in a five-by-seven black notebook, an item he was never without. He had set a further goal of 500,000 words for the entire trip, which he now estimated would take two years, and from these notes he would assemble his first book. He was also jotting down ideas for magazine articles and the first one that occurred to him was a piece entitled "Two Weeks Before the Mast," comparing his voyage to Hamburg with that of Richard Dana's *Two Years Before the Mast* a century before. Not only did he and Dana have the same first name, he noted to himself, but they were the same age when they went to sea, and "we both have the same urge."

Richard's father had succumbed to his son's resolve to some extent, agreeing to finance Richard to the amount of $100 a month until his book was published, or until he changed his mind and entered some other occupation. The elder Halliburton also obtained a commitment from C. P. J. Mooney, editor of the Memphis *Commercial-Appeal,* to buy—for $35 each—all the travel articles Richard could send. Between this and his anticipated sales to magazines, he would somehow make the trip at least pay for itself. He genuinely hoped he would not have to rely on his father's contribution.

The *Ipswich* steamed into the Elbe River on the morning of August 1, a steaming hot day, docking at Hamburg that night. The harbor was congested with ships and excursion boats, and the riverside beer gardens were jammed with holiday crowds. Hamburg, even then the wickedest city in Europe, was bustling with the appearances of prosperity despite a steadily worsening inflation. The mark had plummeted nearly fifty percent in value which enabled Richard and Mike to buy two new bicycles for the equivalent of $15 each in U.S. money. They spent a week in Hamburg, impressed by German affability and generosity, which contrasted with their long-distance impressions of the Kaiser's troops, and Richard conceived of an article on "Life in Republican Germany." However, he found that keeping two sets of notebooks—one for book ideas and the other for magazine article material—was too time-consuming and he incorporated all his thoughts and ideas into one. He now had three notebooks filled with some 30,000 words and he mailed them home to his father. He had also collected several dozen picture postcards and had taken an equal number of snapshots, and he sent them home, too. He was trying to soak up knowledge in volume and his investigations of Hamburg, and then Berlin, were taken up finding out what he thought he would need to know rather than by simple curiosity. He was also determined to spend money only for necessities, a restraint which did not apply to Mike, and they often went their separate ways.

Richard's approach to Berlin was coldly methodical. He bought a street map and memorized it; then he inspected every museum, public building, park and statue. All it did for him, he confessed in a letter home, was force him to the conclusion that there was no good modern art in Germany—only Paul Klee and Andreas Feininger and those other curious expressionists, as they were called—and the architecture of Berlin was "unharmoniously ostentatious." But he was stunned by the gigantic collection of Flemish art in the Frederick Museum.

After a week in Berlin, the days took on an onerous sameness for Richard and the edge came off a portion of his dreams. Was all the world like Memphis, New York or Princeton? Was success only the tedious application of energy to practical obstacles whose conquest was never more than drudgery? There was no romance this far, perhaps none of it was romance. Perhaps life became romantic only after it was stripped of reality by an artist with a private vision. There were moments when Richard felt he had only determination and ambition and he wondered whether it was enough. His departure from Berlin was almost a flight, and he and Mike bicycled the 20 miles to Potsdam in little more than an hour. To rid himself of his own private realities, and to save shipping expenses, Richard sent home collect the small hand steamer trunk he had brought with him. His only possessions now were his camera, his notebook, a raincoat, one suit, one sweater, two shirts, a pair of pants, one pair of shoes, two pairs of socks and one change of underwear. Packed altogether, it scarcely weighed 15 pounds. He felt better.

In Potsdam, they met a wealthy young couple named Ship-King; the husband had roomed with Richard at Lawrenceville. The Ship-Kings took the two boys throughout the city with a car driven by a chauffeur who spoke English. They saw the apartments of the late Kaiser whose gardens were more verdant and colorful and better-kept, Richard felt, than Versailles. They went that night to a beer hall, a long, barren building with a high ceiling which echoed the bouncing rhythms of an unbalanced orchestra playing polkas and other folk dances. The place was filled with soldiers and with plump peasant girls. It was the custom for the men to dance together and let the girls cut in, and then for the girls to dance together and the men would cut in. It was strange to see men dancing together, often in intimate reach.

"They don't look as funny as when they dance with those fat girls," said Richard, but he danced with them too.

Richard's spirits rose after they left Potsdam and began the long trek to Amsterdam by way of Nenndorf and Hanover. They were buffeted by a stiff headwind between Genthin and Mageeburg but one day they managed to bicycle 75 miles in less than eight hours. Richard grew lyrical over the picturesque neatness of the German countryside, and the scrubbed and vivid color of the Dutch landscape with its "canals and cows," and the eeriness of pedaling along the Zuider Zee some twenty feet below the level of the sea. They spent the first night in Amsterdam at a theater seeing newsreels of Jack Dempsey's knockout victory, in the fourth round, over French heavyweight Georges Carpentier in Jersey City a month earlier. The other major event of the weeks was the death of Enrico Caruso, in his native Naples, at the age of forty-nine. The newspapers, even in Holland, were filled with eulogies to the great tenor.

In Haarlem, Richard sent his father a pair of wooden shoes as a birthday gift, and in Rotterdam he and Mike sold their bicycles for $10 each and sailed for London where Richard remained a week doing nothing, he said, but indulging in a giddy social whirl with British friends. He and Mike separated in London, Mike to tour Scotland while Richard returned to the continent to meet Mike in Mayence on the Rhine in a week. Richard went to Brussels and Cologne and Coblenz which was so filled with American soldiers of the Allied Occupation Forces that he resolved to write an article about them. He climbed to the parapets of the famous old German fortress, Ehrenbreitstein, and was thrilled by the sight of a U.S. flag flying from a tower above, and entranced by the view of the Rhine and the Moselle 400 feet below.

At Mayence, he posed as a correspondent of the Memphis paper and was given a tour of French occupation installations there. It was also at Mayence he and Mike agreed amiably to separate for good in Paris in a month. In the meantime, Richard walked alone to Strassburg and to St. Marie aux Mines and the heart of the Vosges Mountains which reminded him of the Blue Ridge in Tennessee. He strode the ridge separating France and Alsace, gazing down alternately at the Rhine on one side and a tiny blue lake on the other, and lingered so long that darkness fell. He strayed off the path and stumbled into a morass of abandoned trenches and barbed wire entanglements and, fearful of falling off a cliff, he curled up in a dugout and spent the night. In the morning he walked on into Schlucht for breakfast, then to Krut where he caught the train for Basel in a pouring rain. He was beginning to feel like an adventurer again for he had decided that the next significant stop in his itinerary would be Zermatt, Switzerland, where he would climb the Matterhorn.

He and Mike reached Zermatt on September 20, 1921, to find

the great mountain swathed in fog and storms and the climbing season ended. Only one small hotel was still operating and they took rooms there while searching for guides. Nobody wanted to take them up the Matterhorn. It was too late in the season and too dangerous. Richard possessed a mixture of disarming charm and perseverance which he applied to two of the area's best guides, Adolph Schaller and Roman Perrone, and in time they agreed. They were appalled to discover that neither youth had ever climbed anything except a flight of stairs and that neither had suitable clothing. They rented cleated shoes from the guides and borrowed mittens, leggings and heavy sweaters from some townfolk who weren't sure whether they were witnessing an heroic undertaking or a suicidal stunt.

Adolph and Roman took the two would-be climbers to nearby Gorner Grat for a day's instruction in climbing technique and two days later the Matterhorn broke free from the weather. The guides said it was as safe as it would ever be until next spring and they set out to scale the peak at 1:30 in the afternoon. It took them five hours to reach the Alpine Club hut, passing, en route, the cemetery containing the bodies of those who had fallen to their deaths from the mountain. It took the party five hours to reach the Alpine Club hut at the base of the peak's diagonal spine and they spent the night there, starting up again at 4 o'clock the next morning in brilliant moonlight shimmering on the fingers of glacier stretching out below, and on the mantle of day-old snow on the Matterhorn looming above.

Richard was roped to Adolph, and Mike to Roman, and they started up the narrow spine, desperately trying to avoid staring down the sheer ice-covered drops on either side. Twice Richard tumbled off and was hauled back to safety by Adolph, and despite this they reached the summit—14,701 feet—in six hours. Their fingers were numb from the sub-freezing temperatures and their faces were raw from the lash of wind-whipped snow and they were desperately out of breath, their hearts pounding wildly, and for a moment Richard thought he might die.

"It was the fiercest moment of intense living I have ever experienced," he said, but Mike took a more mundane view.

"We were hauled up there like two sacks of oats," he said.

Whatever the means, the end was worth it. The air was clear and they could see almost every peak in the chain of Alps, and all Switzerland below. There was Mount Blanc to the west and the Jungfrau to the north, and the lakes of Italy faded into low-lying mists to the south. They remained at the summit only ten minutes, drank a cup of coffee and started down, reaching Zermatt nine hours later. Richard had worn his only grey suit on the climb, the warmest garment he owned, and it was shredded and torn. Both young men were sorely bruised and cut and exhausted, but Richard was too elated to sleep; he was realizing his youth while he still had it and he thrilled to an ecstasy of anticipation that he still had so much of the world to see.

◦§ 2 §◦

Throughout his adolescent gropings for identity, Richard Halliburton anchored his visions to two poetic figures, Rupert Brooke and Lord Byron, the impassioned men of British letters who died a century apart in both the aura and the place of ancient Greece. They were men of arresting physical beauty, although Byron was crippled from birth, and their dominant vision of life was violently romantic. If Richard had private heroes, they were Brooke and Byron.

Brooke had been dead a mere seven years, and to Richard this only served to give life to the tragic legend of this modern English classic hero whose poetry rang with immortal British sentiment. Richard half-expected to find Brooke still alive, somehow; perhaps walking through the mists of an Aegean isle proclaiming the glories of England. With Byron, it was another matter. Byron had hardened into a bronze god in Richard's mind, a spirit to whom one could pay an anguished homage.

He and Mike took the train from Zermatt to Geneva and as it approached Montreux, at the eastern end of Lake Geneva, Richard got off, promising to meet Mike in Paris in a day or two. Richard had remembered that at Montreux, on the shores of Lake Leman, which bulges out of Lake Geneva, he would find the Chateau de Chillon, the setting for Byron's tragic ballad, "The Prisoner of Chillon," and he started on foot down the road toward it like a pilgrim approaching a shrine. It was a time and place to be alone. The tenth-century castle, with its towering white battlements, had long been a museum and Richard wandered through the building, and down the dank dungeon at the water's edge, trying to recall Byron's lines about his doomed but indomitable hero. Copies of the poem were on sale in the museum and Richard bought one, taking it to a tiny

70

gravel beach adjoining the castle and overhung with trees where he sat for a long time reading. The sun had edged behind the Alps to the west, streaking the brilliant waters of the lake with orange and magenta. There was no one else near, and Richard knew he could not be seen from the road above, so he took off his clothes and slipped into the fresh cold waters of the lake, swimming back and forth in front of the castle. When he returned to the beach, it was almost dark and he read until he could no longer see.

> Eternal spirit of the chainless mind!
> Brightest in dungeons, Liberty! thou art,
> For there thy habitation is the heart—
> The heart which love of thee alone can bind. . . .

Richard walked into Lausanne, stealing grapes from a roadside vine along the way, and a passing motorist gave him a ride to Geneva where he caught the night train for Paris, sharing a compartment with the Bishop of London and chatting about theology and church architecture.

He locked himself in his room in the Hotel Wagram in Paris, a room in which he would spend many tortured days during his life, and ground out an 8,000-word article titled "Adventuring in Republican Germany," which he planned to submit to *Metropolitan* magazine. He also expanded his notes on the Matterhorn climb, and his impressions of Switzerland which he had not taken time to record, and sent them off to his father with instructions to turn them over to the Memphis *Commercial-Appeal*. In addition, he was still writing long letters home, letters that revealed both his struggles against an unknown adversary in the realization of his ambitions, and yet which also breathed undiminished confidence.

His books, he vowed, would never have "the set purpose and serious conscientiousness that have dulled so many travel books and robbed them of spontaneity—I've not even a dictionary to corrupt me." His father replied that perhaps the most important thing was for Richard to develop a "jocular tone" and Richard agreed.

He was a month in Paris, until the end of October, finding it increasingly "distracting and stale" and he longed to be off. Loneliness, coupled perhaps with apprehension, gripped him after his final parting from Mike, and he bicycled to Versailles in a spirit that was close to frenzy. From there he went to Chartres to see the Cathedral, then to Mont St. Michel, and on November 2 he was in Tours on a haphazard tour of the Loire Valley. It was so beautiful, he wrote in a letter home, that he thought of getting married just to show it to his bride, "but better yet, I'll show it to my mother." He visited the abbey at Fontevrault, where Richard Coeur de Lion is entombed, and ended his journey at Nantes, the home of his mother's ancestors, and took the train to Bordeaux. He could not seem to remain comfortably anywhere, and from Bordeaux he cycled to Toulouse and then to Aix-les-Thermes, determined to hike across the Pyrenees into Spain. A hotel proprietor warned him he would freeze to death in the high passes and this spurred him on. He rode the mail truck to l'Hospitalet, 2,000 feet high in the foothills and the start of the donkey trail to the tiny and ancient republic of Andorra. Richard neglected to ask the mail truck driver the fare in advance and when he arrived the driver demanded 80 francs, then about $7.00. It was his first encounter with the assumption that he was the rich son of an American millionaire and it would happen many times again. But for the moment he was stunned.

"You've as much chance of getting 80 francs as 80 million," he said. But he had given the driver four letters to mail, one of them a packet of Loire photographs he was submitting to *The New York Times*.

"I won't mail your letters until you pay me," the driver replied.

Richard noticed a spark coil protruding from a battery box on the side of the auto and in a remarkably swift motion he wrenched it free. The driver let go a cry of outrage.

"Give me my letters and I'll give you the spark coil," said Richard, airily, for the driver was far smaller than he, and older, and there was no one else about. Cautiously they traded

ransoms and Richard offered the driver 30 francs which he accepted in surly silence.

Richard rented a donkey for 65 francs and after changing the
animal's name from Josephine to Hannibal, in honor of the
Carthaginian who crossed the Alps in pursuit of Romans, he set
out on the narrow snow- and ice-covered trail for Soldeau on
the Andorran border, ten hours away and 4,000 feet up. Near
the summit of the pass a blizzard hit and it was only the
donkey's infallible sense of direction that got them to Soldeau,
for Richard couldn't see twenty feet. They spent the night in a
primitive inn and started again at dawn. The trail descended
steeply, winding along one gorge after another, until eight
hours later the mountain separated into a gentle tree-dotted
plain. Andorra City, a pathetic cluster of whitewashed
buildings, clung to the lower slopes of the surrounding mountains. The world's oldest republic, it had changed little since
Charlemagne liberated it from the Moors in the middle of the
eleventh century. In the week he was there, Richard grew to
love the place, and all its 6,000 inhabitants, and was reluctant
"to return again to the world, with its complexities, its unhap-
piness and its burdensome wisdom."

Andorrans speak a Spanish dialect and conduct their commerce in the coin of Spain, but their allegiance then was to
France and they were proud to have contributed nine of their
men to the French army during the World War. Three of them
died in the trenches.

Richard spoke no Spanish but many Andorrans also spoke a
French patois and through them Richard discovered the little
country. The president of Andorra, a tall, handsome, grey-
haired muleteer by trade, entertained him in the kitchen of his
home where they sat in their stockinged feet before the fire and
talked of the world and of life.

"We are content," the president told Richard, "because we
have nothing with which to contrast what we think is happiness."

When he reached Barcelona in late November, Richard
could think of nothing but an article on Andorra which he

would describe as a kind of shangri-la where simple people who had nothing were far more wise and happy than sophisticated people who had everything. He worked furiously for four days, often writing steadily for as long as twelve hours, and mailed the piece to *Travel* magazine along with thirteen photographs. He was supremely proud of it and was ashamed of all the other articles that had preceded it. But it, too, would be rejected. He had a sense of true accomplishment now and although none of his articles, except those he sent to the Memphis newspaper, had been published he was sure they would be.

Richard was in Spain six weeks, crisscrossing it like an itinerant peddler, mostly in company with a young Chicago architect named Paul McGrath whom he met during a street dance in Barcelona. They went to Valencia, Richard photographing church towers and Paul sketching them; to Madrid which, apart from a performance of Rossini's "William Tell" at the Royal Opera House and Velasquez' paintings at the Prado Museum, he found "about as romantic as Indianapolis"; to Granada, "the Red City of the Moors," where they explored gypsy caves and spent Christmas Day in the honeycombed halls and verdant gardens of the Alhambra castle, built by the Moors in the thirteenth century; to Seville, where they ate oranges and stared at the gardens of the Alcazar, and finally to the Port of Cadiz where McGrath remained and Richard took the boat to Gibraltar which, when he saw the gigantic rock in all its awesomeness, brought forth "all the restless urges that seethe in my spirit." The urges landed him in jail.

It was dusk when he arrived and dark by the time he had eaten and found a cheap hotel room. He walked up through the terraced city, marveling at the abundance of military uniforms and crisp British accents, and in time found himself at a sentry box barricading the forbidden military fortifications summit of Gibraltar. The sentry box was empty so he walked on through.

"I stood on the very tip of the ears of the crouching lion which the Rock resembles and saw beneath me a panorama that

I have not words to describe. The wind tore at me for tres-
passing but I sat as long as I could stand the elements."

He returned the next day no less enchanted for he saw that
Gibraltar was covered with blooming hyacinths. He took the
official tour of the fortification area, noted the profusion of
signs saying NO CAMERAS ALLOWED and asked what the penalty
was for taking photographs.

"Heaven help the person caught at it," said an officer in a
signal station on the summit, who offered him a cup of tea. "It's
the unpardonable crime in Gibraltar."

Richard had lost his own camera in Valencia or Cadiz or on
the train in between so he borrowed one from the U.S. Consul
and in two days, concealing the camera in his raincoat pocket,
shot five rolls of film of every gun emplacement on the Rock
before he was caught by the very officer who had warned him.

"I don't understand how anyone who has been so repeatedly
warned could be so stupid. . . ."

He was permitted to leave, however, and he took three rolls
of film to a photo shop for developing and hid the other two in
a rain gutter outside his hotel room window. The police came
for him the next morning, accused him of being a German spy
and lodged him in prison. They seized his passport, the three
developed rolls of film and all his belongings.

He was four days in a tiny whitewashed cell in the military
prison before his case was called to trial. Paul McGrath had
reached Gibraltar in the meantime and came to see him.

"Go to my room," Richard hissed through the bars, "and see
if there are two rolls of film in the gutter."

If the police had not found the two rolls, he thought, he
might be able to persuade the court that he was only brash and
innocent. If they had found the undeveloped film, he suspected
he was doomed. He had already heard himself described by the
chief of police as "a very suspicious young man who travels
with only a brown knapsack and whose passport is clearly
forged." The undeveloped film, however, was safe.

His only witness in court was the U.S. Consul who testified

that the passport was not forged and that Richard was, indeed, who he said he was. The prosecution, however, saw nothing innocent in the fact that Richard had "sneaked" into the forbidden fortified area. Richard had no lawyer so he faced the judge alone.

He was a journalist, he said, and he had taken pictures merely to illustrate a magazine article. He knew photographs were forbidden, but because there were so many camera shops near the fortress he assumed the law was not enforced.

"My pictures will not harm your fortress," he pleaded, "but will interest many people who can never visit Gibraltar."

The judge frowned.

"I am convinced you are not a spy, but I think it dishonorable of you to take photographs when you knew they were forbidden. As a warning to all others who have your contempt for the law, I sentence you to pay a fine of ten pounds or spend thirty days in jail."

Richard was shocked. He did not have ten pounds (then about $50) and the thought of thirty days in jail terrified him. His anguish was short-lived, however, for one of the officers who had arrested him offered to loan him the money, out of some unspecified sympathy. Instead, he borrowed the ten pounds from McGrath and hurried to the night train to Marseilles, a dreary, uncomfortable, exhausting ride of 72 hours. There was a batch of mail awaiting him there but it plunged him into despair even though it contained $105 in checks from the Memphis paper. All his magazine articles except one—the story of his Matterhorn climb, which *Travel* magazine bought —had been rejected.

"The world has come to an end," he said in a letter home, "for my trip has been a blank failure."

❦ 3 ❧

The world brightened considerably the next morning under a warm Marseilles sun and Richard remained several days bringing his Spanish and Gibraltar notes up to date, and trying to analyze his failure. He still believed that a chronicle of adventures of a light-hearted traveler who moved by whim would be salable, but he began to realize that his articles had not been light-hearted at all. They had been definitive, thoughtful pieces, reflecting careful research and guarded observations. He was, he feared, working at cross-purposes. Even his father had suggested that the articles were too long and too weighty and he now pressed his father for even more detailed criticisms.

"Please, Dad," he wrote, "when I send you a manuscript, damn it as well as like it."

The effect of this pleading for criticism over the months was to make his father not only his literary agent but also his editor. While most of his articles were typed on a rented or borrowed typewriter, Richard occasionally sent them home in longhand to be typed by his father's secretary after his father had worked them over. But Richard flatly rejected his father's philosophical efforts to console him by saying he should regard the trip as "unusual post-graduate study."

"This trip is my work," Richard insisted. "Some Princeton grads of '21 went into banking, some into theology. I went into traveling and writing and I take it as seriously as they do. It must be my income. You have set me up in business by furnishing me with money for my education. I must make a success of these articles and then of my book."

The rejections of editors had "sadly jolted" him but that was all. He wasn't giving up, yet he wondered why it was so hard to write for magazines and so easy to write long letters home.

77

He spent one of his last evenings in Marseilles attending a concert by the famed French pianist Alfred Cortot who later joined the world-renowned trio of violinist Jacques Thibaud and cellist Pablo Casals. Cortot played the Schumann concerto and Richard added to the "hysterical applause" of the 2,500 Frenchmen filling the auditorium.

He had shipped his bicycle to Marseilles from Carcassonne en route to Andorra and he set out on it now for Nice. He still had few clothes, but he had collected nearly 50 pounds in books which he strapped over the rear wheel of the bike. He left Marseilles in a pouring rain and windstorm which followed him, for the next four days, to Cannes where he gave up in disgust and took the train on into Nice. The sun was waiting for him on the Riviera and after a day his alternating moods of despondency and grim determination left him. When he thrilled to the sight of Sarah Bernhardt walking along the street he knew that he had recovered his perspective. He started to speak to her, then changed his mind and only stared after the great actress, happily.

He met a New York girl, Pauline Frieder, who introduced him to other Americans among whom he became something of a celebrity. His spirits and his outlook were steadily improving when he and Pauline took the train to Monte Carlo and Richard lost all his money at roulette and was deep in despair again. A philanthropic Frenchman who had a long winning streak and who observed his losses staked him to another try and showed him how to play—"never conscientiously and never stay long at one table"—and he recovered his losses and several dollars more. A letter from his "Ammudder," school headmistress Mary Hutchison, contained a check for $100 and this sent him back to Marseilles with renewed determination to keep going around the world, no matter what. And before he left he finished three articles, all about Spain, and mailed them home.

His lack of planning, however romantic, posed certain practical problems; for one thing, he realized suddenly that he would arrive in India in mid-summer when the heat would be unbearable. He debated going home for the summer, or having his parents join him in Italy, resuming his trip in September, but in the end he rebelled at "just killing time" and decided to keep on taking his chances. He booked deck passage, at $7.50, for a seven-day voyage from Marseilles to Cairo. To sustain him during the trip, he bought a wool blanket, three dozen oranges and four books—Mark Twain's *Innocents Abroad,* Dumas' *Count of Monte Cristo* and *The Three Musketeers* and a volume of Voltaire. The trip was starkly uncomfortable, with blazing hot days and freezing nights, and it was only his excitement over reaching Egypt and his delight over Mark Twain— "he had my idea exactly 50 years ago!"—that kept up his spirits.

Richard saw Egypt in precisely fifteen days. He prowled Cairo like a bill collector, spent a moonlit night atop a pyramid and took the train 400 miles up the Nile to Luxor where nine months later in the nearby Valley of the Kings, Britain's Lord Carnarvon and American archeologist Howard Carter uncovered the 3,500-year-old tomb of King Tutankhamen, an event acclaimed as the greatest archeological discovery of all time. Richard visited the area, unaware of the momentous nature of the excavations.

He also swam the Nile at Luxor, after promising his worried mother that he would not attempt to swim the Hellespont. Neither of Richard's parents was altogether sure that their son's heart was sound and they cautioned him repeatedly against strenuous physical activity. His Matterhorn climb had alarmed them because it indicated he might do anything, and they sought to anticipate stunts and warn him specifically against them. He had talked endlessly, for instance, of swimming the Hellespont in emulation of his hero, Lord Byron. Richard's Nile swim was disastrous in another way.

He was returning to Luxor from the Tomb of Kings when he decided to try it. Standing on the muddy banks and staring at the murky water, Richard was reminded of the astonishing assortment of refuse that the Nile carries out to sea from Cairo, and of the almost legendary observation that "never has a river done so much for a country and been treated so badly in return." He also thought of crocodiles.

Nevertheless, he took off his clothes, hid them in some bushes, and waded into the lukewarm water. It was barely a third of a mile across and he made it easily, failing to notice until he had reached the other bank that the current had carried him downstream at least a quarter of a mile from where he had left his clothes. He was resting on the bank, wondering how he could get back to his clothes against the current when a group of Egyptians who had seen him swim came up for a closer look. In panic, he dived back in and allowed the current to carry him even farther downstream, past the Savoy Hotel and the shocked amazement of a group of tourists who were standing on the veranda.

Alarmed now at his downstream speed, Richard finally halted himself beside a moored sailboat, clinging to the gunwale. Richard spoke not a word of Arabic but the owner of the boat, a cadaverous Egyptian with a rollicking sense of humor, understood immediately and was convulsed with laughter. His boat was then being loaded with grain, a two-day process at least, and he could not ferry Richard to his clothes. He did the next best thing; he yanked a pink "nightgown"—the traditional Egyptian garb—from his crewman and gave it to Richard who sat wrapped in its smelly folds in the shade of the deckhouse until darkness came. The crewman, left with only a loincloth, was not amused and accompanied Richard on his ignoble hike in the pink gown back through Luxor. Richard crossed the Nile in a rented skiff and found his clothes where he had left them.

Richard was in Port Said, the Mediterranean entrance to the Suez Canal, on March 22, 1922, wondering how to get to India, when the American oil tanker *Gold Shell* steamed into port in need of an ordinary seaman. With two working voyages behind him, Richard had no trouble signing on. The crew was Greek and, unlike the other crews he had sailed with, an amiable and warm-hearted group. Richard could not pronounce their names so he gave them nicknames such as Slim and Mickey, and they retaliated by addressing him as "Boy." Despite the heat of the Indian Ocean, the month-long voyage was pleasant and restful. When the ship docked at Calcutta on Easter Day, Richard found India hotter than he had ever imagined. The thermometer in the shade of a pier shed stood at 110 degrees. Richard roomed briefly at the YMCA and then spent several days as a guest of a family named Tutweiler whom he had met some years before in Memphis. His host was the general manager of a steel mill at Jamshedpour, a five-hour train ride west of Calcutta, where the temperature was 120 degrees. Late in April, Richard moved on to Dhamtari, 300 miles to the north, and stayed at a Mennonite mission. The countryside was then terrorized by a tiger who had eaten much livestock, and Richard went on an all-night hunt with two missionaries who killed the big cat.

Back in Calcutta, Richard met another young American, David Russell, a twenty-year-old Ohioan, who was also trying to work his way around the world, and they made plans to go into Kashmir together. In the meantime, Richard was off to Benares, Delhi, Lahore, Rawalpindi and Agra where he had an experience that was to haunt him all his life. He took one side trip to Allahabad first because he had heard that Mahatma Gandhi, "the most famous of Hindu political agitators," was imprisoned there and he wanted to interview him. But Gandhi had been moved to Bombay and Richard pressed on to Agra, the site of the Taj Mahal, built three hundred years ago by the reprehensible Emperor Shah Jehan as a tomb for Arjemand, the most beloved of his thousand wives.

"He may have been a scoundrel," Richard observed, "but to have built such a monument of marble poetry he must also have been the world's greatest lover."

He stared for hours at the gleaming white domes and minarets, set like a giant jewel in the arid, barren countryside, and was so tormented by its beauty that he could think of nothing else.

He returned to the Taj that night, soon after midnight, and

found the four guards at its main gate sound asleep. He tiptoed past them and wandered in a near trance through the gardens where the fragrance of roses and lilies and unknown shrubs still clung in the moist night air. He crept up to the very tomb itself, where the torches burn forever over the crypts of the Emperor and his Arjemand, and he waited for the moon to rise. It came out of the eastern sky, three-quarters full, sometime after 2 a.m. and lighted the symmetry of the Taj with an eerie incandescence.

Richard walked about the tomb, aching from its beauty, and he walked along the long and shallow reflecting pools that lead from the Taj to its outside gate. Halfway along its length is an elevated pool, four or five feet deep and perhaps twenty feet long, and he climbed up, his eyes on the glowing dome in the distance, and sat on the rim. First he removed his shoes and socks and lowered his feet into the cool water. Then he took off his shorts and shirt and slid, with scarcely a ripple, into the pool. He lay there naked, the water washing gently over the surface of his body, and how long he lay like that he could not say. When he climbed out and sat on the rim to dry himself it was almost dawn, an arc of pale grey rising from the eastern horizon. And when he walked from the main gate, hurried along by two outraged guards, the day had come and his last view of the Taj was that of its dome covered by the waking sun with a shimmering patina of rose and gold.

Of his moonlight bath in the lily pond, Richard wrote home: "The experience will always be half-lost. The sensations were too unreal to last. I know it happened, felt the weirdness of it, but it was like a dream. Next morning it is hard to recall. It was a taste of paradise."

David Russell, the young Ohioan, joined him in Agra and together they took the train to Simla, 8,000 feet up in the mountains of northern India, and the seat of its government during the hot months. They were bound for Afghanistan, Kashmir, the Khyber Pass and as close to the Himalayas as they could get.

⤌§ 4 §⤍

Richard had learned that it was possible to ride European railroads, and those in Asia, without paying a fare or by paying only a portion of a fare, the latter simply by riding beyond the ticketed point. Conductors were easily confused and often willing to believe they had already collected a ticket. Occasionally, it was necessary to hide in the washroom or in a car vestibule, and now and then Richard would have to get off at a station and dash to the opposite end of the train. It required agility, brashness and steady nerves, but he saved a great deal of money.

Going from Agra to Delhi without a ticket, for instance, was easy. He and David merely avoided the conductor. At Delhi, they lurked in the railroad station near the first-class compartments until the train started. They had seen the conductor collect tickets in one car, which was only half-filled, and as the train began to move they ran for it, jumped aboard and entered an unoccupied compartment in which they slept comfortably and unmolested all night. The train was on the outskirts of Simla late the next day before they were caught and taken before railroad officials who did not believe their plaintive tales of having lost their tickets, especially when both of them looked none too affluent in khaki shorts and shirts and heavy hiking shoes with the remainder of their belongings squeezed into soiled knapsacks. They were detained more than an hour, their identities carefully documented, and Richard worried for weeks whether he would be permitted to leave India without paying the rail fare, nearly sixty rupees (about $20).

Their attire also served to make them social outcasts in Simla which was, at this time of year, dominated by official British colonial and Viceroy society. Even at the YMCA their fellow guests spurned them for dining in their shirtsleeves. They stayed in Simla five days trying in vain to get a visa for Afghanistan (too many killings in the Khyber Pass, the Afghan Consul explained by way of refusal) and then left by truck for Kashmir.

There were a dozen letters waiting for Richard at Simla, one of them reporting that *Travel* magazine had accepted his story of being jailed in Gibraltar. He was pleased but he wondered again what he had to show for his travels. He had been gone nearly a year and it seemed that he still had too much of the world to traverse. Whether he planned it or not, his wanderings now took on an efficient kind of pace and his letters home became fewer and shorter, a fact for which he apologized but he simply didn't have time. He was a month behind in his comprehensive notes and he felt he had to turn out articles immediately after the ideas occurred to him or he would lose enthusiasm.

He and David went by truck—a four-day trip—to Srinigar, in the Vale of Kashmir, stunned once again by beauty that he had to relate:

> Kashmir is so much more beautiful than anything else in the world, everything else looks like back alleys. Myriads of red poppies and iris, lush verdure everywhere, thousands and thousands of poplar trees planted in rows through which the snow-capped Himalayas rise. Every glance is a photograph —a rainbow of color. A poet or artist couldn't stand it. He would perish from too much beauty . . . "an emerald set in pearls" . . . but as I ever reiterate, it's these mountains that awe me most—20,000 to 26,000 feet in a complete circle around us.

They were ten days in the Vale of Kashmir, guests on a luxurious houseboat on Dal Lake occupied by a lonely, wealthy, eccentric American businessman he identified only as Mr. Catlin. Richard did nothing the first few days but eat and sleep and stare at the scenery, but before he left he finished an article on the Taj Mahal and began another on Kashmir. A firm of pack train suppliers offered to provide horses and equipment without fee in return for a promise of being mentioned in Richard's articles and Richard proclaimed that Tibet was really what he had come all this way to see.

Their objective was Leh, some 270 miles northwest of Srinigar, in the heart of the Himalayas. The trip would take at least ten days each way, along narrow and slippery mountain trails still covered with ice and snow, and through passes of 14,000 feet elevation. They made it in ten days, even though they were delayed a day when a horse slipped from the trail and tumbled into the river twenty feet below. Richard and David jumped in and saved the horse and the camping equipment it carried. They were less lucky on the return trip and lost both a pony and all their food. As soon as he reached Leh, Richard was bored with it and wanted to move on.

"Six days here seems like a terrible waste," he said, which was the length of time they would have to remain to witness the year's great religious festival. After three days, Richard had seen everything he wanted to, scorning the 6,000 inhabitants of the frigid rocky wasteland community for allowing the local Lama monastery to "suck the life out of this desert country." He was moved to linger when he learned that the festival would be the reincarnation of the Lama, who had died recently, by a four-year-old boy "who, but for his dark skin, greatly resembles the child pictures of Christ." The youngster fell asleep during the eerie ceremony and Richard later tucked him into bed.

Back in Rawalpindi, in Kashmir, in mid-July, Richard found a month's mail awaiting him but it contained no word of the fate of the magazine articles sent home previously. Traveling by truck and by hitchhiking aboard Indian Army vehicles, Richard and David reached Peshawar on July 20 and boarded a mail truck for Lundi Kotal, an Indian Army post in the approaches to the Khyber Pass. The colonel in charge received them with unexpected hospitality, gave them horses and an escort of Sikh Cavalry for a four-mile ride to the Afghan Border. Richard, just to see what it was like, rode several hundred feet beyond the sign IT IS ABSOLUTELY FORBIDDEN TO CROSS THIS BORDER INTO AFGHAN TERRITORY while his cavalry escort squinted nervously at the rocks and crags about them for signs of Afghan snipers. By recent treaty, Afghanistan had agreed to suspend sniping on Tuesdays and Fridays to allow trade caravans to pass through this back door to India. It was Friday now but the Afghan tribesmen, who did most of the sniping, often did not know what day it was. Apart from the dusty desolation of the Pass, it was hot beyond the accuracy of most thermometers and David was seized with a serious sunstroke three days later in Lahore, his temperature soaring alarmingly to 106. Richard remained with him until his recovery was certain and returned to Delhi. He was almost penniless now and his riding trains free became a necessity and, consequently, much harder. He was caught on the train from Delhi to Jaipur and, to avoid arrest, jumped from the train and walked twelve miles down the tracks to his destination.

He was back in Delhi on August 6, parting finally from David and intensely anxious to leave India. Rather than dodge conductors on the two-day ride to Calcutta, he frankly told the train guard he had no money. The guard allowed him to ride the first day in a coach, the second in the coal tender.

Checks from the *Commercial-Appeal* were in his mail in Calcutta and he sailed, again as a deck passenger, to Rangoon; Mandalay was next—"hardly worth the trip. Kipling made it famous but never saw it"—and then Mergui on the lower Burma Coast, Victoria Point on Burma's southern tip, and north again up the Pukchan River to Taplee to hike across the Malay Peninsula, an adventure that turned into a nightmare. It was preceded, however, by two encounters that set off an agony of introspection that, to his parents at least, was shocking.

On the boat from Mergui, a converted tug, Richard met a young, highly-educated Englishman who owned an island off the Burma coast, an island seven miles square where he lived all alone except for two Chinese servants and one hundred natives who worked his teak and camphorwood sawmill. His name was Ainesworth. Richard found him witty and charming and otherwise delightful and he accepted an invitation to spend several days on the island. It was a typical tropical paradise, with white beaches and green jungles splashed with flowers and birds of every conceivable color. Banana, orange, lemon, pineapple and coconut trees dropped their bounty everywhere. Ainesworth lived in his jungle retreat much as he would have lived in London. He was fastidious and impeccably groomed and he dressed formally for dinner every night, even though he sat there alone, reminiscent of a Somerset Maugham character. Richard was captivated by him and admired him greatly and he stayed as long as he could. It was never clear to him, however, why his host chose such an idle life.

A week later in Chumpon, waiting for the Bangkok train, Richard met another Englishman who was the antithesis of Ainesworth. He was a maintenance engineer with the railroad and he lived with two native mistresses, drank to excess, smoked constantly and insisted he had found happiness by divorcing himself from the hypocritical complexities of western civilization.

Richard spent a day as a guest of the engineer trying to puzzle out the disparity between these two men who were products of similar, if not equal, environment and education.

Perhaps the dissolute engineer is right, Richard suggested in an anguished letter to his father.

"Why seek fame and fortune, why seek anything? You never find it. Ambition is a devil that is never satisfied but only torments one . . . why assume responsibilities if it only makes you bitter and aged and unhappy?"

But Richard's torment was that he could neither accept responsibility nor reject it. He was doomed, he said, "to seek, seek all my life, never content with what I have, despising it after I have it. . . .

"I may get happiness from you and your friends, but from life, never, for it's an overpowering, brooding enemy that I must strain to preserve myself against."

Richard reached Taplee by dugout canoe, 65 miles upriver from Ainesworth's island, and found a guide to take him across the Peninsula. He would have preferred to ride an elephant but could not afford the $6 fee nor find an elephant owner willing to undertake the trip in the monsoon season. Richard slept two nights in a native hut, under relentless swarms of mosquitoes and dozens of tiny lizards crawling back and forth across his body, and started on the 40-mile walk across the Peninsula to the east coast of Siam the next morning with an aged Malay guide, grey-haired, toothless and unable to speak even a word of English. Richard had watched a cobra strike a dog on Ainesworth's island and he was apprehensive about them for the dog had died in a matter of minutes. He had also been warned repeatedly that the Malay Peninsula was impassable during the monsoons. The trail would be under water for vast distances and impossible to follow.

The rain fell in an endless deluge the first day and while the trail was not inundated it was a mud of such sticky consistency that it pulled Richard's shoes off until he tied them on with creepers. They forded swollen creek after swollen creek, with leeches flocking to them like iron filings to a magnet, and Richard expecting every moment to step on a crocodile. They made 12 miles the first day and stayed the night in a village whose delighted inhabitants served them such peppery curry Richard blistered the inside of his mouth and was unable to eat for two days.

The storm did not subside the next morning, either in volume of water or strength of wind which howled deafeningly through the matted jungle. Richard and his silent guide slogged on, through the mud, the maddened creeks, the resisting bamboo thickets. At two o'clock in the afternoon the rain and wind stopped and the sun came out and with it the wildlife that apparently had been in refuge from the storm. Birds, monkeys, harmless green snakes, and deer were suddenly flitting through the underbrush on either side, and it set Richard to worrying anew over the tigers, the poisonous snakes, and an assortment of other hostile animals for which this particular jungle was noted, and Richard was completely unarmed.

He thought, too, about how fear of danger often attracts danger, and how ignorance of it repels it and as he thought he detoured through a patch of grass to avoid the muddy path his guide had taken before him and stepped directly on a cobra. The snake was as startled as Richard but it responded in a flash. A coil of the snake slid up around Richard's ankle and its head reared back as its hood inflated and puffed out. Richard and the snake stared at each other for what seemed to Richard like five minutes during which he suffered not fear of death but only anger at his own stupidity. He was far from help and would surely die. Yet in fact, he reacted more quickly than the cobra, but it was a mechanical gesture for his mind was frozen. He struck at the snake with all his strength with a broken bamboo cane he carried in his right hand and hit it squarely on the tender side of its hood. And as he swung, he jumped. His foot slid free and he shot down the path, stumbling, falling, rising, stumbling and falling until at last he had caught up with his guide who was oblivious of the drama behind him. Richard felt no sensation over his escape for several minutes, then suddenly he was seized with violent trembling, the strength drained from his legs like water from a leaky bucket and he collapsed in the mud, unable to move. And all he could think was that it was wonderful to be alive.

❧ 5 ❧

Back in Memphis, Richard's father and mother bore a thinly concealed anxiety, and one that was growing stronger and more obvious as the months went on. In their letters to Richard, the fear that tragedy might befall him took the form of specific, personal admonitions. Beware "the criminal minds and diseased bodies" that proliferate in the unwashed corners of the world, his mother warned him, and she constantly feared that wherever her handsome son might be, he was never immune to the wiles of scheming and seductive women. Just how she visualized this hazard precipitating a colossal disaster, beyond Richard's appearing in Memphis with an olive-skinned wife, she never said. In time, however, her fears were reduced to one: that Richard would be killed—horribly, painfully and foolishly. And for years an icy band of fear closed about her heart whenever the phone rang or a telegram arrived.

For Richard's part, he was seeing too little of the seamy side of life in strange places, and as far as women were concerned, he had no great desires. His response to a number of contemporary American novels, mailed to him by his family and friends in the States, which took the new moral emancipation of women as their theme, was one of depression. His assessment of two books, *Cytherea* by Joseph Hergesheimer and *If Winter Comes* by A. S. M. Hutchinson was that they were sufficient "to drive any man to celibacy." Letters from his father occasionally contained gratuitous matrimonial counsel but all Richard could say was that he wondered "if I shall ever have the experience of reconciling my eccentricities to the eccentricities of a wife."

Richard turned up in Bangkok something of a hero. His

march across the isthmus was municipal gossip and his encounter with the cobra was a favorite dinner table topic everywhere, especially after he wrote an article about it for the Bangkok newspaper which paid him $20.

Princeton opened an abundance of social doors in Bangkok. The U.S. Consul, Maurice Dunlap, author of *Outwitting the Water Demons of Kashmir*, was a Princeton man, class of 1912, and so was the Secretary to the U.S. Embassy, a Mr. Williams, class of 1917. Richard regaled American officialdom at teas, dinners and luncheons with his adventures and he talked to Williams about a fellow classmate of Williams, F. Scott Fitzgerald, who had had tremendous success with a first novel, *This Side of Paradise*. Richard hadn't read it but promised to. At the time, novels of his age, the Jazz Age, seemed to irritate him; it was as though his contemporaries were achieving undeserved success. He was not envious, he was annoyed. He was further annoyed when his father sent him clippings of his articles in the *Commercial-Appeal* and found that in every one of them he had been identified by the editor as "a Memphis boy."

Richard was one of the first few Americans to visit Angkor Wat, the lost city of Indo-China some 300 miles up the Mekong River from Saigon. Five times the size of Washington, D.C. (in 1922, that is), Angkor is a complex of great carved stone temples built in the fourteenth century by a race of people called Khymers who mysteriously vanished and left their city behind, intact. The jungle swallowed it until 1861 when a French naturalist, Henri Mouhot, stumbled onto it while pursuing rare butterflies. The French government subsequently cleared the jungle from this architectural marvel and opened it to tourists in 1910, but few made the long up-river trip to see it.

Richard was stung on the left foot by an unknown insect while prowling around a cobra- and bat-infested Angkor temple. His foot swelled alarmingly and painfully and, although lanced twice by doctors in Saigon and Singapore, it did not heal until twelve days later when he landed in Surabaya, Java. The voyage and the enforced bed rest, however, enabled him to bring his travel notes up to date, and to complete magazine articles on Bangkok and Angkor Wat. After poking around Java and Bali for a week, Richard wrote to his father that he had seen enough of Asia to fear that the Asiatic's resentment of the Caucasian would one day lead them to sweep over the earth "to the ultimate extinction of the white race."

Broke again, Richard stowed away at Surabaya in an empty cabin on a ship bound for Singapore and was discovered after a day at sea. The captain admired Richard's nerve and did not clap him in irons, but allowed him to do token work to pay for his passage. Among other things, he was asked to read Thackeray's *Vanity Fair* aloud.

Richard still had the $100 his "Ammudder" had sent him, but he was determined to make his way on what he could earn, plus the stipend from his father. Back in Singapore, he went to the U.S. Consul to plead for help in reaching Hong Kong and found the Consul to be a fellow-Tennessean from Jackson, who knew the Halliburton family. As a result, he sailed as a deck passenger for $15 on the liner *Van Overstraten* whose purser took pity on Richard and gave him a second-class cabin without charge. In Hong Kong on November 16, Richard found a large bundle of mail, including several checks, and he calculated he had made $730 on his newspaper and magazine articles and that his trip was actually paying for itself. And the next day he had a cable from his father that the *National Geographic* magazine had bought his article on Tibet for $250. It gave him nearly $500 in cash which he spent on jade jewelry in Canton, saving only $100 to get him back to the U.S. by way of China, Siberia and Japan. He spent a weekend on the Portuguese island of Macao where he won $45 playing fan tan, and was on his way back to Hong Kong on the British excursion liner *Sui An* when it was sacked by sixty pirates who had been aboard disguised as passengers. Halfway between Macao and Hong Kong, they whipped out pistols, shot and killed two of the ship's four armed guards and wounded the captain and stripped all the tourist passengers of their money, clothing and valuables which they loaded into a fleet of junks that had been standing by.

Richard lost all his money, his shoes and coat. He tried unsuccessfully to sell an eye-witness account of the mass holdup to local newspapers but in Shanghai a week later he was offered a job as a reporter on an English-language newspaper there. He declined. In Peking he stayed at Princeton Court with Lenning Sweet, brother of a Lawrenceville classmate, Channing Sweet, and the manager of the YMCA in Peking. On Christmas Day, 1922, Richard was in Harbin, Manchuria, where the temperature was 20 degrees below zero, waddling about in a borrowed fur coat, his feet wrapped in burlap, and where he was shocked at the poverty and suffering of the White Russian refugees who had fled the Bolshevik terror. In Vladivostok, he saw enough of Communism to report:

> The Reds rule like iron and are a thousand times more autocratic than the autocrats they destroyed. They are giving up their wild theories one after another. They see it's impossible to enforce them, that the economic laws against which they revolted must prevail in the long run . . . Communism will resolve itself into a sane sort of government like England or America.

On January 9, 1923, his twenty-third birthday, Richard was in Kyoto and eight days later he was scaling Mt. Fujiyama after being warned that it was impossible to climb the 12,700-foot peak in mid-winter. He went alone, thirteen hours each way, and nobody would have believed he had done it if he had not taken a photo of the summit's crater. Broke again, he sold the story of his climb to the Tokyo *Advertiser* for $50. He also cabled the *Commercial-Appeal* in Memphis for a $50 advance on the story and got it. On January 31, he signed on as a seaman aboard the liner *President Madison* and sailed for Seattle where he was a house guest of the widow of a former Lawrenceville headmaster.

In Portland, he sold his Fuji story and pictures to the *Oregonian* for $35 and caught the train for Denver where he visited classmates and sold the same story to the *Rocky Mountain News* for $15. He stayed a day in Denver as a guest of Colorado

Governor William E. Sweet, father of his Lawrenceville room-mate, and moved on to Kansas City for a reunion with Mike Hockaday, his fellow-traveler when he began the great adventure twenty months before.

Another Princeton classmate, Edmund DeLong, was working as a reporter on the *Kansas City Star* and Richard took his Fuji story there. DeLong introduced Richard to the city editor who said, "It's a lousy story but I'll give you $25 for the photograph." Richard shrugged and held out his hand.

When he got to the railroad station, he had $40 in cash and he spent it for a compartment to Memphis aboard the Florida Limited, and on March 1 he arrived back in the red brick house his father had built at 1916 Central Avenue.

By the time the checks had all come in from the Memphis newspaper and various magazines (*Travel* published his Malay Peninsula adventure), Richard figured he had earned exactly $300 more than the trip had cost him and on April 23 he went to New York to make his further fame and fortune.

IV

The Making of a Celebrity

Provided a man is not mad, he can be cured of
every folly but vanity.

—JEAN JACQUES ROUSSEAU
(*Emile*)

◦§ I §◦

THE New York of Richard Halliburton was not the New York of the tough, languid and hedonistic New Generation that Scott Fitzgerald was writing about. Richard took a certain pride in the literary successes of a fellow Princetonian, but Fitzgerald's stories of jaded youth had no reality for him. Richard's world was still enchanted and success and fulfillment were natural consequences of talent and energy, both of which he possessed in abundance.

He stopped in Flint, Michigan, after leaving Memphis and bought a new Buick roadster, a gift from his father, and drove it to New York where, even in 1923, parking was impossible. He put the car in a public garage at $1 a night, took a room for himself in the YMCA on West 57th Street and went to work confident that the literary market place of the universe would soon recognize him. He spent a day sorting the boxes filled with his notebooks, his rejected magazine articles, and his hundreds of photographs and then began the heartbreaking rounds of magazine and newspaper syndicate editors and publishing houses, all of which alternately encouraged and rebuffed him. By the end of May he had been everywhere and was grimly deflated, even though in his letters home he assured his father, "We'll get there yet—you and Mother and I. Who can resist our united determination?"

Aching with nostalgia he drove to Princeton one Friday night to a dance, and spent the weekend at a classmate's summer place on Long Island. He went to Washington in a futile effort to sell some pieces to the *National Geographic* which, although it had published his Gibraltar story nearly a year earlier, was not in the market for Fujiyama or Bali. The only

bright note was that he had decided on the title for his book.
He would call it *The Royal Road to Romance*.

Richard had taken courses in public speaking at Princeton
and his father had frequently suggested that he consider becoming a lecturer, a special breed of public figure then receiving the adulation a later generation would lavish on popular vocalists. A kind of intellectual vaudeville, lecturing was
then blossoming into its second century, its origins credited to
Josiah Holbrook, a Millbury, Massachusetts, educator who
launched what became the lyceum movement in 1826. And
from that day forward, waves of authors, social commentators,
poets, travelers, pundits of all description and qualification,
spread over the nation to cajole, berate and occasionally educate the public. Sex and psychology became the most popular
topics, travel a close second, and then self-help and politics.
Lecturers, too, were the originators of the Great Questions of
the day—Where Are We Now? Where Do We Go from Here?
What's the Matter with Us? or Why Be Afraid?

Authors whose books sold poorly could make a decent living
on the lecture circuits, if they could endure weeks of living in
Pullman cars and saying the same thing over and over again,
trying to make each lecture sound like the first.

Talking authors reached their zenith during the 1930's when
there were as many as 200 of them almost simultaneously on
tour, ranging in stature and earning power from first novelists
who were paid $25 fees up to Sinclair Lewis who collected
$1,000 per lecture and gave twenty-three of them one year. Dale
Carnegie, whose pitch was how to be successful, negotiated
what was believed to be a record contract for a single tour—
$33,000 for fifty-five talks.

Lecturers also wrote their reminiscences, some of which sold
better than the books on which they lectured, and they wrote
books on how to be a successful lecturer, how to make after-
dinner speeches, how to develop word power, how to speak
effectively, and guide books which provided usable speech texts,
easily adapted to any speaker, situation or subject by a few
simple changes in wording.

The phenomenon of lecturing lured a number of foreign celebrities who made a great deal of money telling Americans how rude and provincial they were. It was after a U.S. speaking tour that Oscar Wilde observed that Americans were the only people on earth who would pay to hear themselves insulted.

Nearly all the lecture circuits were controlled by about three dozen high-pressure New York agents who had a nationwide network of representatives. They took twenty-five percent of the fee, or fifty percent if they had to advance the lecturer's travel expenses. In return, they sold the speaker to the sponsors, published vivid advertising brochures, handled all the bookings and arranged travel schedules.

Richard soon came to discover the truth of the Broadway axiom, subsequently attributed to A. J. Liebling, that New York is a town for winners, not for losers. His assaults on the temples of publishing were ill-organized and inconsistent. He went from place to place, from McClure's to the Bell Syndicate to King Features to Scribner's to Doubleday-Doran. He was flatly rejected at some, his wit and energy admired at others, and those who could bring themselves to assess his writing had one word for it: immature. *American* magazine wasn't even remotely interested in his exotic adventures, but he later had a note from editor H. L. Mencken saying that if Richard ever wrote any pieces about the U.S., Mencken would like to see them.

"I abominate this life here," he confessed in a letter home. ". . . New York has been inhospitable. It's every man for himself here. They trample on those that fall down."

His book, which he hoped to assemble out of the rejected articles and his voluminous notebooks, was an awkward project for publishers to envision for there appeared to be a vast gulf between the rumpled assortment of manuscript Richard displayed and his accompanying description of the book which he articulated so enthusiastically.

Finally, it became clear that he would simply have to sit down and write. But this would take time and, for reasons which eluded him, he had the sensation of time running out, and of the need to do something immediately realized. He set aside his hopes of literature and presented himself and his bundles of photographs at lecture agencies. It was the first of June when he did this, and most of them told him he was too late for the coming season, that bookings were filled and promotion too far under way. The only agency that seemed interested in him at all was one named Feakins, but in the absence of experience they doubted anything would come of this interest.

The oldest agency in the business, if not the biggest, Feakins was run by its founder, burly, enterprising William B. Feakins, known to his friends and acquaintances as "Pop." Fame and fortune, it was said, awaited the speaker he chose to include in his stable.

Richard hurried back to the YMCA where he was staying, remembering that the lobby boasted a speaker almost every night, and persuaded the manager to let him give a talk the following week on a Tuesday night. He invited a representative of the Feakins Agency to attend and was surprised when he did. Richard had decided to tell the story of his arrest in Gibraltar and he rehearsed it with a diligent zeal. But when the night of his lecture arrived, conditions could hardly have been worse. Richard had a high-pitched and somewhat strident voice that was drowned out by the constant movement through the lobby, by someone playing a piano in an adjoining room, and by a bagpiper on the street outside advertising a restaurant.

However, the Feakins man was impressed and hopeful that Richard would amount to something if he could get more experience. He sent him over to *Boy Scout Magazine* whose editors took days of his time discussing a lecture-writing job that never materialized, and to the Child Welfare Association which was desperate for speakers to appear—without fee—at various welfare shelters and orphan asylums.

His first talk was at a Queens home named "Sheltering Arms" and once again Richard persuaded Feakins to attend. Richard dazzled the 200 youngsters with animated stories of Gibraltar, the Matterhorn and the Malay Peninsula. He be-

came absorbed with his ability to hold their interest and forgot
about his hard critic in the back of the room. But when it was
over, the Feakins man shook Richard's hand heartily and said,
"that's the best talk I ever heard given to children" and signed
Richard up. Feakins would book him wherever possible at
whatever fee was available, and take twenty-five percent commission. The first talk was at a New Jersey women's club and it
paid $25. There is no record of its success.

In the meantime, Richard sought out other platforms himself
simply to gain experience and to develop his stories and style.
He drove 200 miles up the Hudson to a Hoosac Falls boys
school where a former Lawrenceville teacher was now headmaster, and scored a hit with the students. Stimulated by this new
success, Richard returned to his book with furious concentra-
tion and in less than two weeks he had converted his rejected
magazine pieces into 14 sample chapters which he submitted to
Scribner's. It only took the publishing house a week to reject it,
but the pain of failure was lessened by what Richard regarded
as the best "constructive criticism" he had yet received. He was
also receiving an abundance of advice from his mother at this
time on how to avoid the snares of the wily and seductive
women she was sure he was meeting every day. His repeated
declarations that he had "no time for women" failed to reassure
her. His parents came to Princeton in August and rented a
house there and Richard spent a leisurely, pleasant month with
them. They also drove his car back to Memphis for clearly he
could no longer afford to keep it.

It was the summer of President Warren Harding's death in
the Palace Hotel in San Francisco, and Vice President Calvin
Coolidge took the presidential oath of office at midnight from
his father, a notary public, in a farmhouse near Plymouth, Ver-
mont. It was a bizarre turn of history, and the staunchly democratic Halliburtons reflected on its significance. They had little
confidence in Harding, and less in Coolidge, and their uncer-
tainties were sustained a year later with the exposure of the oil
graft scandal of Teapot Dome and the publication of a book,
The President's Daughter, by one Nan Britton who accused the

late President Harding of having fathered her illegitimate child.

The Feakins affiliation seemed to be the turning point for Richard. By the end of the year, he had been booked for $2,500 worth of engagements, he had been offered the job (which he refused) as secretary of the Asia Society, he was sharing a comfortable East 39th Street apartment with Cecil Crouse, a Princeton classmate and talented pianist, and had been admitted to membership in the Princeton Club. But he had no more time for his book.

He was speaking now before a wide variety of audiences and he was surprised to discover that an animated talk which moved a lower East Side boys club to thundering applause and shouts of "More! More!" was frequently just as effective with a staid Newark church group or even the profound Ethical Culture Society in Manhattan.

He developed a repertoire of seven stories, to give himself variety rather than his audiences, and he rotated them, telling two or three at each lecture. But he also acknowledged that his performances were inconsistent in quality and interest and it troubled him. There were times when he was so nervous he could hardly talk, and other times when he could hold 500 people apparently spellbound for two hours. Despite this, his popularity on the Feakins circuit by midseason sent his name from 45th to 6th place on the agency's promotional circulars. This stiffened his self-confidence somewhat, but he still wasn't sure that his early success was not an accident of some kind. When he went home to Memphis for Christmas of 1923, he was seized periodically with fits of trembling and nausea that alarmed his parents. They all attributed it to nerves and agreed that he would slow down for the remainder of the tour.

Lectures in St. Louis, Kansas City and Culver, Indiana, followed New Year's end and he was back in New York by late January. His roommate Cecil Crouse had returned to Philadelphia so Richard took an apartment on 73rd Street just west of Central Park and for a time was caught up in a fashionable social digression. He attended the theater or the Metropolitan

Opera with the regularity of a patron with one of two new friends, music critic Alan Houghton or actor George Gaul, a fellow Lawrenceville alumnus then appearing on Broadway in *Seventh Heaven.*

Even then, Richard had no active attitude toward current affairs, but when former President Woodrow Wilson died in early February, Richard went to Madison Square Garden with 10,000 other New Yorkers to hear Rabbi Stephen S. Wise, among others, in a tortured eulogy to the thwarted advocate of the League of Nations, "the hope-bringer of mankind."

"New York is the coldest-blooded place on earth," said Richard afterward, "yet no other city can be as emotional when the occasion arises."

Richard made no further efforts that winter to work on his book. His plan now was to give the summer to it and send the manuscript, as fast as he could write it, to his father in Memphis who would edit it and have it typed for him. He was more confident now about the book, but he was also more confident about everything. By the first of May, Richard had given a total of 48 lectures for fees ranging from $15 to $100, and the last one was the hardest—an audience of 300 matronly women at an Eclectic Club luncheon at the Waldorf-Astoria Hotel. It was even harder than the one preceding it, the Boston membership of the Harvard Club. But the ladies loved him.

Toward the end of May Richard went to Siasconset on Nantucket Island where he had taken a room for the summer and where, he was determined, he would finish his book, find a publisher in the fall and see it in the bookstores by Christmas. He had written more than 300 pages of manuscript—three-fourths of the book—by August 8 when he suffered a crippling recurrence of trembling, nausea, rapid heart beat, and weakness and was told by a Nantucket doctor that he had a goiter and that it would have to be removed. He went into New York to a specialist instead and received a diagnosis of hyperthyroidism.

By mid-August he was in the Battle Creek Sanitarium, the scene of recovery from his boyhood illness, and despite the treatment and the enforced bed rest he managed to finish the book before he went home to Memphis in October. It was nearly 150,000 words—almost twice too long—and he was relying on his father to help him cut it. The Feakins Agency, meanwhile, had booked him into some $3,000 worth of lecture engagements beginning in Chicago November 10 and the pressure of the schedule gave him considerable anxiety.

His father returned with him to New York and in two weeks they had cut the manuscript by almost one-third, making the book less of a chronological chronicle of Richard's two-year vagabond journey.

His father hired a team of stenographers to re-type the manuscript and on the afternoon of November 9, moments before catching the train for Chicago, Richard boxed the book and sent it off with high expectations to Boni & Liveright, one of the more daring publishing houses, but they rejected it almost overnight. Between November and April, while Richard barnstormed the Eastern Seaboard and the Midwest with the frenzy of a one-man medicine show, a total of ten publishers turned down *The Royal Road to Romance* with remarkable unanimity of reaction: it was just too giddy and juvenile.

The deflation that Richard had suffered during his first weeks in New York was nothing compared to his new mood; it was one of absolute despair. He read and reread the unwanted manuscript, dog-eared and rumpled from its constant movement in and out of publishing houses, but he could find no way to improve it.

Early in April, Richard gave a talk at the Princeton Club in New York, of which he was a member and whose atmosphere and associations were vital to his self-respect. In the audience that night were Thomas R. (Tim) Coward, a New York editor with The Bobbs-Merrill Company, who later founded the firm of Coward-McCann, and David L. Chambers, the Bobbs-Merrill editor-in-chief from Indianapolis. Chambers was a Princeton graduate (1900) and had once worked as private secretary to Henry van Dyke, the famed author-educator-clergyman who had described Chambers as "the smartest man who ever came out of Princeton."

Richard's lecture platform performance had developed into one of rapid-fire delivery, wild gesticulations and pantomime, with a high-pitched voice that vibrated with enthusiasm. Chambers and Coward were both impressed with it and sought Richard out afterward. Bobbs-Merrill was then the only major house to which Richard had not sent his manuscript and he began to tout it slyly during his talk with the two editors who finally asked to read it.

Richard went home to Memphis in mid-April and stayed with his parents who had taken an apartment in the Parkview Hotel while the elder Halliburton was building a new house. Richard had been there less than a week when the following letter arrived from Coward in New York:

> Dear Mr. Halliburton:
> We are all enthusiastic about your manuscript and want to publish it. However, our entire editorial force and the outside readers are unanimous in thinking it should be cut to about 80,000 words. I shall be away this Saturday and Monday, so I wonder if you could come in Tuesday at some time convenient to you and we can talk it over.
> > Sincerely,
> > Thomas Coward

The letter had been delayed by being forwarded from Feakins in New York and it was followed by a telegram from Hewitt Hanson Howland, an editor with Bobbs-Merrill in Indianapolis.

BECAME SO INTERESTED THAT HAVE BEEN DOING SOME OF THE WORK I INTENDED ASKING YOU TO DO. SHALL MAIL TOMORROW A NUMBER OF CHAPTERS THAT WILL GIVE YOU A LINE ON THE JOB AND FROM WHICH YOU CAN DECIDE WHETHER TO GIVE ME THE GATE OR THE BROWN DERBY.

Howland was widely recognized in the publishing business as the discoverer of such talents as Mary Roberts Rinehart, Booth Tarkington, James Whitcomb Riley, George Barr Mc-Cutcheon and Gene Stratton-Porter. He remained with Bobbs-

Merrill barely long enough to finish editing Richard's book before he moved on to become editor of *Century Magazine*.

Richard left immediately for Indianapolis and spent ten days reducing the manuscript by nearly one-third under Howland's guidance. Richard was delighted with Howland, and with his wife who was the sister of humorist Irvin S. Cobb, because Howland allowed him to retain in the book "the singing, capricious spirit I value so highly."

However, neither Howland nor Chambers approved of the title, *The Royal Road to Romance,* which they considered hopelessly sophomoric, and it was the only point in which Richard would not yield.

"I'm sorry," he said, after hours of argument, "but I won't change the title. It's the whole point and aim of my book. Romance. If you don't want to publish it under my title, then it won't be published."

His argument expressed a belief, which he developed to a science in later years, that most people lead drab and uninteresting lives and that they want romance more than anything else. They are unable to "chase the horizon" themselves, by circumstance or nature, he contended, and they will settle for the vicarious experience because it is their only chance.

While Chambers was confident the book was salable, he was equally confident that it would take a more dramatic title to attract attention to it. However, in the end, he capitulated to Richard, with great misgivings. And before Richard left Indianapolis, the cover and jacket had been designed and 48 pages of photographs selected to illustrate the book. They also decided it would sell for five dollars which Richard feared was too high.

"I don't think it will sell over 5,000 copies unless you bring out a cheaper edition," he said. But he also shot off a thrilled note to the editor of the Princeton Alumni magazine for inclusion in the news notes of the class of '21.

"Bobbs-Merrill has signed on the dotted," the item said, "and it's all over but counting the royalties."

᪥ 2 ᪥

Richard had what one critic described as a "groveling admiration for creativity," and while he himself had a flair for lyric and purple phrases, his only inspiration came from history books and to them he turned, devoutly, whenever he was in need of an idea.

When Richard made his first trip around the world, he was following in the footsteps of his own fancy, and it occurred to him that it might be fun (and profitable, from the standpoint of a lecturer and author) to follow the trails of some historic figure whose exploits were popularly familiar and which he could use as the thread for his own narrative. He considered Napoleon's various marches of conquest, the route of the Crusades, and the Homeric adventures of the legendary Ulysses, who was vanquished in the Trojan war and who wandered for ten years through the Mediterranean before returning home to the island of Ithaca as its ruler. The last had at least two attractions; the irresistible romance of the legend with its ancient gods and heroic myths, and the fact that such a journey would take him to the land of his twin heroes, Lord Byron and Rupert Brooke. He made the choice almost without thinking about it and apart from a few New York conferences with his lecture management, delighted over the forthcoming publication of his book, he spent the weeks before sailing July 4, 1925 on the *Mauretania* soaking himself, as he put it, in Homeric lore, Greek mythology and maps of the Middle East. He also found two companions to sail with him—Roderic Crane of Omaha, a classmate from Lawrenceville, and actor George Gaul who was only going as far as Paris. Crane planned to spend a month with Richard, or perhaps two, depending on how amiably they got along. Crane, a school administrator on leave, was openly apprehensive about the unpredictable aspects of Richard's nature. Coincidentally, Richard's mother also sailed on the *Mauretania* for she was chaperoning seven Memphis college girls on a month's tour of Europe.

Richard and Crane hurried through Paris to Innsbruck and Vienna, then down the Danube to Budapest and, a day later, to Belgrade, "the full, dirty capital of Serbia," as Richard described it, where they caught the Orient Express for Constantinople.

Unlike the first trip, the second was organized and scheduled. Richard had promised his lecture agency he would be back before the end of the year, and he also wanted to visit Rupert Brooke's mother in England before returning for he had a half-formed idea of writing a biography of the British poet. His itinerary was simply that of Ulysses in *Homer's Odyssey,* a 10-year journey compressed into five months—from Ithaca to Ithaca by way of Troy, the isle of Jerba off North Africa, Cyclops in Sicily, Circe on the west coast of Italy, Charybdos and Scylla, Malta and Corfu. Richard would omit one adventure of Ulysses—the trip to Hell and back—but he would add some others. He would climb Mt. Vesuvius and Mt. Olympus and he would also visit the grave of Brooke on the isle of Skyros where, it was said, Ulysses had gone in search of Achilles. He would also swim the Hellespont, in tribute to Lord Byron who had done it a century before, and he would duplicate the 25-mile run of Pheidippides who brought the news from Marathon to Athens in 490 B.C. that the Persian armies invading Greece, 20,-000 strong, had been defeated on the beach by a mere 10,000 dedicated Athenians. The exertion of it all, of course, killed Pheidippides.

Outlining this last project to Crane, who was willing enough to watch his friend swim the Hellespont but who balked now, Richard could give no reason for his desire beyond saying, with alarming ardor, "but I want to FEEL what it was Pheidippides felt." He also longed, in braving the Hellespont, to be as near to Byron as he could get, and to the mythical Leander who swam the current to his death, all for the love of Hero, the vestal virgin.

Although Byron poked fun at these two tragic lovers in an irreverent verse, he changed his mind after swimming it himself and living for a time in a whitewashed cottage on the shore.

The Hellespont has not been called that since antiquity, but Richard, for romance's sake, would not refer to it as the Dardanelles, the name which appears on modern maps. It is a 40-mile salt water strait through which the Sea of Marmora flows into the Aegean Sea at the rate of two or three knots at slack tide and double that at flood or ebb tide. The Dardanelles also separate Asiatic Turkey from European Turkey and the Gallipoli Peninsula where 30,000 British soldiers died in 1915 trying to bridge the Dardanelles and seize Constantinople. As the sea route between the Black Sea and the Mediterranean, the Dardanelles and the Bosporus Straits have been a military strategic waterway since Alexander the Great took his troops across on a bridge of boats. Turkey lost the Dardanelles after the First World War but regained control in 1923 at the Conference of Lausanne, provided the strait was not fortified. When Richard and Roderic arrived, the Asiatic shore was heavily patrolled by Turkish troops who regarded every fair-skinned stranger as a British spy. They went to Abydos on the Asiatic side and stayed in the cottage Byron had occupied at a point where the Dardanelles is only a mile wide and where Byron, and Leander, made their famous swims.

Bad weather and nagging Turkish soldiers, who refused at first to give them permission to cross to Sestos, on the Gallipoli side, forced Richard to make his swim sooner than he had planned and very nearly ruined one of his first publicity stunts. He had arranged with a friend in Athens to report to *The New York Times,* where the friend had contacts, that Richard had drowned in mid-swim. He wrote his father and his publisher and informed them of the stunt, advising them to feign a grief mixed with uncertainty. But he made the swim before the letters reached the U.S. and both his publisher and his father said the story was preposterous.

Richard and Crane crossed to Sestos on August 10, 1925, in a Turkish fishing boat. The next morning it sailed upstream nearly two miles to allow for the distance the current would carry Richard downstream before he could reach Abydos which is on the tip of a peninsula jutting into the strait. Richard ate a can of sardines and, stripping to his shorts, waded in. The sun was bright and the air balmy but the water was so cold that in a few minutes he was numb. A wind arose and whipped up white caps which broke over his head, forcing him to swallow so much salt water that he was nauseated as well as numb. Crane and the fishing boat tagged along behind him, Crane taking photos all the way across, and two hours and five miles later Richard's knees, now blue with the cold, struck the rocky bottom not far from Byron's cottage. While his knees were blue, his back and arms and head were crimson from sunburn and the trip by steamer back to Constantinople was agony.

The story of Richard's drowning did not appear in the *Times* until September 6 and by that time he was in Athens, having covered all of Ulysses' tracks in Greece. He had been up Mounts Olympus and Parnassus, through the Vale of Tempe, the sacred haunt of the god Apollo, and he had been to Delphi and to the Acropolis and the Parthenon. He was deep in research on ancient Greece and he was consumed with rough chapters of his new book which he mailed home to his father to be edited and typed.

Crane had returned to the U.S. and although their months together had been more harmonious than Crane expected, there were many heated arguments. Crane was openly appalled over what he considered Richard's frivolous abuse of his talent.

"Why are you writing this romantic nonsense?" he asked, repeatedly. "The world needs serious writers and you have the intelligence and talent to write important books."

But Richard only laughed.

"The world doesn't really want philosophers and intellects," he argued, "the world wants escape—it wants romance. Life is hard and dreary for most people. They want to believe that there is something else and to wish they were lucky enough to enjoy it."

"But you're not doing anything worthwhile," Crane retorted, "you're throwing your own life away."

"No!" cried Richard, "I'm living life more than you or anyone else. Before I die I will have experienced every emotion and tested all my senses while you won't have lived at all."

The New York Times reported that Richard perished while making a return crossing of the Dardanelles, and it was only this that indicated to his father that the story was not true.

"There was no return swim planned," he told reporters who came to see him, but he didn't really know where Richard was and couldn't confirm his belief. The *Times* of September 6 reached Athens toward the end of the month, along with copies of the Memphis *Commercial-Appeal* which had also carried the story. Richard cabled an apology and an explanation to the Memphis editor, realizing that the world had thought him dead, assuming anybody cared, for nearly three weeks, but he lied his way out of it.

. . . EXHAUSTED, I WAS PICKED UP ON SECOND SWIM BY SAILBOAT, LANDED AT TROY REMAINED THREE DAYS UNAWARE SPREADING RUMOR . . . WENT INTO WILDERNESS ON MT. OLYMPUS, NO MAIL RECEIVED OR SENT FOR MONTH. MY OWN CARELESSNESS TO BLAME FOR MISINFORMING STORY. TERRIBLY SORRY.

He also sent an embarrassed letter to Chambers at Bobbs-Merrill. The story had gone too far, he said, as "I only wanted to remain dead for a week or 10 days."

Richard went out to the island of Skyros, on a holy pilgrimage to the grave of Rupert Brooke who died there in 1915 of blood poisoning at the age of twenty-eight while serving as a subaltern in the Royal Navy. He climbed the rocky hillside to the olive grove and stared at the raised marble slab gravestone, remembering the memorial tablet that hangs in Rugby Chapel with its familiar inscription, "If I should die, think only this of me: that there's some corner of a foreign field that is forever

England. . . ." He wanted to cry, but all he could manage was a lump in his throat.

That night, he wrote a touching letter to Brooke's mother in Rugby and begged to be allowed to visit her. Her reply, which he received a month later in Naples, was neither an invitation nor a rejection and he resolved to call on her.

Before he left Athens, Richard took the bus to Marathon and walked the 25 miles back, over the hills, just as Pheidippides had done. He stopped at a wayside bistro for water but drank wine instead and when he finally reached his hotel he was staggering slightly.

From Athens he went to Sicily and its western coast where Ulysses battled the Cyclops, then to Malta and to Jerba, half-way along the north African coast toward Tripoli, where Ulysses lingered with the lotus-eaters but where Richard went sponge fishing and lounged on the beach in a bower of lavender crocuses.

The trip had been a heady one for Richard immersed himself, as he said, in the personalities of the characters he emulated and in this mood of rich reflection and experience he thought of the title for his next book. He would call it *The Glorious Adventure* and no publisher would talk him out of this one, either.

He was in Tunis on Thanksgiving Day, hoping to find some American newspapers with reviews of *The Royal Road to Romance* which had come out in late October, but there were none. Nor did he see any in England when he arrived there December 6 but he scarcely had time to look before catching the last afternoon train from London to Rugby. He had written to Mrs. Brooke that he was coming and he could only hope that she would let him in, which she did. He arrived in Rugby at 7 p.m. and checked into a hotel where he dressed and had dinner and got to the Brooke home at 8 o'clock. The cottage was almost in the shadow of the famous school, where Rupert received his education, on the sloping hillside above the banks of the Avon. Although Mrs. Mary Ruth Cotterill Brooke had lost her husband and all her three sons (one by illness and two in the war), she was less a figure of tragedy to Richard than a personification of stern reticence. She was brusquely cordial, in that she permitted him to remain with her before the fire in her living room for two hours; she looked with interest at his photographs of Skyros, and listened in a politely diffident way to his boyish praise of her dead poet son, but she told him nothing. He found it hard to assess her, beyond hoping that he had made inroads on her reserve without knowing the precise reasons for it.

"She is much as I expected," Richard said later. "Sensitive poets often have such mothers, vital, domineering, strong." In any event, she had not discouraged him, and he left England the next morning aboard the *Mauretania*.

Richard was in Memphis for Christmas before he found out what the critics thought, generally, about his book. They were slow to review it, which annoyed him, and opinion was so extremely divided that their comments seemed useless.

"*The Royal Road to Romance* is evidence that its author had a riotously happy time," said the New York *Herald-Tribune*, deploring his "bumptious juvenility" and adding, "but it is a book that lacks the perspective of good taste . . . Only doting acquaintances will be interested in a travel document of this sort. . . ."

The *Saturday Review of Literature* was kinder: "Mr. Halliburton writes vividly and much of his description is painted in warm romantic colors. Of course, his observation is superficial . . . but one cannot deny the intrinsic interest of his picturesque story."

The *Dallas News* dismissed him as one of those "college boys from wealthy families who occupy the boring intervals between social seasons by acting as amateur international tramps. Only one thing saves the book from being completely worthless. That is the impudence of the author. . . ."

The Los Angeles *Times* reviewer was spellbound. "The enjoyment derived from reading [it] may be likened to the enjoyment of small children watching a magician who brings rabbits from empty hats and does all sorts of mysterious things . . .

Between the drab covers of this fascinating book comes even more wonderful things. . . ."

Sunset magazine eventually termed the book "a signal service, proving that novels are not the only books that can sell more than 50,000 copies in these unregenerate days. . . ."

The New York *World* praised it as being full of "life, swift movement, unending variety," and the Detroit *News* ecstatically rated it "a story of amazing adventure told with captivating charm."

But it took the Columbia College *Spectator* to put its editorial finger on the heart of the matter. *"The Royal Road to Romance,"* it said, prophetically, "is the best substitute available for those unable to make a similar trip." Perhaps it was this, above all the elusive intangibles of the book business, that inched the book onto the best seller lists at the end of January, 1926. In April, sales had reached 30,000, and by the end of 1926 the book had set what became its annual sales total—100,000 copies. And with the book's success came Richard's ascent into and across the heavens of public adulation, and later through the brimstone of ridicule from the hard core of literary criticism. Although high-placed scorn troubled him at the outset, Richard soon took a perverse delight in it and made as much fun of his critics as they did of him. He was safe, he believed, within an impregnable armor of popular fame and money. The only threat to his peace of mind came from himself, for he wanted the approval of the literary arbiters, yet he saved his ego by reminding himself that few of his critics, at the age of twenty-six, were making $70,000 a year.

◈ 3 ◈

With his sudden fame, Richard saw himself as the vicarious fulfillment of the daydreams of the little man and he began to act the part with the same gusto that ignited his writings and his lectures. He had taken to wearing a derby hat toward the end of his last lecture tour and he now embellished this trademark with a black silver-tipped cane, spats, a double-breasted Chesterfield overcoat, pearl grey suede gloves and an assortment of flamboyant neckties. When he appeared in this regalia on the railroad platform of some Kansas prairie town, he had to admit he was also attracting attention which, he knew, was a factor in the sale of books. To the amused reproaches of his friends, some of whom were a trifle embarrassed by this vagrant showmanship, he was apt to reply, with his little boy grin, "I don't care what people say about me, as long as they buy my books." He didn't mean it, but he clung to success as a good substitute for respect.

He set out from Memphis on his 1926 tour in mid-January, making a broad sweep through the Midwest on his way to Chicago where he heard Mary Garden sing "Louise" and where he discovered that perhaps he was more important than he even imagined. Fanny Butcher invited him to write a piece for her "Confessions" column in the *Chicago Tribune* and he did so with more self-revelation than he may have intended. "I wish, instead of *The Royal Road to Romance,* that I had written *Don Quixote.*"

Marshall Field's department store gave him a huge reception, with most of Lake Shore Drive's female society in attendance, despite a raging blizzard, and for the titillated matrons thronged about him, Richard inscribed copies of his book as follows: "Here's all that's fine, books and old wine, boys be divine to ————." Brentano's main store on Michigan Boulevard filled its show window with copies of *The Royal Road* flanking a giant photo of Richard and a poster which proclaimed "The Outstanding Travel Book of the Year."

The Chicago Adventurers Club toasted him at a 60-cent plate luncheon and in Cleveland he was the guest speaker at the annual Rotary Club convention. A Baltimore bookstore promoted a forthcoming lecture by touting him, in letters sent to hundreds of its customers, as the author of "the best travel book that ever was, is or will be." He dashed back to Memphis for a lecture at the South Side High School and was irked at a commentary which appeared the next day in the school newspaper: "Some may be skeptical, but throw it aside and hope Mr. Halliburton hurries back."

He had not yet ceased to worry about critics, or even ordinary readers, detecting incidents in the book which, while not altogether invented, took certain liberties with reality. Many of the people Richard met in his travels, for instance, he would describe as he wished them to be, rather than as they were. His purpose was not deception, or even self-glorification, but a determination that his only chance for success lay in making travel synonymous with adventure and adventure—no matter how unpleasant—synonymous with romance. In relating his ascent of the Matterhorn, he described himself as being struck dumb by the beauty and magnificence of the scene, and Hockaday as being so irreverently indifferent to the majestic surroundings that all he could think of to say was, "Gee, Dick, I can actually spit a mile." In truth, both of them were so exhausted, and not a little frightened, that they could hardly speak at all. But why climb a mountain, Richard reasoned, if glory isn't the goal?

Ironically, the only portion of the book anyone ever challenged was his moonlight swim in the Taj Mahal pool which he recorded with as much accuracy as he could muster. His sole departure from the truth was in failing to mention, to avoid diluting the romance of it all, his anxiety that he would be caught and ignominiously ejected, if not jailed.

Richard's Taj Mahal swim was disputed for years by other travel writers who said there was no pool in the Taj more than three inches deep. This was untrue, and an astonishing accusation, because the four-foot-deep pool in which Richard had immersed himself is clearly visible in most standard tourist guide photos of the Taj.

Richard dismissed most of these criticisms but one—an article by humorist Corey Ford in *Vanity Fair* was so stinging that Richard and Bobbs-Merrill threatened a lawsuit. Ford investigated the matter, found he had indeed made a mistake and apologized in a subsequent article.

The momentum of Richard's ascent in the world of authorship now was reflected in his lectures which drew ever-larger crowds. More than 1,500 people cheered him at the Philadelphia Forum in April and he received an equally enthusiastic reception from the membership of the National Geographic Society in Washington, which paid him $400, his highest fee to date, even though he appeared in the wake of explorer Roy Chapman Andrews just back from one of his famed expeditions into the mysterious regions of Central Asia.

Perhaps some of his platform popularity stemmed from the brochures mailed that year by the Feakins Agency to thousands of clubs, schools, colleges, museums, town halls and assorted societies, describing Richard as "a refuge from reality, an adventure genius who brings with him the beat of the sea and the sweep of winds and the glamor of far places." Not everybody felt that he lived up to his advance billing. After telling the Buffalo Historical Society all about the Hellespont, Mt. Olympus and his Marathon run into Athens, he found the *Buffalo Express* off-handedly reported it all in a story headlined QUEER FEATS DESCRIBED BY GLOBE TROTTER.

But after a particularly polished performance before the Brooklyn Institute of Arts and Sciences, a *New York Post* reporter in the audience confessed he was enthralled. "The

North Pole hasn't seen him yet, nor has Mars, but he is still young," he wrote in a review thick with superlatives. And it was much the same everywhere, from Principia College in St. Louis to New York's exclusive Spence School for Girls. A Boston department store was paralyzed when three times the capacity of its 600-seat lecture hall sought admission and when he appeared at Princeton, in whose campus and alumni publications the book had been heavily advertised, he was hailed as "Princeton's vagabond extraordinary." To a reporter who interviewed for the *Daily*, Richard was a pillar of modesty. His first book was a trifling thing, he said, and did not merit a place in literature. He was, however, working on four other books which he described as "important." Princeton President John Grier Hibben, to whom he had proudly sent an inscribed copy, wrote him a note of appreciation and oblique praise. "I almost read your fascinating book in one sitting and I congratulate you upon the remarkable opportunities you yourself created to see this wonderful world of ours."

Richard was now being interviewed constantly by newspaper reporters and magazine writers, including one from *Physical Culture* whose editors were amused at Richard's arrogant dismissal of physical fitness. "All an athlete needs," he said, "is inspiration. That's what enabled me to swim the Hellespont. I didn't train at all." *American* magazine interviewed him as "a slender blue-eyed boy who has dared to live his dreams, who has fought and laughed his way from Spain to Siberia" and later asked him to write an article about "The Romantic Corners of the World."

His fame, too, had crept abroad. Princess Murat invited him to come to her suburban Paris estate for the summer, as did Alex Thiers, grandson of the French President. Playwright John van Druten wrote from England suggesting that they tour Norway together.

Mixed in with all the other praise was a modest accolade from somebody who counted although Richard, with characteristic bravado, paid it slight attention. It was from Burton Holmes, the grand old man of travel lecturers, then in his thirtieth year. Although Holmes had never met Halliburton, "I believe he's the real thing and his writings are interesting. Right now, I'm puzzled as to how to put the romantic touch to my lectures."

Although *The Royal Road* was technically a best seller, it appeared at the bottom of most lists and it wasn't until after the American Booksellers Association convention in St. Louis in April, 1926, where Richard charmed the membership, a majority of whom were women, that his book moved upward toward the heights dominated by Carl Sandburg's *Lincoln* and John Dos Passos' *Manhattan Transfer*.

Richard had been something less than frugal about the money he was earning. His stipend from his father had ceased, because it was no longer necessary, and Richard resolved not to end up broke like so many celebrities he had heard about who spent all their short-lived fortunes. He instructed Bobbs-Merrill to withhold the first $2,000 of royalty payments and buy a bond "for self-protection." But two months later he was borrowing from his publishers against unearned royalties. How he had managed to spend everything, he could not say.

⤜§ 4 §⤐

Richard ended his lecture tour in New York and stayed there until the end of July, 1926, writing magazine pieces, being interviewed by magazines and radio, sunbathing on Fire Island, and attending an endless round of parties and dinners with the result that he made very little progress on his book which was due at the publisher in November. Early in August he went home to Memphis and moved in with his parents at the Park View Hotel. He slept until 10 o'clock every morning, breakfasted, walked four miles round trip to the Memphis City Club for handball or a swim, had dinner with his mother and father and worked until 2 a.m. on a rented typewriter. This routine enabled him to complete all but two chapters of *The Glorious Adventure* by the end of September when he returned to New York.

Among the Halliburtons' neighbors at the Park View were Louis N. Geldert and his wife, Grace, who as Grace Duffie Boylan had been one of Chicago's leading newspaperwomen. She had been a reporter for the famed and short-lived *Inter-Ocean,* and later a columnist for the *Post* and for the McClure Syndicate and she was the first woman the Chicago Press Club admitted to membership. Following the death of her first husband, Robert J. Boylan, she had married Geldert, who was publisher of the *Cotton Oil Press* and moved with him to Memphis where she began writing novels, poetry and juvenile books with impressive prolificacy and success.

Mrs. Halliburton, who was an intensely active figure in the literary club life in Memphis, soon cultivated the friendship of this accomplished writer and when Richard arrived, she intro-

duced them. Like most women of late middle years, Mrs. Geldert was enchanted with handsome Richard, with his gentle
southern manners, his sprightly conversation, and his conspicu-
ous devotion to his mother.

Mrs. Geldert discovered that Richard was contemplating a
trip to California and she immediately began writing a series of
glowing letters of introduction to her son, Malcolm Stuart Boylan, who had ascended through the ranks of newspaper reporting, press agentry and screen writing to become executive
producer of the Fox Film Corporation and a member of the
triumvirate then in command of the studio in what was still its
halcyon period. If Mrs. Geldert's intent was to give Richard
entree to Hollywood, her efforts missed. With each succeeding
eulogy to "this darling young man," Boylan's antipathy
mounted to heights that alarmed even him. "I haven't met the
sonofabitch," he said, "and already I hate him."

Richard delivered *The Glorious Adventure* manuscript in
person to Chambers in Indianapolis in mid-October and
begged for stringent criticism. "It's a true narrative," he told
Chambers, "with buckets of bright paint flung over it." But he
was worried, he said, that his readers might think it was fiction.

He went on to Chicago for a lecture before a mammoth audience in Orchestra Hall, then to Fort Wayne, St. Louis and
Pittsburgh, returning to Indianapolis in late October to hear
Chambers' critique of the book. Chambers wanted less Homer
and more Halliburton, and the two of them argued for a day
and settled on a series of compromise revisions.

Richard had his first genuinely unpleasant lecture in Stamford, Connecticut, a few days later. The aggressive personality
of the women's club president there irritated him and he struck
back by saying he would only talk, he would not show slides.
The woman, who had obtained a screen, projector and an oper-
ator, threatened to call off the lecture. Richard threatened to
give his lecture in the park. The woman backed down but
when the lecture was over she refused to pay Richard.

Bobbs-Merrill gave a reception for him in mid-November at

the Waldorf where he was introduced to the assembled New York literary throng by Thomas Crowell, the owner of *Colliers*, the *Woman's Home Companion* and *American* magazine.

Richard rented a cottage in East Orange, New Jersey, and finished the revision of *The Glorious Adventure* in a month and resumed lecturing. He went home for Christmas and left for California the day after New Year's, stopping briefly in Tucson to visit his mother's sister.

He had several lectures scheduled in California but his first objective was the Fox Studio offices of Malcolm Stuart Boylan. Richard had received some inquiries, through his publisher, about the sale of film rights to *The Royal Road* and he erroneously assumed from this, and from the head-swelling attention he had received on the lecture circuit, that he was a celebrity of national importance upon whom Hollywood was only waiting to dance attendance.

Boylan, who was known throughout the industry as Mike and as a man whose innate graciousness was the biggest threat to his career, detested Richard on sight but concealed it fairly well. Richard had the notion that his derby and cane would attract no attention in filmdom so he enriched his appearance with a red cummerbund that nearly provoked Boylan into throwing him out in the street, but instead he took Richard on a tour of the studio. There were no films shooting at the moment, and Boylan apologized for the absence of stars, but he did introduce Richard to Saul Wertzel, the terrible-tempered president of Fox, and to Winfield Sheehan, the third member of the ruling troika. Boylan also took Richard to lunch at Montmartre on Sunset Boulevard, a restaurant that was the 1920's forerunner of the Brown Derby, and Richard's crimson-streaked appearance on the threshold shocked the otherwise suave maitre d', known only as Alex the Mexican, into an open-mouthed stare, and the assembled diners into silence followed by laughter.

Montmartre, too, was temporarily bereft of stardom and the red-faced Boylan could only point out to Richard, who was totally unruffled by his reception, such lesser luminaries as screenwriter Waldemar Young, the grandson of Brigham Young, and actor Marshal (Mickey) Neilan.

Boylan told Richard that Fox wasn't the least interested in *The Royal Road,* although it did buy the rights several years (and managerial hierarchies) later for $15,000. Richard was plainly crestfallen and before he left Los Angeles he called twice at a miniature hacienda in west Beverly Hills where Boylan lived with a cream-white Lincoln convertible, a Negro chauffeur and 16 great Danes. These surroundings intimidated Richard and he later reported that Boylan was "an odd sort, with none of his mother's peculiar sensitiveness, but very bright and good company." Hollywood, said Richard, was "demoralizing."

He spent an evening in Pasadena with his millionaire cousin, Erle Halliburton and his family, and in Culbertson Hall there he delivered one of his more outrageous lectures which began:

> Don't be steady, women; don't be steady, men. God made the world so large for restless people that when you feel that urge to be off on the Royal Road to Romance, rebel against the prosaic mold into which you are being poured and fare forth in search of the beautiful, the joyous and the romantic.

And it was in Pasadena that intense lionization set in. Richard was deluged with dinner, luncheon and party invitations from prominent Pasadenans and the socially-significant from adjoining San Marino. He accepted several, including one given by Carrie Jacobs Bond, enjoying the fortune such songs as "A Perfect Day" had earned her, and another where he met Scott Fitzgerald for the first time, a brief and superficial encounter.

Richard barnstormed his way north, often making two appearances a day, to San Francisco where he lectured in the authors series at Paul Elder's bookstore and where he met novelist Charles Norris, the husband of novelist Kathleen Norris, who was openly admiring and took Richard to lunch at the Fairmont Hotel.

"I read your book," said Norris, "and I enjoyed it thoroughly." It was substantial praise and Norris followed it by inviting Richard to spend a few days on the family ranch at Saratoga in the coastal mountains south of San Francisco.

Los Angeles had been a kind of early courtship by California for Richard's affections and after he had spent a few days at the Norris ranch, he was enraptured with the golden state, with its eternal sunshine, its breezy informalities, its friendly inhabitants, its gentle pastoral scenery knitted to the grandeur of the Pacific coastline.

The Norris ranch was teeming with children and Richard became one of them. He romped through orchards and vineyards and over the hills like a schoolboy on vacation and delighted in the Norris custom of breakfast at dawn, cooked over an open fire on a mountain ridge above the valley.

Kathleen and Charles Norris had only one child, a son, but also living with them were Kathleen's brother, Mark, and his wife and children, and poet William Rose Benet and his three children. Benet had been married to Kathleen's sister, Teresa, who had died. The Benet children were not motherless, by definition, but Benet's second wife was novelist Eleanor Wylie who didn't hide the fact that she had no understanding of, and little patience with, children.

Richard spent most of his time with the youngsters, roaming the countryside like a pack of pixies, and it was only merest chance that Kathleen Norris discovered Richard masterminding construction of a tree house in the crotch of an aged oak, some 20 feet off the ground.

"You'll all fall out of there and break your necks," she said, and no one was more disappointed than Richard. "You're like a little boy," she admonished him, more than once.

Richard told the youngsters stories by the hour, and later proposed to the older ones that they accompany him on a trip around the world. He was halfway serious, visualizing himself as the leader of an expedition of moppets traipsing through strange and faraway places, and they all trooped up to Kathleen to gain her consent.

"Who'll take care of you?" she asked them.

"I will," replied Richard, confidently.

"I know," Kathleen retorted, "but who'll take care of you?"

His San Francisco visit concluded with a temporarily disastrous luncheon in his honor in the Oak Room of the St. Francis Hotel, attended largely by booksellers and reviewers. Richard was still piqued over the reviews of his book and his talk was, perversely, a tribute to booksellers, a gaffe which drove several reviewers from the room. And when he lectured that night in the Scottish Rite auditorium to a mob of 2,000—200 of them sitting on stage with him—Richard's mind went blank. After several moments of embarrassing silence, Richard staring panic-stricken toward the ceiling, the audience began to leave. Richard immediately fainted and was carried into the wings where he regained consciousness but became violently ill. He recovered completely after a night's sleep and, despite everything, the San Francisco *Examiner* headlined him: HERO AUTHOR IN TOWN—HAS MADE OVER $1 MILLION. It was a pardonable exaggeration.

Richard returned to Los Angeles for an overnight visit with a new friend, actor Rod La Rocque, a silent screen idol, and then resumed his western tour, his health and composure apparently restored.

He took Salt Lake City by storm on February 3, and was annoyed over a newspaper article linking his popularity with that of writer Elinor Glyn, the novelist who coined the word "It" as the synonym for sex, and whose racey sophisticated novels were then selling out of all proportion to their quality.

"People think I'm a sort of male Elinor Glyn," he peevishly told a reporter who buttonholed him at the railroad station. "People think my book is ten short cuts to the grand passion with sixty illustrations. That is not me nor my book. My book is only the story of my attempt to realize my romantic dreams— dreams of climbing romantic mountains, swimming romantic rivers. To me, sex and romance have nothing in common."

It was standing room only in Seattle where his lecture was reviewed by the *Town Crier* as two hours of holy writ.

"Mr. Halliburton sent us back home to dust off the red hot

shoes lying in the closet and to fare forth, for to see and for to admire. So easily we fall into ruts, mentally and physically . . . laying up no treasures for the future. . . ."

In Pocatello, Idaho, the *Tribune* thought he merited a front-page editorial: "A wonderful thing . . . to have as our guest . . . a young man who has no special message beyond taking us outside our own smug personalities and leading our imagination to those far-off places of which we have all dreamed and sometimes hoped to see. . . ."

Working his way east from Portland, he appeared to be gathering momentum in terms of audience appeal, and in Washington in March he spoke before the National Geographic Society to a mob of 4,000, his biggest yet.

Richard had been preceded to the Denver lecture season by journalist-adventurer Lowell Thomas and he would be followed by Count Felix Graf von Luckner, the World War I German Naval hero who was then regaling Americans with accounts of all the U.S. ships he had sunk. Either of them, apparently, would have been preferable to a Denver *Post* reporter assigned to follow Halliburton about for the day. "Never before have the feminine hearts of Denver fluttered so flutteringly," the reporter later wrote in describing a frantic bookstore autographing party, but he relented somewhat in relating Richard's advice to youth with nomadic yearnings.

"One needs the proper background for vagabondage. Otherwise, to wander willy-nilly around the world would be a fruitless and unenjoyable task. . . . My books are nine-tenths an appreciation of the arts, not just the rambles of a tramp."

It was the reporter's further observation that Richard was a "modern writer who refuses to starve in a garret for the sake of his art. He knows his verbs and adjectives and everything about a writer's craft, and he also knows his dollars and cents."

In Lincoln, Nebraska, he had been a dinner guest of the governor, and in Rochester, Minnesota, Dr. and Mrs. Charles Mayo gave a luncheon in his honor. From there he had zigzagged back and forth across Illinois, Indiana, Ohio, New

Hampshire, Pennsylvania, giving 60 lectures in as many days, arriving in New York in mid-May for the publication of *The Glorious Adventure* and a staggering round of cocktail parties and assorted social exercises. He lectured at Smith, Wellesley and Vassar, where he attended the graduation prom and danced every dance—each one with a different girl, several of whom were briefly infatuated with him.

Because of his popularity, the reviews of the new book appeared immediately after publication and they were equally as extreme as before.

"The author is too exuberant, too cheerful, too narcissistic," said the New York *Evening Post*. "But the picture of the author posing happily and with infectious grin against a column of the Parthenon makes a reviewer realize that youth must be served. . . ."

The *Saturday Review of Literature* said the book contained less information about the Greek lands than a dozen average volumes on the subject, "and as for the spirit of the countries, that is so swamped in the high spirits of Mr. Halliburton that little of it reaches the reader. Yet if you want an animated narrative, here it is."

The Glorious Adventure is a bore, suggested *Time* magazine, and its author is a "romantic, poetic, enthusiastic, dauntless, sparkling, bubbling, impetuous, adventurous, dramatic, enthralling, etc., playboy." *Time* deplored Richard's tendency to "substitute romance for violence and when he mentions a female companion, he always assures us that they stayed in separate hotels."

The Catholic Vigil, in contrast, was ecstatic. "I wonder if readers understand that it is at least five times as difficult to produce a charming book like this than it is to produce an immortal masterpiece of mere erudition on the same general theme of exploration. Any drudge can do the second thing, but it takes a sublime blend of charming gentleman and clown to do the first."

The New York *Herald-Tribune* had similar praise. "The

most amusing, consistently readable, original book of travel
. . . (and) an effective blow against the tedious volumes
which travelers write. . . ."

Some critics didn't really know what to make of it.

"There is rather too much author and too little experience,"
said the Springfield *Republican*, "but Mr. Halliburton is so
convinced of his power to transmute self-conscious adventure
into words that the reader is almost overwhelmed by his breezy
self-assurance . . . the narrative is spirited and amiable and for
the most part is at least as much worth reading as most movies
are worth seeing."

Richard may not have expected to be hailed as a literary
giant, but he hoped for better treatment than he got and once
more he took refuge from the critics in his undeniable success.
He toured the eastern states briefly, holding endless autograph
parties in bookstores, most of which were mobbed by clamoring
fans. At Halle's in Cleveland he autographed—and the store
sold—500 books in one afternoon. It was the same afternoon
that Charles Lindbergh made history of another kind by flying
alone across the Atlantic.

The bookstore autograph party has long since gone the way
of other quaint, and slightly incredible, American customs, but
in the 1920's, it was a standard bookselling device. Most bookstores were run by women who, to a large extent, dictated their
customers' reading tastes, or at least knew what they were. New
books were automatically shipped to a large list of regular customers who were simply billed on a monthly basis. And a mass-
mailed note from the store proprietor, advising of the immi-
nent appearance of a real, live author was frequently enough to
start a riot.

A substitute for this was what was called the autograph tip, a
sheet of paper the same size as the pages of the book, which the
author signed at his convenience, usually by the hundreds.
These were gummed along one edge and were inserted by booksellers into the book. Richard signed thousands of "tips" and
mailed them off to Bobbs-Merrill for national distribution.

Although Richard was already thinking about his next book,

torn between emulating the adventures of Napoleon and Richard Coeur de Lion, he still cherished the hope of writing something important. He abandoned his self-promotions abruptly at the end of June and sailed aboard the *S.S. Melita* for Scotland. He was going to spend a few weeks in the Hebrides with John van Druten, who had a cottage on the Isle of Skye, and then he was going to London to pursue his researches for his biography of Rupert Brooke. His mother was escorting another group of college girls to Europe and they sailed on the same ship.

Richard stayed less than two weeks with van Druten but the two of them went to London where they met Richard's mother and for several evenings took her to dinner and the theater.

Richard had a photograph taken of himself and van Druten and he sent it to his publisher to be distributed for publicity purposes. Whether he and van Druten had a falling-out was never revealed, but Richard cabled Bobbs-Merrill only a few days after the photograph had been received in Indianapolis and frantically requested that the photograph be withdrawn from circulation. It was all horribly embarrassing, he said.

And he never saw the young playwright again.

But for the next two months he was grimly pursuing Brooke's family and friends. Brooke's mother was no longer evasive, she was unfriendly; and although she continued to see Richard and to answer many of his questions, she became increasingly hostile and finally forbade him to write anything about her dead poet son until after she, herself, was dead. In ferreting information from Brooke's friends, Richard found the going almost as frustrating. John Masefield, the poet laureate of England, met Richard but volunteered nothing, only answering Richard's half-formed questions with monosyllabic grunts.

He sought out Francis Cornford, a fellow (later professor) at Trinity College where he was regarded as the best Greek scholar in Cambridge, and his wife, Frances (the daughter of Sir Charles Darwin), both of them close friends of Brooke. The Cornfords invited him to lunch and afterward he went upstairs where their fourteen-year-old daughter, Helena, was ill with a

reaction to a vaccination. Brooke was her Godfather, a distinction she did not fully appreciate at the time.

Richard sat by her bed for two hours or more, telling her
stories about himself and his adventures, and relishing it, as he
always did when he talked with children, as much as she.

"He was so very handsome," she recalled years later, "and so
very nice to an unattractive little girl of fourteen."

The Cornfords sent him to Sir Geoffrey Keynes, who was
then editing Brooke's letters, and to Dudley Ward, a Cambridge classmate. He met fellow poet Walter de la Mare, "the
most charming man in all England." He had tea with Cathleen
Nesbitt, the actress who had been Brooke's sweetheart, and he
interviewed Sir Edward Marsh, Brooke's lifelong friend and,
for a time, literary executor.

He was two months in this painstaking probe and it proved
profoundly fruitful, producing several hundred letters written
to, and by, Brooke, ten notebooks filled with summaries of
Richard's interviews, scores of photographs, and a dozen books
by and about Brooke.

Richard's determination to write Rupert's biography in spite
of Mrs. Brooke's now adamant refusal to permit it, was sustained partly by his new proximity to his hero, and by his private desire to have the respect of his betters in literature. He
had not yet achieved the popularity in England that America
had given him, and London reviews of *The Royal Road* had
expressed more annoyance than criticism because of the flip-
pancy of the book, which was construed as anti-British. The
people he had met in his Brooke quest had been kind and cour-
teous, but Richard suspected it was no more than they would
have shown any other inquiring American.

He confided his discomfort to his father who suggested he
was "satiated with success, praise and publicity," an observation
with which Richard morosely agreed. Even the news that both
his books were now on the national best-seller lists failed to
soothe him. *The Glorious Adventure* led the non-fiction list in
1928, followed by Lee Simon's *France on Ten Words a Day* and
T. E. Lawrence's *Revolt in the Desert*. In sixth place was *The*

Royal Road. Sinclair Lewis' *Elmer Gantry* was the fiction best-seller of the summer.

The Royal Road had been bought for publication in Denmark, Holland, Sweden, Norway, Germany, Hungary, Italy, France and Czechoslovakia, and Richard's fame and popularity began inching its way around the world.

⊸§ 5 §⊷

Richard arrived back in New York aboard the *Majestic* on October 11, just five hours before he was scheduled to lecture in Lancaster, Pennsylvania, and he barely made it. And for the next few months, Richard was imprisoned by the demands of his fame, all the while tortured by self-doubt that it would continue, and by frustrations over the fact that he could not write the things that, deep in his heart, he believed he wanted to write.

"I must stop glorifying myself," he wrote to his father, "I'm getting sick of it and so is the public."

The public, however, was far from sick of him, and they continued to mob bookstores, lecture halls and railroad platforms in ever-larger numbers as he ricocheted back and forth across the U.S. giving as many as 50 talks a month through the spring of 1928. Women hovered under his gaze like butterflies in the spring sunshine, small boys and adolescents trailed him through the streets and autograph hounds invaded the lobbies of his hotels. The press, although manifestly annoyed with what it considered his impudent vanity, treated him as though he were from another planet and he began to feel, in truth, like a vaudeville performer with a bizarre and probably short-lived talent.

His fan mail, pouring into the offices of his publisher and his lecture agent, was counted by the sackful. He tried to answer some of it, out of a sense of courtesy, but had no time. One especially carping letter from a woman was forwarded to him for comment. Richard scrawled across the face of it that he suspected the writer was a lesbian with goggles, and mailed it back.

A woman in Iowa, whose first name was Mary, wrote him in

shocked protest over his progressive drunkenness during his run from Marathon to Athens. Richard went to a bookstore, bought a copy of his own book and mailed it to her with the inscription "To Mary, a good girl, from Richard Halliburton, a good boy when sober." He enjoyed the joke immensely because his capacity for alcohol was minimal and liquor of any kind frequently made him sick.

The Dallas Forum was jammed to the rafters and, in fact, turned away some 2,000 persons whose resentful milling in the street in front of City Hall Auditorium alarmed the management into calling police. It took a squad of patrolmen to disperse the crowd. And when the lecture was over, 200 copies of *The Royal Road* were sold from a foyer bookstall.

In what seemed a rebellion against his popularity, Richard now began scorning both himself and his public.

"What are all you silly people doing?" he said, dismissing a throng of admirers in the Russell-Lamson Hotel lobby in Waterloo, Iowa, and to a local newspaper reporter who pursued him to his room, he declared:

"I don't find the U.S. romantic. People say to me 'didn't you like Kansas City?' and I say 'no, I didn't even see it.' Oh, I was there a day but all I saw was brick buildings and smoke Chesterfield signs.

"I've been in England collecting material for another book. It's a secret, but it's a complete departure from my previous work. I'm writing it to save my literary skin. You may say that a man with two best sellers going strong who talks that way is a silly ass. My publishers urge more travel books, my public clamors for more travel books, but I won't let myself get into a groove. I never intended to be a travel writer.

"I have seven different lectures and I re-arrange and re-assemble them to suit the intelligence of my audience. My audience here was intelligent enough for the stories I told.

"I look out over the audience and I say to myself, 'look at those fools, paying good money to hear me rave.'

"But I know it's perfectly safe to tell my audiences to be unsteady. I'm a stirring-up influence, an exciting force.

It's good for folks to be stirred up and excited but nothing will ever come of it."

He also loosed a few snide snipes at other authors, among them Catherine Mayo whose book, *Mother India,* a monumental socio-cultural dirge, was a raging best seller.

"When Catherine Mayo went to India," hissed Richard, "she kept her eyes fixed on the gutter. If she had raised them once, she might have seen the Taj Mahal . . . she might have seen all the beauty and poetry, the romance and wonder, that India held for me."

To a letter from film producer Cecil B. de Mille inquiring about film rights to *The Royal Road,* Richard replied that he wouldn't consider it for less than $50,000 plus a major role in the movie for himself. De Mille did not answer the letter.

To the foreign editions of *The Royal Road* was now added a transcription in Braille. It was published by Taylor, Thorne & Co. in six volumes of 703 pages each.

In Chicago, he told a Union Station trackside press conference:

"The American public is starved for romance. That's why it goes to the movies. That's why it reads my books. Romance is doing what one wants to do. Is there anybody in this country who is doing what he wants to do? They drudge, that's what they do."

The turmoil in Richard's private thoughts was aggravated by the frantic logistics of his public life. Books, and autographed ones at that, had to be shipped to the sponsors of his lectures, often the chairman of a club or the principal of a school, so that they could be available for sale following his talk. If he failed to visit the bookstores in any town where he appeared, to pay his respects and autograph whatever unautographed books were in stock, usually dozens of them, he ran the risk of being boycotted. He was constantly reminded of this by his publisher whose salesmen lived under eternal threat of ostracism by slighted bookstore proprietors.

Christopher Morley's great novel, *Kitty Foyle,* for instance, was barred from Youngstown, Ohio, for a year because Morley forgot to call on one of the two bookstores in town. Nothing could persuade the offended merchant that it wasn't a deliberate snub and she prevailed on the other bookstores to join in the boycott.

Bookstores often demanded that Richard hold an autographing party before or after a lecture, and he had no alternative despite physical exhaustion, missed trains or anything short of a fatal illness. He was even asked by his publisher to detour as much as a hundred miles to soothe the ruffled dispositions of a bookstore owner suffering from some long past affront, real or imagined.

Since Richard was selling quantities of books on his lecture circuit, Bobbs-Merrill agreed to pay half of his travel expenses. This enabled him to hire a traveling secretary, a recent Harvard graduate named Albert Shattuck whom Richard had met in New York and who traveled with him throughout the spring of 1928. Shattuck was frequently described in the press as "a rather picturesque young man."

It all involved the most detailed daily correspondence by mail and telegram with Bobbs-Merrill headquarters or with its various sales and promotion representatives around the country. Sandwiched between these urgent missives were even more urgent ones from Richard for money, for advances against royalties or for outright loans. "I am broke again," he would say, which was as much of an explanation as he was ever able to offer.

And the apparent futility of it bore down on him from time to time as he dropped his weary body on the sixth strange hotel bed in a week, without bothering to undress or pull down the covers, and fell into a dead sleep. It drove him at least once to write a plaintive letter home.

> I'm lonely. My affections are starved. I've no time to care about people. I wish I would fall in love. It would add some sweetness and sparkle to all this brass materialism. I lead an absolutely loveless life. Friends and acquaintances—too many —all of them could disappear and I wouldn't know it.

Yet the very next day, when some newspaper reporter would ask him about the women in his life, he would smile sardonically and say, "Matrimonially speaking, I'm still the last of the Mohicans."

And to his lecture audience, women fresh from sinkfuls of dirty dishes, unmade beds and squealing children, and men bone weary from another day of sameness at the office, he would appear as a real, live harbinger of hope that they, too, had a chance, undeterred by the realization that few working Americans had the price of international travel because Richard had an answer for that, too.

"Romance doesn't travel de luxe. I could not find it in the salons of ocean liners, but in the crew's fo'c'sle; not in Pullman drawing rooms, but on the brake rods."

And the women would sigh and the men would dream.

Richard had been plagued with throbbing headaches since fall, and after seeing his editors at Bobbs-Merrill he went into the hospital in Indianapolis for a painful sinus drainage. He was groggy with sedatives, which barely suppressed the subsequent searing agony, but he was unwilling to remain in bed and, airily dismissing the protests of nurses and interns, he dressed himself and went to a hotel.

The clerical staff at Bobbs-Merrill had long responded to Richard's courtly manners and somewhat coquettish airs by referring to him, behind his back, as "Dick Darling," a custom which became less amusing after they saw him, the day after his operation, playfully breezing through the offices, obviously wracked with pain but stubbornly refusing to admit it.

Richard was frequently mistaken for a daredevil and expected to undertake some impromptu stunt like scaling the sides of a building. The nearest he came to this was to admit that he would like to climb the Empire State Building, by the stairs, "so I could feel what the building feels." Once, in Austin, Texas, the daughter of a faculty member at the University of Texas, where he was appearing, drove him from the railroad station to the campus and genuinely terrified him by racing down a residential street at 40 miles an hour.

The erosive pace of his life was relieved only by occasional social encounters with people he admired and whose respect he sought. A meeting with novelist-critic Glenway Wescott at a New York party inspired him for days and in California he lunched with novelist Gertrude Atherton who became a lifelong friend and his staunchest fan. "People who criticize Richard are just jealous," she said, repeatedly.

He was less impressed with actor Douglas Fairbanks, the original swashbuckler, who rejected Richard's relentless urgings that he buy *The Glorious Adventure* for a film. "Not my cup of tea," said Fairbanks.

Richard also made his debut that winter in the celebrated Thursday evening salon of art and book connoisseur Emily Francis in her East 10th Street town house in Manhattan. There he met and mingled with such diverse contemporary notables as poet Don Blanding and the recently-deposed Grand Duke Alexander of Russia.

He was in a snappish mood when he got to Charlotte, North Carolina, and presuming the ear of a lone reporter meeting him to be a sympathetic one, he complained about everything.

"Some kind ladies have invited me to tea. Wonder how much I'll have to drink and think of all those little cakes. I'd rather have a ham sandwich. I haven't had any lunch. I did get here in time to attend the Rotary Club, but I don't have any message for those luncheon clubs and they don't interest me. Who ever heard of a Rotarian who read books, anyway?"

In Asheville, North Carolina, the *Citizen* welcomed him with a three-column front page editorial cartoon. It showed a matronly woman unlocking the giant gates to "the Land of Romance and Adventure" with a key labeled "Halliburton lecture."

Richard desperately needed a literary grubstake to free him from the tightening coils of his success and give him time to try his literary wings for the self-respect for which he hungered. But his lecture management was offering increasingly higher fees—guaranteeing him $750 a week—and his publisher was bombarding him with proposals that his next book be in the wake of Napoleon, Richard the Lion Hearted, Marco Polo, Alexander the Great, Sir Francis Drake or Charlemagne. In the midst of his indecisions he met Loring Schuler, editor of the *Ladies' Home Journal*, who wanted him to write a series of articles about romance in the U.S.A. The idea did not captivate him, but he looked upon Schuler as a potential source of steady income and began to hope he could negotiate something. Anything but another trip and another book now seemed like an escape for him.

In the meantime, he received a letter from Rupert Brooke's mother reiterating with seemingly hopeless finality her refusal to allow a biography of her son.

There was no letup in Richard's need for money—it was still being spent faster than he could make it—and in April he went to Philadelphia determined to close a deal with Schuler who was already the object of a campaign of persuasion by Bobbs-Merrill. Their meeting resulted in Richard being offered a contract to write a series of ten articles—at $3,000 each—for the *Journal* on Latin America, and the articles could later become part of his next book. Richard decided to title both the series and the subsequent book *New Worlds to Conquer*. When the title was circulated around Bobbs-Merrill for a reaction, one editor said he felt the title would only add fuel to the blazing fire of Richard's conceit.

But there was little conceit in Richard's heart as he bought armloads of books on Latin America, about which he knew nothing, and manfully decided to make the best of his new entrapment. "I have to go to Mexico and South America and like it—and I will," he told his father. After all, he would be reveling among the ghosts of Cortez and his fellow conquerors and somewhere in those Latin lands he would find a deserted island where he could live like Robinson Crusoe.

V

A Vagrant Conquest

There is nothing more tragic in life than the
utter impossibility of changing what you have
done.

—JOHN GALSWORTHY
(*Justice*)

❦ I ❧

RICHARD estimated that his two books would sell a total of 100,000 copies by the end of 1928, thus yielding at least $50,000 in royalties. With a guaranteed income of $30,000 from the *Ladies' Home Journal* he should be able to save—and possibly invest to a profit—all his book royalties. He so instructed his publisher which began to deposit his earnings in the Central Union Trust Co. in New York for cautious, long-term investment. He was also blessed that year with such unexpected riches as a fee for a Lucky Strike cigarette endorsement which he wrote with as much enthusiasm as if he had been a smoker. He decided, too, that smoking was a debonair trait worthy of frequent inclusion in his books. In reality, smoking repelled him; it made his throat raw and triggered his sinusitis.

He made one final lecture swing through the East and South before heading for Latin America. In Macon, Georgia, where he spoke before the Macon Writers Club, he became arrogantly candid to a reporter who nabbed him in the lobby of the Dempsey Hotel. He was only going to South America because he needed the money, and declared he hated writing travel books. "I have never wanted to be anything but a poet," he said, "but my publisher won't let me. It took me two years to write my first book, three months to write my second and it will take only a few weeks to write the third."

He wanted a companion for his trip, and had selected a young man named Fred Healey, who worked for G. P. Putnam's Sons publishing house in New York, but who was unable to leave until July, so Richard took his father with him as far as Mexico City. They sailed from New Orleans to Vera Cruz in late April and walked the 230 miles to Mexico City, following approximately the route of Hernan Cortez when he landed there in 1519 and with a mere 400 soldiers set out to annihilate the Aztec Empire. Mexico City's newspapers gave the Halliburtons a hero's welcome.

Richard arrived in Mexico at a time when he might have been denounced or even stoned rather than praised with the Spanish equivalent of "indefatigable adventurer."

It had been scarcely six months since the United States considered sending its troops across the Rio Grande to protect American oil and mining interests, to halt the pogrom against the Catholic church and to save Latin America from "Mexican Bolshevism." Anti-American sentiment was still strong among Mexicans who had learned to distrust the "Yanqui" speculator and mineral concessionaire. That Richard looked like a hero to Mexicans was due probably to two men—U.S. Ambassador Dwight Morrow, of the J. P. Morgan banking house, who gave Mexico a new and benevolent image of America, and Charles Lindbergh, whose historic flight gave the world a new image of Americans. Halliburton, the Mexicans felt, was another Lindbergh, even if he wasn't engaged to marry, as Lindbergh was, Morrow's lovely daughter, Anne.

With the help of a burro he named Virgie, Richard and his father made the hike in less than three weeks and then scaled Popocatapetl. The elder Halliburton returned to Memphis and Richard went on to Progreso on the Yucatan coast where Healey was waiting for him. Healey apparently told Richard stories of Putnam authors who received higher rates and it made him suspicious of his own publisher. He sent off a long, carping letter to Chambers demanding proof that the firm was actually spending as much on advertising as the contract specified and all but demanding a raise. Richard's contract called for payment of 12½ percent royalties on gross retail sales, with 2½ percent returned to Bobbs-Merrill to be spent on advertising. Richard said he wanted 15 percent, with 2½ percent for advertising.

Other authors did nothing to promote their own books, Richard argued, yet they received higher royalties. Richard said he believed he sold more books than his publisher's entire sales force.

The letter was not the first of petulant indignation, nor the last, and Chambers was always able to mollify his top money-making author. Either that, or Richard would suffer severe lapses of self-confidence and hasten to apologize, acknowledging that Bobbs-Merrill was, after all, responsible for his success.

Richard's assignments from the *Journal* included articles on Cortez, Emperor Maximilian and on the climbing of Popocatapetl. He finished the first two in his room at the Hotel Regis in Mexico City, and he made three copies of each. He sent one to Schuler at the *Journal,* one to his father and he kept one so that he could revise it. He was disappointed in their quality, and believed he might be out of practice. And as his self-confidence waned, so did the sense of security he derived from the *Journal.*

In Merida, Healey became violently ill from inoculations so Richard went on alone to the Mayan ruins at Chichen-Itza where he became obsessed with the "well of death" into which maidens were thrown to appease the rain gods. The well was a 400-foot-wide crater in the jungle, with sheer rock walls down to the surface of the pale metallic green water about 70 feet below. The legend was that as a young girl was hurled to her death by the priests presiding at a rock altar on the brink, a Mayan warrior, weighted with armor and weapons, leaped in with her in a ritual marriage of death. Richard remained alone at the altar until nearly dusk, his Indian guide having wandered off to gossip with friends. He stared in morbid fascination at the still water, wondering what incredible secrets it held and wondering, too, what it was like to die in such a mystic way. A delicious thrill of expectancy surged through him and without thinking about how he would get back out, he jumped.

It seemed many minutes before he hit the icy water. The impact stunned him senseless for an instant and then as he plummeted deeper, he felt squeezed almost to the point of suffocation. He struggled furiously for the surface, for the shock had knocked the breath from him and he was terrified that he would drown. At last he broke into the air, gasping and thrashing, and he knew that he had been spared by only a second, or less. He swam to a rock ledge protruding from a tangle of vines that hung down one face of the rock wall, and lay there several minutes, panting and shivering and curiously satisfied. A crowd of Indians had gathered around the rim of the well in a frenzy of excitement, uncertain as to whether Richard had dispelled or renewed their superstitions about the once-sacred well. They made no move to help Richard as he removed his moccasin boots and began climbing up the tangle of greenery, laboriously inching his way to the rim.

Back in Merida the next day, no one believed his story of the leap and he suspected his readers and his lecture audiences would be similarly incredulous, so he offered to do it again for the benefit of an American archeologist, Arthur Rice, who would photograph the event with a motion picture camera, and for a photographer and reporter from the Merida daily, *La Semana Justrada*. Richard had gone in the first time fully clothed, but for the second jump he stripped to his trousers. He jumped feet first, his arms held out like the wings of a descending angel, and the shock of impact sprained his shoulder. He was hauled out this time by ropes and was the village hero for the week he remained in Merida. The film of his sacrilegious leap was shown nightly in the local theater.

Richard and Healey left Progreso aboard a 60-ton coastwise sailing vessel, the *Xpit*. It was so crowded with Mexican laborers recruited for work in the chicle fields to the south that Richard and Healey got off on the island of Cozumel and spent five days lounging in the surf. Another sailboat loaded with sea turtles took them to Belize, in British Honduras, then by steamer to Guatemala and Bluefields, Nicaragua, where Healey came down with malaria. He was so sick, Richard appealed to the battleship U.S.S. *Cleveland,* then in port, to take them on to Panama where Healey could receive proper medical care. After depositing Healey in a hospital in Colon, Richard called on General M. L. Walker, the Governor of the Canal Zone, and asked permission to swim the length of the canal. He was armed with letters of courtesy obtained for him by Chambers from

Richard and Wesley Halliburton at eleven and eight respectively.

Halliburton at Lawrenceville

Halliburton at Princeton (*second from right*)

Halliburton after his plunge into the Well of Death

Halliburton at Chichen-Itza

Halliburton enters
the Hellespont

Halliburton with pris-
oners at Devil's Island.

Halliburton with
Ramon Novarro.

Culver Pictures, Inc.

Halliburton flies up-
side down over the
Taj Mahal.

Culver Pictures, Inc.

Halliburton in 1931

Wide World

Halliburton autographing for San Francisco schoolchildren in 1934

San Francisco Chronicle

Halliburton autographing his books in Cossitt Library, Memphis,
1940

Halliburton and *The Sea Dragon*

assorted federal officials, including Secretary of State Frank Billings Kellogg, co-author of the recent Kellogg-Briand pact which proposed to bring peace on earth by having 63 nations sign the document as a repudiation of war.

General Walker received Richard with grace and amusement but then, too, Richard's fame had preceded him. Richard put his request, as earnestly as he could, and was prepared to meet only the most obvious objections.

"The canal is 50 miles long," said Walker.

"I know," Richard answered, "but I'll only swim a few miles a day and spend each night ashore."

"The water is full of typhoid, alligators, sharks and barracuda."

"I've been inoculated against all diseases," said Richard, "and maybe the Army would lend me a sharpshooter to protect me from those other hazards you mentioned."

"Perhaps they would," said Walker, his brows furrowing. "But it seems very foolhardy at best. Still, I know of no law that forbids it." And he shrugged.

"I know that," said Richard, "but I'll need your permission to go through the locks."

Walker was now genuinely shocked.

"That's impossible! You'd hold up traffic. And who would pay the lock fees?"

"I would—on the same basis as ships—according to my tonnage."

Walker laughed at this, and laughed even more after he had calculated the fee for Richard's 140 pounds—36 cents.

In the end, he gave Richard the following letter:

Mr. Richard Halliburton
Hotel Tivoli
Ancon, Canal Zone
Sir:
With reference to our personal conversation of today, you are informed that there is no objection on the part of the Canal authorities to your projected swim from Colon to Panama. In this connection you are advised to take a course of anti-

typhoid vaccinations. You are also informed that alligators have been observed frequently in Gaillard Cut.

You are authorized to have a rowboat containing a rifleman accompany you. You are also authorized to swim through the locks.

It is understood that any expenses in connection with this expedition will be borne by yourself, and that the Panama Canal will not be held responsible for any damages sustained.

Respectfully,

M. L. Walker

Governor

Everyone Richard met in Panama told him he was insane to contemplate such a feat, and after sailing through the Canal aboard the battleship *Cleveland,* Richard concluded that it was indeed too long and arduous a stunt, and far too dangerous. He was on the verge of giving it up when he heard that he would not be the first man to do it, that a postal clerk named Wendell Greene had paddled 45 of the 50 miles of the Canal in 1915 without mishap, and in only six days. He had avoided the barracuda by diving in the channel rather than Colon Harbor. There were no alligators in the canal then, for it had been opened only a year and the garbage from ships had yet to lure them down from the Chagres River. Richard sought out Greene, who turned out to be a big barrel-chested man, and Greene encouraged him, giving him advice on the tides, currents and sharks. Then Richard learned that another swimmer, an Army captain known only as Brown, had negotiated 30 miles of the partly-finished Canal in 1913, and he began to feel committed. He realized finally that he had to try it because wire service stories announcing the swim were appearing on the front pages of the daily newspapers in the U.S.

There were at least 500 people standing on the Colon dock near the Limas Bay Foreigners Club when Richard dived in and started across the harbor. A rowboat containing Army Sergeant Thomas Wright, a gangly six-foot-eight-inch professional soldier with an unwavering record of dead-eye marksmanship, proceeded immediately in front of him, his eyes searching the water for barracuda. Richard crossed the harbor uneventfully, a distance of four miles, in about six hours and his triumphant emergence and return to the Washington Hotel was sullied by a biting lampoon of the whole stunt in the daily *Panama-American.*

The author of the piece was Fred Cole, the paper's sports editor, who described the swim as "an installment marathon" and a disappointing one at that. "Anybody could swim the Pacific Ocean at that rate," sneered Cole, declaring that Richard owed a more sensational effort to the Bobbs-Merrill Company. This last remark made Richard furious and he called Cole on the phone. "Don't say things like that," he protested, "I'm not swimming the Canal for Bobbs-Merrill any more than Lindbergh flew the Atlantic for the *Saturday Evening Post.*"

"I thought you were going to swim the Canal," Cole answered, "not swim AT it."

Cole not only continued to poke fun at Richard, he wrote a hilarious article which appeared in the *New Yorker* magazine almost two years later.

Richard was in the water seven hours the second day, but covered less than three miles up the channel, his progress impeded by a deluge of water from the Gatun locks every time they were opened to let a ship through.

A mob of several hundred lined the locks the third day, as Richard slipped over the side of the rowboat and paddled through the double 70-foot gates into the chamber. He nearly drowned when the water surged and bubbled in through the giant inlet tubes like a whirlpool in reverse, and the crowd of onlookers was vocally critical of his lack of swimming style. When he finally emerged into Gatun Lake at the end of the third lock and hauled himself up on a pier, he was loudly jeered by a score of spectators. Richard winced and dived back into the 24-mile-wide lake which took him two and a half days to cross.

Richard's head, shoulders, arms and back were now crimson with sunburn and on the fifth day he wore a sailor hat with the brim turned down and smeared himself thickly with vaseline.

He also collided with a dozing alligator near the shore of the lake and Sergeant Wright gave him a bayonet which he wore on a belt around his waist.

Richard was continually saluted by the whistles of passing ships whose rails were lined with cheering passengers, for progress reports on the swim appeared daily in the press. He was nearly run down by a freighter in the channel near Bohio Point when a squall separated him briefly from his rowboat escort.

Sergeant Wright shot three alligators in eight-mile-long Culebra Cut, all of them sound asleep along the shore. Better safe than sorry, he said, when Richard protested.

Half the population of Panama City was at the waterfront on the morning of the eighth day as Richard was catapulted from the single Pedro Miguel lock out into Miraflores Lake, a mile wide, then through Miraflores lock and into Balboa Harbor. The tide hurried Richard along the last six miles of the swim and when he was less than a quarter mile from the Balboa docks, swarming with people, the barracuda struck.

Two of the vicious fish, "as big as elephants," said Wright—stalked him like bobcats stalking a rabbit. Wright could see them from time to time, circling ominously, and when he could not see them he flayed the water in front of, and alongside, the boat with a parasol and shouted at the top of his stentorian voice. When at last Richard was hauled victoriously ashore at Pier 15 to the applause of several thousand onlookers, he was weak from anxiety more than from the swim. But he chatted merrily with a delegation of reporters and then took them all back to his suite at the Tivoli Hotel and served them ginger beer and soda.

✑ 2 ✑

The Canal swim received its due attention in the newspapers of the world, and earned Richard a whole new string of headline sobriquets—Daring Dick, Romantic Richard, Handsome Halliburton. The *Natal Mercury* of Durban, South Africa, was so impressed that it bestowed editorial praise on the Panama Canal officials for having the wit and humor to allow the stunt "especially when one considers that Mr. Halliburton required the same amount of water, in passing through the locks, as does the battleship HMS *Hood*."

Richard's swim, which he completed on August 24, 1928, was a bright strand in a rather vivid fabric of events. The *Graf Zeppelin* was making its round-the-world voyage, an achievement that implied a fantastic future in air travel. The first all-talking motion picture, *Lights of New York*, was premiered, of course, in New York. August was also the month of the great Times Square subway crash which killed 18 persons and injured nearly 100, and a little later the notorious underworld czar Arnold Rothstein was fatally shot to death by an unknown assassin in a Manhattan hotel room. On the outskirts of Los Angeles, the St. Francis Dam collapsed and let loose a deluge that drowned 450 persons. Neophyte dictator Benito Mussolini saved his nation's straw hat industry by requiring all Italian adult males to wear one.

America's moral revolution was still going on, epitomized by the violence and scandals of prohibition and by the emergence of literature such as *Well of Loneliness*, by Radclyffe Hall, a bold and sensitive novel about the tortures of lesbianism. The book, oddly, was suppressed in England, a country which had been among the strongest critics of American "puritanism, provincialism and pruriency." Herbert Hoover was in the White House and the nation, as well as the world, was economically sound, despite four million unemployed Americans and periodic stock market panics which were always quickly dissolved by reassurances from John D. Rockefeller or one of the other U.S. billionaires.

Richard was temporarily oblivious of the state of the world. He was reading his way through a pile of texts on South America and rejoicing privately over the ecstatic letters from his publisher. Chambers was delighted over the publicity the swim had received, the Hearst newspapers had bought *The Glorious Adventure* for serialization, and several Sunday rotogravure magazines were giving their front pages to the Panama Canal feat as they eventually came to do with almost all of Richard's stunts.

Richard, however, was broke again. Although he had completed three of the *Journal* articles, he had not been paid as they all required rewriting. The original versions he had torn up in disgust, and it was only after pleading letters from Chambers and Schuler that he began to write them anew. To pay his Panama Hotel bill, meanwhile, he borrowed $200 from a Balboa bank on the strength of his name and fame, and set out through the jungles for Darien Peak where, in 1513, Spanish Admiral Vasco Nunez de Balboa first gazed upon the Pacific Ocean. Bobbs-Merrill, meanwhile, paid the bank loan and cabled $2,000 to Lima, Peru, which was Richard's next scheduled port of call.

Richard's pursuit of the magic of Balboa's historic discovery took him by steamer to San Miguel, 100 miles south of the Canal, and then by dugout canoe 40 miles up the Tuira River to the base of Mount Piri which, Richard had been assured, was the summit Balboa had climbed. Richard was spared the hostile Indians which had wiped out half of Balboa's band, but he had to hack his way up 15 miles of mountainside jungle, tormented by clouds of mosquitoes and swarms of tiny red bugs which bit him viciously. He took slight comfort in the observation that,

The Bridge of San Luis Rey, which Peru regarded as a vicious libel, Richard was still the unsullied hero. "El Infatigable" the newspapers called him, and the dictator president of Peru, the 98-pound strong man, Augusto Leguia, who had read both of Richard's books, summoned him to the palace to hear all about the Panama Canal swim.

Healey was still in the hospital when Richard left Lima and sailed south to Mollendo where he caught a freight train and rode a box car three days to Arequipa and Cuzco, shivering with cold and gasping and nauseated with altitude sickness. From Cuzco, the last great Inca capital, Richard hiked over the 14,000-foot-high ridge of the Andes and down the Urabamba River canyon some 60 miles to the lost Inca stronghold of Machu Picchu, an immense stone citadel in the mountains, built in the ninth century and abandoned and forgotten in 1300. Peruvian history contains no record of Machu Picchu and consequently no clue as to how or where its gigantic stones were obtained. It took an American archeologist, Dr. Hiram Bingham, to discover the city, intact and empty, in 1911. Richard rummaged futilely about the place, desperate for some novel encounter he felt would make a "story," then boated across 12,-500-foot-high Lake Titicaca to Bolivia. A train took him from La Paz to the Chilean coast where he boarded a southbound steamer for Santiago to meet Healey. He was headed for the island of Juan Fernandez, 400 miles off Valparaiso, where the British seaman Alexander Selkirk had been marooned for nearly five years in 1704 to inspire Daniel Defoe's saga of *Robinson Crusoe.* A fishing schooner took them there in three miserable days, both of them prostrate with seasickness, and they remained on the wild and mountainous island for a week eating lobster and gathering courage for the trip back to the mainland. Richard decided that since Defoe had set his famous story on Tobago in the West Indies he would do the same.

A train took them across the shank of South America to Buenos Aires where, despite local laws to the contrary, Richard bought a monkey named Nino and a hurdy-gurdy hand organ. He was determined, as he so often said, that when adventure failed to appear, he would create one. He and the monkey would earn their passage north. Healey had another attack of altitude sickness and went directly into the hospital again. Richard and the monkey begged around the streets of Buenos Aires, in defiance of pleas by police to desist, and found he could make four or five dollars a day. The police, who knew full well who he was, refused to arrest him for fear of offending the American colony, although Richard urged them to. He thought a night in a jail cell with the monkey would make an entire chapter in his book.

Healey went on to Rio by boat, but Richard and the monkey went inland, by train to Posados in the northeast tip of Argentina where he boarded a steamer going up the Paraná River into the Brazilian jungle, past the Iguassa and La Guayra falls, both of them bigger than Niagara. Normally a 36-hour voyage, the ship took four days because a passenger died en route and the ship turned back to return the body. A train took him to São Paulo and then on to Rio de Janeiro.

In Rio, Richard and Nino teamed up with a sidewalk troubadour, a baritone with a mandolin, and split the profits which exceeded what either could make separately. But Richard grew bored after three days of this and felt he had wrung the stunt dry. He and Healey, and the monkey, lived on the Copacobana beach during the day, with Richard writing furiously every night, until January 9 when they boarded ship for New York. He had finished the Cortez article for the *Journal* and when he docked in New York on January 15 the first check was waiting for him. He needed it.

Richard had taken the monkey aboard ship, intending to give it to the Memphis girls' school where he had been a student and where his mother still taught, but the engaging little animal, stuffed with sweets by the admiring passengers, died two days out of port of acute gastritis and was buried at sea. Richard dropped the hurdy-gurdy overboard, too.

Richard had canceled the first ten days of lecture engagements by cable from Buenos Aires, creating some ill will for himself, but he started right in on a grinding schedule the day

after he arrived. He managed to turn out all nine remaining
Journal stories in hotel rooms while on tour, but one 9,000-
word piece on his Panama Canal swim he had to rewrite from
memory because the air mail plane carrying it to Philadelphia
had crashed and burned. He began to make carbon copies after
that.

Richard felt the Latin American series was more heavily contrived than anything he had written, but Schuler, the *Journal's*
editor, thought they were excellent inasmuch as they were
clearly responsible for a jump in circulation. Richard had hired
young Shattuck back as his traveling secretary and this eased
some of his burdens. Although he had been away from the lecture platform for almost a year, he was in better form than ever
and his tour was so successful, with ever larger audiences, that
he resolved to demand a $900 weekly guarantee from his agency
the following season.

His books, too, were more popular than ever, with sales
climbing steadily and his New York trust fund building into a
substantial stock holding. The American Library Association
reported that *The Royal Road* and *The Glorious Adventure*
were two of the 12 books most in demand at public libraries
during 1928. Among the others were Lindbergh's *We,* Will Durant's *History of Philosophy,* Emil Ludwig's *Napoleon,*
Wilder's *The Bridge of San Luis Rey* and *Death Comes to the
Archbishop* by Willa Cather.

❦ 3 ❧

Richard's return from South America also marked an extreme change in his relationship with his father and mother. While he was as attentive, dutiful and loving as he had always been, he no longer shared his intimate problems with them. For one thing, the criticism of his writing that he received from his father was often totally opposed to that he received from Bobbs-Merrill which was, after all, the criticism that mattered. He stopped sending his writings home to Memphis and he told Chambers, after admitting it was Bobbs-Merrill's editors who had saved his books from oblivion, to ignore any letters from Memphis. The elder Halliburton was in the habit of discussing his son's work at length with Chambers.

Early in 1929, Richard was plagued by an impersonator who, while keeping half the country between himself and Richard, gave several lectures which apparently were very good and cashed numerous checks which weren't any good at all. He and Richard came within a month of each other at Lafayette, Louisiana, and Richard was asked to redeem several checks his double had cashed there. "He must be good," said Richard, "I'd certainly like to meet him."

Richard also had his imitators, none of them serious. His swim of the Hellespont, for instance, triggered almost a mass bathing invasion of the tricky current. A group of seventeen college boys did it first, one backstroked round trip in 54 minutes one way, 58 minutes returning. Then a second group of college boys, including two Princeton seniors, was followed by the noted journalist Leland Stowe, then of the New York *Herald-Tribune,* who made it in 54 minutes and 30 seconds. The first girl to swim the Hellespont was Eleanor Studley of Boston, a Wellesley student. Another girl, twenty-two-year-old Anita

156

Grew, daughter of U.S. Ambassador to Turkey Joseph C. Grew,
swam the entire length of the Bosporus in five hours. Her
father accompanied her in a rowboat, feeding her chocolate
bars and playing music on a phonograph.

Richard also began to feel the sting of ridicule and parody, a
sure sign of success. He was included, for instance, in a relent-
lessly funny book, *Meaning No Offense,* by Corey Ford, along
with such substantial public figures as H. L. Mencken, Sinclair
Lewis, Fannie Hurst, Eugene O'Neill. Ford had Richard swimming the Hudson River, from Hoboken to Manhattan,
threading his way fearlessly through orange peels, cat carcasses
and other refuse, after addressing a worshipful multitude on
the New Jersey waterfront.

> Harken girls, I represent the spirit of bubbling youth!
> Youth at its maddest, youth at its gayest. I give you adven-
> ture, dreams, surcease and a severe pain in the neck. I am the
> Don Juan of Romance, the slightly Pied Piper of Weltsch-
> mertz, and I am only a boy, if that. Wheee!
> Harken Girls, I place to my lips the magic flute of adven-
> ture and sound the call of the gypsy trail. Who will wander
> with me, hand in hand, down the Royal Road to Romance?
> Harken, middle-aged suburban housewives, impressionable
> girl graduates, Thursday afternoon bridge clubs, sex-starved
> librarians, and the rest of my fluttering middle-western audi-
> ence. Look, I'm calling you!

And when his South American book, *New Worlds to Conquer,* was published late in 1929, it was widely referred to in
the press as "New Ladies' Clubs to Conquer."

The famed cartoonist, John T. McCutcheon, lampooned him
on the front page of the Chicago *Tribune,* showing Richard, a
stenographer and a photographer falling together through space
with unopened parachutes, with Richard saying, "like some
great winged bird I am plunging downward through the
vast. . . ."

Richard inspired an uncountable number of cartoons over
the years. One of the more memorable ones appeared in *Judge,*
the humor magazine. It showed a tramp clinging to the side of
a box car, staring fearfully up at a railroad detective who, club

in hand, looms menacingly. "No kidding," pleads the bum, "didn't you ever hear of Richard Halliburton?"

Helen Hokinson, a cartoonist whose fame derived from her ruthless satirizing of the women's club world, caught Richard's influence, too. In a cartoon which appeared in *Collier's,* one suburban matron is showing off a tiny garden fish pond to a visitor. "We're very proud of this pool," the matron exclaims. "Richard Halliburton jumped over it."

In one of a variety of vain efforts to defeat his frivolous image, Richard joined the special committee of artists and writers of the Association Against the Prohibition Amendment, along with Irvin S. Cobb, screen writer Nunnally Johnson, writer Channing Pollock, poet Stephen Vincent Benet and Richard's good friend, novelist Gertrude Atherton.

His lecture tour in the spring of 1929 was not only more successful, his audiences were more important. He gave a lecture on Rupert Brooke to 2,000 Notre Dame University students and he talked on writing to the annual sales conference of The Curtis Publishing Co. His travels were also more hectic than ever, for in his spare moments he was rushing to finish the *Journal* series and his next book. These, together with the still booming sales of his other books, would give him enough of a nest egg to be able to take a year off and, perhaps, to write that important book that was festering away in the back of his mind. And instead of demanding $900 a week from his lecture agency, now Alber-Wickes of Boston, he told them he would not be available at all the following season. The agency was acutely distressed and pleaded with him, especially when the extravagant press notices of his current tour began to roll in.

"Not since Fannie Hurst and Ruth Draper appeared here," said the Boise, Idaho, *Statesman,* "has there been so prominent a personage as Richard Halliburton. . . ." He was, the newspaper added, "the social attraction of the week."

In Seattle, he was challenged both to swim Puget Sound and climb Mt. Ranier. He couldn't be bothered with either. "Puget Sound is only 16 miles wide," he said, "and I wouldn't climb Ranier except in the winter when there's some challenge."

Notices like the one in Boise galled him. "I am trying to kill the women's club legend," he would confide to reporters but they were unable to regard him, apparently, in any other light.

In Birmingham, Alabama, the *News* was ecstatic. "The thing that really caught us and made us a greater worshipper at his shrine than anything else is his adoration of his mother . . . And the next nicest thing about this young fellow whose name resounds all around the civilized world is that he is just that southern that he says, 'yes ma'am.' Don't you love that?"

An irritating percentage of Richard's fan mail was either from young people who wanted to travel with him or be adventurers themselves, or from older people who sought advice on how to get a book published.

"I have no message for anybody," Richard declared on more than one occasion when his admirers trapped him after a lecture. "They are the world's most useless commodity. There is no way to learn but by living, by trying, by failing. The only message I have is to ignore all messages."

He stopped briefly in Memphis in May of 1929 and received a reception worthy of a chief of state. It went slightly to his head, apparently, for he told a press conference that he was through with adventuring and had now committed himself to matters of literature and the spiritual side of life. But the stunt he enjoyed most, he admitted at last, was swimming the Panama Canal.

"I held up traffic for three hours," he said, "and the canal is infested with sharks. I had a sharpshooter with me. The water was black with alligators but my man shot hundreds of them." Like most of his exaggerations, it seemed forgivable. He was expected to swim through waters teeming with alligators; anything less would be a disloyalty to his believers.

His father, who was frequently interviewed on the subject of his son, saw Richard in the light of dismal reality. "He is an ordinary human being," he would say, "with light hair, blue eyes, light complexion, five feet nine inches tall, weighs about 140 pounds. He has the general appearance of a lounge lizard and also the manner." It made Richard more comprehensible, he believed.

ᦄ 4 ᦅ

Devil's Island had been a recurring cause célèbre for U.S. newspapers, periodicals and books, ever since the French Army Captain Alfred Dreyfus was falsely imprisoned there for four years in 1894. Americans—judging from magazine and book sales—were unfailingly shocked, horrified and titillated by the repeated disclosures of an almost prehistoric brutality and oppression in France's island penal colony of French Guiana off the northeast coast of South America. The Sunday rotogravure magazines never tired of first-hand accounts, both genuine and false, of life and death on, and escape from, Devil's Island whose infamous conditions had been exposed by the Dreyfus case nearly thirty years before. But apart from Blair Niles' classic volume, *Condemned to Devil's Island,* little had been written by journalists of professional stamp. Richard was determined to claim the distinction and, further, he believed the subject irresistibly commercial, both for the *Journal* and for his own book. The only obstacle to a fresh exposure of the dreaded place was that French authorities would not admit inquiring writers. Richard knew it was useless to apply for permission to inspect the colony and he didn't try. Instead, he took a freighter from Brooklyn to Trinidad, a tedious twelve-day trip that enabled him to catch up on his *Journal* deadlines, and in Trinidad he wangled a seat aboard the flying boat *Washington* making its inaugural flight from New York to Buenos Aires. The plane made a refueling stop at Cayenne, the capital of French Guiana, and Richard disembarked to be mistaken for a member of the aircraft's crew. Cayenne is just inland from the mouth of the Maroni River and the three island prisons, and is itself a prison town. Cayenne's population included several hundred *libérés,* convicts who have served their term but who were forbidden to return to France, on the implausible theory they would colonize Guiana. But they had no source of income and they simply lingered on as beggars until they died of disease or starvation.

Richard, for all his vanity, had an outgoing charm that weakened the wills of convicts as well as it had that of chiefs of state and he made friends with a number of the *libérés* and with the inmates of a prison barracks there who worked in the town. He also gave them money and cigarettes and listened to their tall stories. That he was not robbed or murdered or both was doubtless due to his total ignorance of its likelihood, or to the fact that he held a genuine admiration and sympathy for the convicts.

But hearing their stories wasn't enough; he had to experience what it was like to actually be a convict, so he purchased a convict's striped shirt and trousers and bribed two guards to let him spend a night in a convict barracks. He slept in the filthy canvas hammock, used the wooden toilet bucket, ate the half-rotten prison fare, breathed the foul barracks' air, heavy with the odors of sweat and excrement, and allowed himself to be tormented by mosquitoes and lice.

With his liberal dispensations of cash and tobacco, he became something of a pied piper in both Cayenne and Saint Laurent, some twenty miles up the Maroni River, the site of barracks housing some 3,000 convicts who worked in the jungle lumber camps. It was also home to a thousand *libérés* and a shifting population of bush Negroes whose ancestors were runaway slaves from the U.S.

Richard spent a week between the two river towns, and then headed for the Ile Royale, one of the three island prisons, to personally apply to the commandant for permission to inspect everything. He had written a letter to the commandant embodying his request and, by insisting to the guards that he had to deliver the letter in person, he was permitted to land on Ile Royale.

The commandant, a genial and lonely French Army colonel

serving out the few remaining months to retirement, also assumed Richard was an aviator, greeted him warmly, opened a bottle of champagne and invited Richard to be his guest.

Richard lived in the commandant's house for two weeks and not only was able to inspect every part of the prison, but he so insinuated himself into the life of the place that he intervened in behalf of several convicts and, in one instance, saved one of them from two months of brutal solitary confinement for calling a guard "mon Cheri."

"That's an appropriate greeting," Richard whispered in the commandant's ear during a disciplinary hearing, and the colonel laughed.

"Charges are dismissed," decreed the colonel, "as a favor to my guest."

The irony of it all, of course, was that everything Richard saw and heard would find its way into print, and some of those whose hospitality and friendship he now enjoyed would suffer by it.

Richard toured Saint Joseph Island, site of the concrete blockhouses whose dark and suffocating cells held dozens of convicts who had recently tried to escape, and as many more who had gone insane. Among the latter was an elderly Frenchman, a *libéré*, who had been swimming off the island and had been set upon by sharks. Great chunks of flesh had been torn from his legs and hips and while his body had miraculously survived, his mind had not.

Richard was privy to the interminable escape plots, which were so unrealistic in their casual assessments of the jungle, of the nearby Dutch and British Guiana police who hunted the escapees, of the cruel distances by sea to Venezuela or Brazil, the nearest sanctuaries, that even Richard knew they would not succeed. He was also acutely aware of the homosexual courtships of the young and new prisoners by veteran convicts, and he was frequently the object of some crude seduction efforts. As in all prisons, sex in the *Iles de Salut* was the unseen torment and the only relief was another man unless a convict were young and handsome and virile enough to entice the wife or sister or daughter of a guard into an affair. At one time, Richard was told, older women in the guards' families would pay for a convict's attentions and some of them made enough money to escape successfully. In these steamy, animalistic surroundings, Richard was pleased that his view of everything was so clinical.

Those who could not escape altogether, could escape from the worst of it into the hospital where the food was no worse and there were only rats to contend with. They did this largely by small self-inflicted wounds which they encouraged to become infected, or they feigned ailments, such as appendicitis even though it meant painful and rudimentary surgery. Richard worked for the prison's only doctor for almost a week, draining abscesses, bandaging knife wounds, holding the convicts to the table during minor operations, and pressing his friendship on a growing circle of convicts.

His closest friends were a twenty-one-year-old French youth, who had already served three years for robbery and for whom he pleaded in vain with the commandant to permit an escape, and a convict named Henri, in his sixties, who had been confined to this tropic hell for thirty-four years. What Richard could not discover for himself, these two told him. Richard also became friendly with the executioner, also a convict, whose fees for operating the guillotine would enable him to buy a fishing boat and escape, and with the convict undertaker, who acquired by virtue of his job the money every convict kept secreted in a *plan*, a metal capsule carried in the rectum. The undertaker was busy, even though his job consisted only of weighting the body with a rock and feeding it to the sharks, for at least 1,000 convicts died every year.

Richard's only sensation when he finally left the *Iles de Salut* was that he had no right to go, that by turning his back on 5,000 suffering men he had somehow betrayed them.

Richard went from Trinidad to Tobago by schooner and spent barely two weeks there. He took up residence in a cave by the beach, and acquired from the natives in a nearby village the props to play Robinson Crusoe—two milk goats, a cat, a dog, a parrot, an old musket, some sheepskin garments and a young

Negro goatherd who thought he was crazy but who agreed, for a fee, to be his faithful servant, Tuesday. The two of them built a lean-to, a goat corral and a dugout canoe which, when finished, was too heavy for both of them to push to the water's edge. Most of his time, Richard spent trying to write the adventure in parody of Daniel Defoe's archaic style. When the schooner came to pick him up, Richard gave his pets and livestock to Tuesday who loaded it all in the rear of his old Ford and puttered happily home to his village.

Richard was back in New York by the end of August, telling the horrors of Devil's Island to all the newspapers. Even before the *Journal* article appeared, the repercussions of his reportorial memory had set in. The commandant of the prison had been brought back to France, court-martialed, and drummed out of the service in disgrace. Letters from his wife and daughter, bitter with recrimination and stained with tears, reached Richard, who realized now that he could have protected the kindly, hospitable colonel in his disclosures. But a score of grateful convicts also wrote him, for his outraged revelations had precipitated reforms on the island and conditions were much less severe. For one thing, a new commandant had stopped graft among the guards which left more money for better food. One convict sent him a crucifix. When the story appeared in the *Journal,* heavily illustrated with Richard's own snapshots, it came as something of an anticlimax.

Richard spent the fall of 1929 in New York, compiling the *Journal* articles into his next book, and in Philadelphia trying to negotiate a new *Journal* series. When he needed solitude for writing, he took a hotel room in Atlantic City and locked himself in, often writing for as long as eighteen hours at a stretch. The *Journal* stories had been so successful, from Schuler's viewpoint, that he paid Richard a $2,000 bonus which Richard sent to his mother to help build a new family home in Memphis.

Richard's social life was focused in New York where he was still the most wanted single man at Park Avenue dinner parties, and at theater and opera parties, and his name and picture appeared at least weekly in newspaper society page columns whose authors speculated endlessly on the absence of women in his private life.

"When a man marries," said Richard, with what he hoped was a convincing tone of bitterness, "he becomes domesticated, interested in making money and he likes the smugness of his home. His wife, in nine cases out of ten, is arresting and irresistible to other men and he is afraid to travel without her. It would be unwise for me to ever marry."

On October 28, 1929, Richard went to opening night at the Metropolitan Opera to see Lucrezia Bori and Giuseppe de Luca in *Manon Lescaut,* escorting Marian Wilson, daughter of the socially-prominent Richard T. Wilsons. There was a party afterward and Richard drank too much bootleg champagne. He awoke at noon the next day and immediately made two distressing discoveries: he had a monumental headache and the stock market was undergoing its worst decline in history. Richard didn't know it then, but it was the beginning of the great American depression. He telephoned his banker who turned him over to a broker who convinced him there was nothing to worry about, that the $100,000 he had thus far invested may have slipped a little in face value, but the market would recover as it always had. "Don't join the panic," the broker warned, and Richard agreed he was never one to panic. The broker did not tell Richard that sixteen million shares of stock had been sold that day, that losses in the market since September were now close to $50 billion—or five times the World War I debt. Richard could have read it in the newspapers, but the complexities of high finance eluded him and he dismissed the matter from his mind. He was still on the best seller lists, the royalties were still pouring in, Garden City Publishing Co. would issue a cheap edition of *The Royal Road* guaranteeing at least 250,000 sales, and he could hit the lecture trail again if necessary. He did, however, halt any further investment of his royalties.

New Worlds to Conquer was officially published on November 27, 1929, the day before Thanksgiving, and Bobbs-Merrill threw a party for Richard in the Gold Room of the Savoy Plaza

Hotel. Among those present was a reporter for the *New Yorker* magazine who may have been disturbed by the contrast between this frivolous opulence and the nation's crumbling economy, for the magazine's report on the party was as follows:

> No matter where a young man might turn, he would find fresh tracks in the dust—the marks of Richard Halliburton's boots; and he would find signposts pointed down sideroads to publishing houses. The paths of glory still lead but to the grave but they lead first to the Savoy Plaza; there one finds Halliburton, the snows of Popocatapetl still clinging to his coatsleeve, the waters of the Panama Canal still gathered in little beads on his eyelashes, young adventurer home on schedule, surrounded by his memories, his little sandwiches and his bookchat ladies.

Accompanied by his mother, who was puzzled by the estrangement of her son from his parents, Richard went on to Indianapolis, Chicago and Cincinnati for other book-launching parties, and then alone to Bermuda for a week's vacation. When he came home to Memphis for Christmas, he discovered that his father's business had suffered, indirectly but severely, from the market crash, and he realized he would have to contribute to his parents' support. There was nothing to do but begin lecturing again, for the slump in book sales had set in. And if books were not selling, neither, he learned, were lecture tickets. His agency agreed to sign him up for another tour, despite his arrogant refusals of four months ago, but they could offer no guarantee at all. Business was terrible. Vassar College, for example, had always paid $500 fees but now was unable to offer more than $300. It was the same everywhere and Richard barely earned enough to cover his expenses which remained, admittedly, higher than necessary.

Richard ended his tour in California in April. He spent several days with Noel Sullivan, a wealthy bachelor patron of the arts and nephew of ex-senator James Phelan, and in early May he had installed himself in the Roosevelt Hotel in Hollywood, determined now that his only financial salvation was in selling his books to the movies.

VI

The Flying Carpet

He who serves the public is a poor animal; he
worries himself to death and no one thanks him
for it.

—JOHANN WOLFGANG VON GOETHE

~§ I §~

NEW *Worlds to Conquer* joined Richard's other two books on the best seller lists, but it was a stunted achievement, for sales in the first four months following publication had barely topped 30,000. Now he was worried. Had his meteor run its course? Were people too poor, or too preoccupied with harsh economic realities, to seek the escape he offered them? Was it a new age and was he a leftover from the other age, the Jazz Age? Of the dozen ideas he had submitted to the *Journal*, none had struck Schuler's fancy, yet Schuler assured him repeatedly that something would turn up. His publishers had communicated a certain despair, thinly concealed in the otherwise hearty letters of encouragement. What about another book? But Richard felt he could not undertake a new intercontinental jaunt without a corollary commitment from a magazine. He didn't really understand the royalty statements from Bobbs-Merrill and he was uncertain as to how much money they owed him, if anything. In the meantime, he was out of cash again and he telegraphed a plea to Chambers for $2,500 advance. It arrived promptly but Chambers was beginning to wonder what on earth Richard did with his money.

He made the rounds of the film studios, beginning with Fox where he had been welcomed so cordially by that friend of his mother's, Mike Boylan, three years earlier, but Boylan was no longer there. Neither, for that matter, was anybody else he had met. But instead of being coolly rebuffed, he was warmly received and negotiations opened immediately for the purchase of the film rights to *The Royal Road*. But rather than turn the whole thing over to an agent, or to his publishers who had a half interest in the film rights, Richard saw himself as the consummate businessman and breezily suggested $50,000 as a suitable price, plus a role in the film. Fox countered with $5,000 and no role.

And there the matter lay. But the fact that Fox was at all interested bolstered Richard's confidence and his anxieties about his career and the great depression were relieved. He visited the Fox studios daily, but had been clearly outwitted. Nobody at Fox would talk about money. They had made their offer and that was that. If Richard didn't want to take it, they were above any form of persuasion. He was unable to reopen the negotiations and melancholy settled on him again. It was preposterous, he thought, and grossly unfair. In spite of the depression, Hollywood was throwing money about as though it grew on trees as profusely as the oranges that were everywhere. "People of the commonest, stupidest types are getting $5,000, $7,000, even $10,000 a week," he wrote his father, bitterly, and began to nourish a resentment against the Fox studios.

Never one to brood for long, Richard was lured from his gloomy reveries one morning by a phone call.

"Mr. Halliburton?" said a crisp voice. "Captain McGuire here. John McGuire. Royal Air Force. I'm flying the Atlantic in a small ship and thought you might like to come along. I'm a great fan of yours."

"Let's have lunch," said Richard.

McGuire was in fact a former RAF pilot who had been working in Hollywood as technical advisor on a movie and was returning to England. The only obstacle to his trans-Atlantic flight was that he had no plane and no financing, but was frankly confident that with Richard's backing he could get it. McGuire was a dark, handsome, dashing young man with a waxed moustache. Richard liked him immensely, was sold instantly on the idea and saw himself as another Lindbergh. He gave McGuire $500 as fund-raising expenses and never heard from him again.

The loss of the money dismayed Richard not at all, for McGuire had given him the idea he needed to pull himself and his career out of the doldrums. But instead of merely flying the

Atlantic, he would fly around the world alone in a tiny airplane, and he had visions of himself swooping heroically down in some remote corner of the earth where no plane had ever been before. He didn't know how to fly but he could learn. He went out to the Burbank airport the next day and enrolled as a flight student. After two days of instruction, he realized flying was too complicated and would only clutter his mind with technicalities that would be burdensome for an author. And learning to fly took too much time. He would find someone else to pilot the plane.

He had already written to Schuler and Bobbs-Merrill about the idea and received enthusiastic replies. The *Journal* was willing to commit itself to another series with emphasis on the French Foreign Legion, Sahara Desert slave traders, Borneo headhunters and other raw, bold adventures generally. When could he leave? As soon as he made some money.

Richard's income was enriched slightly by a fee from Chase & Sanborn's coffee for a series of magazine advertisements in which world-traveler-adventurer-author Richard Halliburton had tasted the finest coffees and it was all inferior to Chase and Sanborn.

Richard's mother received some testimonials of her own that year, 1930, when she was named the Most Distinguished Mother by the Memphis Cooperative Club, an honor attended by a good deal of publicity in the Memphis press, including Mrs. Halliburton's advice to all mothers:

"Give your best to the child while it is young, so with the impression made and the seed planted then, he may be permitted to feel his own responsibility in adolescence." In later years, she said, "parents should direct or assist as necessary."

Richard hired a press agent at $750 a month and began lecturing around southern California. The depression was as severe here as elsewhere, but he managed to average $400 fees at such places as the snob-ridden Hollywood Breakfast Club, the American Library Association convention, and a breakfast benefit for Hollywood Bowl. His social life ascended to a kind of local zenith, too. He was a frequent dinner guest at the home of actor Basil Rathbone along with novelist Louis Bromfield, and he dined several times with U.S. Senator William Gibbs McAdoo and his wife, Eleanor Wilson, the daughter of Woodrow Wilson under whom McAdoo had been Secretary of the Treasury. As head of the California delegation two years later, McAdoo would become a key figure in turning the tide for Franklin Delano Roosevelt at the Democratic National Convention.

Richard was also toasted by the Hollywood Women's Press Club, in company with Lawrence Tibbett, Jeanette MacDonald and Grace Moore, three illustrious voices of opera, concert and films.

Richard was also invited frequently to the opulent San Marino home of Florence Barnes whose husband, the Reverend Rankin D. Barnes, was executive head of the Episcopal church social service. Mrs. Barnes was a lusty, adventurous woman known to her friends and acquaintances by the nickname Poncho, the result of a lengthy voyage aboard a commercial fishing vessel as a member of the crew, posing as a man. Mrs. Barnes entertained on a large and lavish scale and Richard met an assortment of people there, among them Paul Mooney from Washington, D.C., a young writer who had at least one book to his credit under a pseudonym. He had also done some professional ghost writing. Their meeting seeded a close friendship that flowered two years later.

He spent a weekend at the famed Bohemian Grove on the Russian River north of San Francisco, a fellow guest with Charles Chaplin and violinist Mischa Elman. He also took to wearing crimson silk pajamas emblazoned with green dragons.

Richard's notion of flying the Atlantic in emulation of Lindbergh crept into the papers in various distorted forms and he was steadily besieged with propositions, by telephone, mail and in person, from promoters, confidence men, unemployed aviators and people who wanted to go along. One of them, from a man named Harry Halley, intrigued him. Halley showed up at the Roosevelt Hotel in the uniform of a U.S. Marine pilot, his breast heavy with wartime decorations. Halley reminded Richard of his disappointing encounter with the missing Captain McGuire but Halley had infinitely more charm and assurance and, frankly, had nothing to offer but his services as an experienced pilot. He did not ask Richard for money and was otherwise convincingly earnest. And the more he talked with Halley, the more Richard was certain he had found his pilot.

"Don't worry about money or a plane," Richard assured him, "I can get all that."

The two of them toured southern California together, inspecting airplanes, Richard introducing Halley everywhere as the man who would pilot him around the world. Halley was somewhat vague in his recommendations for a suitable ship and Richard decided to seek other expert counsel in the matter. He had met Major C. C. Mosley, the World War I ace and founder of Western Airlines, and he invited Mosley to lunch. Halley was there, too, resplendent in his Marine captain's uniform, and the three of them talked airplanes and flying for two hours. As they were leaving the restaurant, Mosley took Richard aside.

"Where did you meet Captain Halley?" he asked.

"He's an old friend of mine," Richard lied.

"Well, I suppose it's none of my business," said Mosley, "but he's wearing some of his decorations upside down."

Richard swore Mosley to secrecy on the subject and later that afternoon confronted Halley who admitted, sheepishly, that he was not a Marine and had never flown a plane in his life. But instead of dismissing Halley, Richard offered to pay the cost of training him as a pilot. He not only liked Halley, he was embarrassed to publicly admit that he had been taken in—again.

To prove his sincerity, Richard had Halley obtain a passport and he enrolled him in a flying school in San Diego, far enough away from Los Angeles to escape notice. But Halley had no aptitude as a pilot and the school, after barely two weeks of training, refused to allow Halley to further endanger their planes or their instructors. Richard and Halley parted, regretfully.

Richard renewed his efforts to sell *The Royal Road* to Fox and, fearful that he would impulsively kill the sale, Bobbs-Merrill President John Curtis came out from Indianapolis to take over the negotiations. Richard had dropped his demands to $25,000 plus a contract at $1,000 a week to write the screenplay, but Fox was unwilling to offer more than a flat $5,000. Curtis was able to drive their offer up to $15.000 and persuaded Richard to accept it. He did so with considerable bad grace, resentfully turning half of it over to Bobbs-Merrill and declaring that in his next book contract he would retain all the screen rights. But he sent $1,000 home to Memphis and, stung by guilt over his neglect of his parents, he brought them out to Los Angeles for a visit. He had written briefly of his airplane plans and had received only alarmed protests from his father. He wanted to reassure them that it was all perfectly safe.

Fox had no sooner disclosed the purchase of *The Royal Road* than it announced the hiring of a screenwriter, William Counselman, and the casting of two stars—George O'Brien and Maureen O'Sullivan. Winfield Sheehan, who would produce it for Fox, had decided on a unique blend of a love story and newsreel footage. Hollywood gossip columnist Louella Parsons raved repeatedly about the idea, and about Richard and his books, triggering no end of speculation by other columnists around the country that Richard Halliburton, the great vagabond and story teller, had sold out to Hollywood, personally, financially and morally. He was engaged to various actresses, it was said, he was having affairs with the wives of various male celebrities, it was also said, and he was giving Hollywood parties of such hedonistic abandon that the police were frequently obliged to break them up. In time, the rumors died out and so did the movie. *The Royal Road* was never produced.

Through Colonel Mosley and a friend of his with the Civil Aeronautics Authority, Richard finally found his pilot. He was Moye W. Stephens, a member of an old southern California family, a tall, handsome, mild-mannered young man who had quit Stanford University Law School in his second year to fly Ford Tri-Motors for Transcontinental Air Transport, the forerunner of Trans World Airlines. Stephens, who was twenty-four, six years younger than Richard, had been flying for eight years and had held a commercial license for four. He was obviously competent, level-headed and after meeting him, Richard's parents withdrew their objections to the trip. The only obstacle was that although Stephens wanted to make the flight, he had severe misgivings about Richard personally and even after several meetings was unwilling to commit himself. This provoked Richard to a campaign of persuasion to which Stephens eventually succumbed—with conditions. He insisted that their relationship remain a formal one of chartered pilot and client to the extent that they would separate on landing and stay in separate hotels.

"I don't think your interests are mine," Stephens said, with a directness that amused Richard. Stephens was, however, willing to forego salary if Richard would provide the plane, the gasoline and all necessary expenses, and Richard heartily agreed.

Richard went about stalking an airplane alone, confident he knew what was needed even though Stephens told him the only suitable ship was a Stearman two-place open cockpit biplane with a 225-horsepower J-5 engine, the same engine that had taken Lindbergh across the Atlantic.

Richard left Los Angeles for Wichita, Detroit and Chicago to inspect aircraft, but all that came of the trip was that an impacted wisdom tooth which had been nagging him for weeks was finally extracted in Chicago. The Windy City left a mark on him for other reasons. It was in the full grip of the depression and although official estimates of unemployed were about 400,000, it seemed that everywhere Richard went the streets swarmed with bums and beggars, as he described it. When he returned to Los Angeles he bought a new Packard touring sedan, as if to prove he was immune from the blight of poverty sweeping the nation, and drove out to Riverside to show off the car to his millionaire cousin, Erle Halliburton. A serviceman at the Packard agency had neglected to tighten the oil drain plug and the crankcase emptied itself during the 60-mile drive. When he pulled into the driveway of his cousin's ranch, the engine of his new car had burned itself up. The car remained in the driveway as a plaything for the Halliburton children for nearly a year until Erle Halliburton angrily ordered its removal to a junkyard.

Richard was a mixed blessing to the Halliburton family. Erle, who was the son of Richard's father's brother, had left Memphis as a penniless youth to seek a fortune in the Oklahoma and Texas oil fields. He worked some years as a rigger before inventing a cementing device to cap gushers, and it had earned him the fortune he sought. He had a grudging admiration for Richard's achievements and frequently remonstrated with him to invest his money while he had it. "You'll end up broke, the way you're going," he would say, "no matter how much money you make. You just spend it all."

Erle's wife grew increasingly annoyed with Richard and threatened periodically to bar him from the house. She had invited him to three formal dinner parties and he had arrived wearing flannel slacks, tennis shoes and a sweater. When she remonstrated with him, he chided her for being a snob. He was, as always, simply trying to attract attention to himself. Invariably, one or two young women guests at the dinners would fall desperately in love with Richard who, even without his gauche attire, could monopolize the conversation. Erle thought these infatuations were funny and occasionally teased Richard, to no effect.

"Women are the cross most men have to bear. I am free of them," Richard would say.

Halliburton's two young daughters, Vida and Zola, thought Richard was the most wonderful man in the world. He played with them, told them stories, and took them for rides in a car through the orange groves which he magically converted, in all their imaginations, into the jungles of Africa, the orchards of Valencia, or the forests of Switzerland. Erle believed that Richard did not like children, in the way adults do, but that Richard himself was a child. The theory was not unique to Erle, but came to be widely expressed over the years. In one rare piece of adverse hinterland publicity (they might sneer at Richard in New York, but they worshipped him in Cedar Rapids), the

Tulsa *World* reviewed one of Richard's 1930 lectures as the incredible utterances of an "outgrown adolescent." It was the same year that the American Library Association reported Richard's books were by far the most popular among teen-age borrowers.

Richard's purpose in shopping personally for an airplane had not been solely an issue of ego, but because he hoped to obtain one free in return for the publicity the trip would generate for an aircraft manufacturer. That he failed in this was not due to any lack of his powers of persuasion, but to the high rate of small plane crashes and he was warned repeatedly that his proposed flight had less than a fifty percent chance of success. The only offer of a free plane came from Erle Halliburton who had purchased a new Ford Tri-Motor and no longer needed his twin-engined Lockheed. "Go ahead, take it," he told Richard, "it's all yours." But Stephens vetoed it as too unwieldy for small, unknown airstrips and too expensive to operate.

Early in November, Stephens found a Stearman at Burbank airport and Richard bought it. The ship was completely overhauled, and Richard ordered the fuselage painted a brilliant scarlet with the words, in black, "The Flying Carpet," on a gold stripe that ran along each side. The wings were silver and the struts black. The Shell Oil Company, after some consideration, agreed to sell Richard gasoline around the world at a wholesale price and then, in return for whatever publicity it might derive, to refund the money—if Richard survived the trip.

Stephens was a month getting the plane ready and Richard went on another California lecture swing to shore up his forever dwindling funds. And everywhere he appeared—from the University of Southern California to the League of Western Writers in San Francisco—he touted his forthcoming trip as a feat to outdo Lindbergh.

Stephens and Richard underwent the full spectrum of inoculations against all tropical diseases and on December 22, 1930, they took off from Burbank planning to make Memphis in time for Christmas dinner, but a fog grounded them in Fort Smith,

Arkansas, and it was December 26 before they reached Richard's home.

The Flying Carpet and its two occupants limped east from Memphis in mid-January, hopping from town to town under a canopy of nasty weather, and in Philadelphia, Richard discovered, to his anguish, that the *Journal's* enthusiasm over the trip had waned markedly and Schuler was almost noncommittal. "Let's see what you send us," he told Richard. "If I like it, I'll publish it."

"And if you don't?" asked Richard, but Schuler only shrugged.

Without a *Journal* commitment, Richard's finances were in lean shape and during the five days he and Stephens were in New York before sailing, he began selling off some of his stocks but they had shrunk to a fifth of what he had paid for them. On top of everything else, his mother fell ill with pneumonia and Richard sent $1,200 home.

The Flying Carpet's wings were removed and crated with its fuselage and lashed down on the forward deck of the White Star liner *Majestic* which charged Richard $450 in freight plus $270 each (first class) for him and Stephens. In addition to selling stocks, Richard had spent considerable time in New York gadding about. He was wined and dined by, and with, film star Mary Pickford, novelists Frank and Kathleen Norris, Fannie Hurst, and Edna Ferber, columnist O. O. McIntyre and Maxwell Aley, the noted literary agent who was also sailing on the *Majestic*. Aley and his wife became Richard's friends but never represented him. Richard feared Chambers and Bobbs-Merrill would view a literary agent as a symbol of distrust.

Richard met the press on the *Majestic's* deck, perched jauntily on his crated airplane. He was wearing a black homburg and black chesterfield coat, pearl grey gloves and spats, and carrying his silver-topped cane. He outlined his plans expansively. He was flying around the world, from France to North Africa, across the Sahara to Timbuctoo and . . .

"Why Timbuctoo, Mr. Halliburton?"

"Well, everybody talks about the place—'from here to Timbuctoo,' people say—but nobody ever goes there."

Why had he chosen an airplane, the reporters asked?

"An adventure not in the air," declared Richard, imperiously, "is obsolete."

ᕁ 2 ᕗ

Stephens reassembled the Stearman at a small airdrome outside London while Richard made the dreary and interminable rounds of consulates and embassies for the several visas required for the flight and discovered, among other disappointments, that the U.S. had never recognized the French occupation of Morocco, an obstacle removed finally by an avalanche of international red tape. Richard also learned that Rupert Brooke's mother had died, thus freeing him from his promise to suspend work on Brooke's biography, but his earlier enthusiasm for the project was gone. In any event, he had no time for it.

Crossing the English Channel, the Stearman developed a serious vibration in her controls and it took three weeks before a Wright aircraft engine expert, passing through Paris on a vacation trip and snagged by Stephens, found the trouble—the aileron control rods had been installed upside down when the ship was built.

Richard had arrived in London on February 6, 1931, but it was the end of March before he and Stephens landed in Rabat, French Morocco, where the Foreign Legion and the general population gave them a tumultuous welcome. They were in Rabat two days, basking in the adulation, then they flew cross-country to Fez and over the Atlas Mountains, still severely infested with tribesmen dedicated to French annihilation; to Colomb Bechar, a major Legion stronghold and the last fragment of civilization north of the Sahara.

Richard's desire to traverse the desert by plane, over a hostile, trackless, uninhabited, burning wasteland of 1,300 miles, was regarded by the French authorities as foolhardy. There were gasoline dumps every 400 miles but they were marked merely as wayside stops on a rutted truck route frequently obliterated by sandstorms. If they were unable to find either of the dumps, they would crash-land in the desert and perish. The French Air Force was reluctant if not unwilling to search for them, and the French troops who rode the truck run twice a month were under orders not to stray more than one hundred yards from the road in the belief that they would either get lost or be captured and tortured to death by nomads. Richard and Stephens were on their own and with that understanding, the French military gave them permission to make the flight.

Apart from anxiety over following the truck ruts and finding the gas dumps, Stephens and Richard had no trouble on the 1,300-mile flight from Colomb Bechar to Gao on the southern rim of the Sahara. A sandstorm assaulted them the first day, and even at 5,000 feet they could not escape it, and the heat throughout was so intense that Stephens suffered burns in his bronchial tubes from the superheated air and dust. They had intended to make the flight in two days, but a stiff headwind the second day forced them to spend an extra night on the desert, in the midst of a bleak, bitter cold emptiness. Richard later rhapsodized over that night in his book, but in reality it was never more than supreme discomfort, lying on the lifeless sand—too arid to sustain even insects—with only an unfurled parachute for warmth.

They landed uneventfully at Gao, a mere military outpost on the Niger River, spent three days cleaning the Stearman's engine of sand, and flew 300 miles upriver to Timbuctoo.

A 300-year-old market place in the heart of a wasteland, Timbuctoo was a dirty, crowded village of 5,000 persons, most of them Moslem Negroes, and at least as many storks who nested in what seemed like colonies on every rooftop. Richard and Stephens slept in a mud hut amid stork droppings, clusters of bats and millions of flies. They ate their meals at the Foreign Legion officers' mess and in the crude home of a French Catholic missionary who had come to this primitive heart of the Sudan 30 years before to abandon his faith, take a native woman into wedlock and beget eight children. He had, however, traded religion for scholarship to become the sage of Timbuctoo. He was an authority on the languages, dialects and cultures of north central Africa, and his erudition saved him from social as well as religious ostracism. Stephens spent his evenings with the French officers, singing and drinking champagne on the roof of their quarters, but Richard chose to prowl the strange town alone. He was never molested, except by veiled black women seeking husbands, and although Timbuctoo was dying, bereft of its ancient commerce in slaves and salt, it held for Richard the enchantment of a mysterious eternity, or so he chose to think.

He and Stephens managed to buy two adolescent slaves from a wily Taureg chieftain who charged them $10 each as a purchase price and another $5 a week later to take the two little black children off their hands.

Except for the heat and the same old anxiety, the return flight to Fez was even less eventful. Richard was now hurrying to get to Sidi-bel-Abbes, the training headquarters of the French Foreign Legion, to complete the story for which the *Ladies' Home Journal* had partly committed itself.

The long low approach to this legendary bastion of romance, brutality and ruthlessness was over the green wooded hills, the wheat fields, the crimson acres of poppies of northern Algeria. Sidi-bel-Abbes was a camouflage of poplar trees, flower gardens and vast green lawns, and its only function was the training of the world's fiercest army. Its several thousand inhabitants—legionnaires and Algerians who made their living off the legionnaires—were then wildly celebrating the Legion's 100th anniversary. A massive monument to the Legion's dead, financed by donations from all over the world, had just been unveiled, a stone and iron symbol to the Legion's motto, *Honneur et Fidélité*. The town was full of Legion veterans, 2,000 or more, from some twenty-seven countries other than France, and their unmistakable affection for their old outfit took the obvious edge off any exposé Richard may have had in mind. Like most Americans, Richard was painfully misinformed about the Legion through the tawdry, highly-publicized confessions of Legion deserters, Hollywood movies and several popular novels, not the least of which was *Beau Geste,* by the British writer, Percival Christopher Wren, and which the Legion itself regarded as a curious slander.

The Legion, Richard learned, to his growing concern, was not bestial nor were its ranks depraved. The Legion was an almost incredible assembly of rootless men—predominantly German, Russian, Swiss, Italian and Greek—shaped by relentless discipline into proud, dedicated soldiers of a supernational cause—the fraternity of the Legion. The food was good, the beds comfortable and the barracks clean, and apart from the low pay ($2 a month) and the hazards of fighting dissident Chlur tribes in the cruel Atlas Mountains, life was pleasant and purposeful. This was not the kind of story the *Ladies' Home Journal* was likely to buy, Richard thought, or was it?

He decided that perhaps no one had ever told the simple truth about the Legion, and that a rather vivid fabric of stories, bright with valor but stained with sin, might be the best approach of all. He would tell the tall legends and also report the alcoholism, the homosexual rampages, the assaults on the Arab brothels, all as elements of an incomprehensible mix that had solidified itself into an army unequaled for courage and self-sacrifice, from the sands of Morocco to the jungles of Indo-China and the mountains of Mexico.

He and Stephens spent two weeks in the barracks and barrooms of Bel-Abbes, gathering up the stories and observing the transformation of dispirited men from every known nationality into Legionnaires. The depression had infected Europe, too, and Legion enlistments were at a new high—nearly 600 a week. A goodly portion of them were rejected as physically unfit, and of those who remained, almost a third tried to desert during the first two weeks of training. It wasn't brutality from which they fled, only the grueling monotony of soldier life. In later years, the Legion would install swimming pools and recreation centers at its posts, but in 1931 the Legion left morale up to the intangibles of its reputation.

Stephens went off to Oran to an air show, and Richard, wearing cotton slacks, tennis shoes and a sweater, hiked off across the desert on maneuvers with the recruits. He suffered mercifully unrecallable agonies from thirst and the heat and on one 30-mile hike, had it not been for the compassion of the mess wagon driver, he might have well dropped in the sand and died there. But the Legionnaires admired his spirit anyway, for he had no reason beyond journalistic curiosity to endure the training. He seemed a slight, mild-mannered young man to many of the Legionnaires, but he bought them their *Pinard,* the Legion's fiery red wine, by the gallon and he listened in rapt attention to their stories.

Richard and Stephens moved on to the Legion's fort at Colomb Bechar but found it tame as Bel-Abbes and headed for Rich, 150 miles due west in the hostile Atlas Mountains. Rich was a center from which Legion columns went out periodically to subdue the murderous Chlurs. Morocco was, officially at least, at peace, but a 100-mile long link of the Atlas, called Le Sagho, was what the Legion described as "a redoubt of dissidence." At Rich, the two Americans bought burros and joined a convoy of three mounted native policemen, Goumiers, escorting two prostitutes to an outpost deep in the mountains. It was a long day's slow journey over winding mountain trails and Richard never expected to arrive alive. The Chlurs were noted for their exquisitely painful and unspeakably depraved torture of captured Legionnaires and it was the custom for a wounded soldier facing capture to kill himself. This was one explanation for the fact that in Legion casualty lists, the number of dead far exceeded the number of wounded. The other reason was that a Legionnaire fought as long as he was alive.

Richard, Stephens and the two prostitutes were warmly welcomed in the mountain outpost, and their arrival was the occasion for a party which lasted two days with numerous fist fights and two men in the guardhouse for homicidal assault on each other. Their common plight united them, however, and they became the best of friends. The officer in charge of the

fort, a French lieutenant, conceded he had jailed the pair because of his own savage hangover and he freed them.

The fort was at an altitude of nearly 5,000 feet and although
it had been under deep snow all winter, May had brought the
long paralyzing hot summer with a vengeance. There had been
few encounters with tribesmen, except for an occasional sentry
decapitated silently in the night by a lone stealthy Chlur, and
this and the heat and the interminable monotony kept everybody's nerves on edge.

The stories of Legion gallantry told in this perilous place
were richer than the ones Richard had heard before, but the
newest story—and one which everyone applauded—was altogether true. It had happened that very winter on the summit of
Bou-Gafra peak, a natural fortress held by 500 heavily-armed
tribesmen. Captain de Bournazel, known on sight throughout
the Legion for the red burnous he wore, led 100 Legionnaires
on the final assault and reached the top. But of the 100 men
who began the attack, only four remained alive, and Captain de
Bournazel was not among them. Two Legionnaires, armed with
a machine gun, had held the peak throughout the day, under a
bone-chilling cold rain, while other volunteers gathered up the
Legion's dead and wounded and returned them to the main
force, most of whose officers had been killed.

While the majority of Legion officers were French, it was
engagements like this that made officers out of enlisted men and
in almost every instance where a Legion officer was not French,
his had been a battlefield promotion. Of some 5,000 Russians
who had served in the Legion up to 1931, more than 100 had
become officers through hair-raising gallantry and sacrifice in
action. The proportion in all nationalities, however, was about
equal. Denmark had contributed only 80 men to the Legion
up to that time, but 10 of them became officers.

Richard wrote his Foreign Legion article in Fez, in an ancient Moorish house he and Stephens rented for three weeks,
and it may have been the first to approach the truth. Floyd
Gibbons, the famed war correspondent, came out later and told

the story straight, but Richard paved the way. Legionnaires, he wrote, "may be sunk up to their eyes in all the sins the devil ever dreamed of, but by the very Gods they mock, I know that when at last an Arab bullet gets them, their souls . . . will go marching up into the blue African sky . . . into the Paradise of the brave."

He failed to finish the articles, but he and Stephens and the Flying Carpet soared off anyway, back over Casablanca, Gibraltar, Seville, Lisbon and Biarritz to Paris where Richard locked himself in the Wagram Hotel to wrestle with it. Paris proved too diverting so he moved down to an inn at Villers-sur-Mer on the Normandy Coast where, in mid-July, he sent the piece off to Schuler in Philadelphia.

⤙ 3 ⤚

The silence from Philadelphia and the *Journal* gnawed numerous holes in the thin armor of Richard's self-confidence and, still worse, gave him more money worries. He had sent Schuler two articles by early August, one on the Legion and one on Timbuctoo, and heard nothing. Finally he asked Maxwell Aley, his literary agent friend, to intercede for him and Aley cabled reassurance. Richard anticipated rejection by the *Journal* because he feared he was losing his gay romantic touch. He attributed this outwardly to the grimness of his new subject matter, but he suspected the real reason was that he no longer felt gay and romantic.

He communicated little of his anxieties to Stephens because they seldom saw each other. Richard had numerous friends in Paris with whom he spent most of his time and to whom he did not introduce Stephens.

Flying from Paris to Geneva, Richard looked down on the lovely French landscape he had explored in such a carefree way so many years before and it was like looking at a painting; it no longer enchanted him. He was old and jaded, he believed, though only thirty-one, and he felt the first of the cold fears of failure, of being a has-been, that haunted him to his grave. Even flying past the Matterhorn, whose summit he had so perilously reached on foot, was a minor thrill. How to write about thrills one did not feel, he asked himself, and was terrified there was no answer.

Vienna failed to restore his spirits, but flying through fog-shrouded Simplon Pass into Italy, with the prospect of grisly obliteration on some ragged peak, so exhilarated him that he arrived in Venice the same old capricious Richard Halliburton.

Seated in Harry's Cafe, a hangout for displaced Americans, Richard challenged a young man named Jimmy Lownes, who went under the nickname Whoopee, to a swimming race in the Grand Canal which, for all its visual magnificence, was still the recipient of the outflow of Venetian sewers. The race was for two and a half miles, from the railroad station to the front door of Harry's Cafe whose proprietor promised a bottle of champagne to the winner.

The two of them, with Stephens as an unwilling referee, hired a Gondola and, stripping down to their undershorts, dived in. The race was neck and neck through floating offal and the conglomerate of canal boats whose operators made such a clamor that the police were summoned. They had barely reached the Rialto Bridge, about half the distance, when a police launch collared them. They were taken, dripping wet, to the police station and fined ten lira, then about fifty cents. The police were amused to have arrested such a famous person and afterward everybody went to Harry's Cafe and had a drink.

Richard was in Budapest, sipping beer and nibbling radishes in a Danube cafe, when Schuler's cable arrived, late in August. It was not an outright rejection but it alluded overmuch to hard times and high costs and Richard recognized it as the handwriting on the wall. He sold the remainder of his brutally deflated stocks and bonds and obtained another advance from his publisher who, in spite of anything, remained confident that the public appetite for Richard was insatiable. Even a lawsuit threatened by a nobleman whom Richard had mistakenly included in his account of the Peruvian insurrection in *New Worlds to Conquer* failed to curtail Chambers' long-range expectations.

And when Schuler finally turned Richard's articles down flatly, on the grounds people were too preoccupied with the depression to be interested in international frivolities, Richard heaved what he hoped sounded like a sigh of relief. He wrote Chambers at Bobbs-Merrill that being under the *Journal's* yoke had been "one long grief" and he was glad to be free of it. His only concern, he assured Chambers, was to turn out another best-selling book.

In nearly every European city where the Flying Carpet landed, Richard and Stephens were pulled into the ranking social orbit, their presence at cocktail parties, formal dinners, embassy lawn luncheons fought over by wealthy widows and divorcees and the wives of government officials and business barons. Richard was no more an itinerant stranger in Cairo than he was in Sioux City. His first three books had been translated into nine languages, in addition to the British editions which were sold throughout Europe and the Middle East. The press frequently met him at airfields and spread reports on the progress of his flight via the wire services and the effect of it all was cumulative. By the time he got to Constantinople, for instance, the first dinner invitation came from the U.S. Ambassador who doubtless had been nagged into it by his wife. Until they had met Richard, men usually recoiled from him in scorn and disbelief. But after a few minutes' exposure to Richard's ingenuous charm—which consisted chiefly of Richard quietly convincing them that he was far more interested in them than in himself—detractors became fans who not only liked him but believed that he had actually done all those stunts.

From Constantinople, Stephens piloted the Stearman along the Bosporus to the Black Sea, skirted the southern shore and headed inland some 700 miles to Aleppo. He flew low, 1,000 feet or less, the strident roar of the engine unheard in the barren, uninhabited desert below. After the Sahara, neither of them was troubled by the possibility of a forced landing in some hostile wasteland. Richard had purchased a pair of .38 revolvers in the U.S. before they left, but they had declared both weapons to French customs officials who impounded the guns and failed to return them when the Carpet departed from France. Stephens had obtained a .45 automatic and a shoulder holster in Algeria and he wore it constantly when in flight. But he never offered it to customs inspections, nor did he ever have occasion to use it.

They saw the twelfth century castles built near Homs by the Crusaders, whose saga Richard hoped yet to exploit, and the Greek ruins at Palmyra and they flew directly across the desert to Damascus where Richard considered insinuating himself, somehow, into the legend of T. E. Lawrence, the Lawrence of Arabia. It had been thirteen years since Lawrence had led the British-Arabian amalgam into the last stronghold of Turkish-German aggression, and Richard could find no remnant of his glory there. He realized, too, that Damascus had been merely a symbol of a dream—Lawrence's dream of a united Arabia—and that the ancient capital of Syria had seen the destruction of the dream. Damascus had fallen to diplomatic perfidy and inter-tribal bickering among the Arabs and Lawrence had gone home in self-mortification.

Richard pressed on to Tiberias, on the shore of the Sea of Galilee. Richard had not dismissed Lawrence, but he wanted to swim the Sea of Galilee, and he did the day after he arrived. Accompanied by a fishing boat, he covered the seven miles across in just five hours, but when he climbed into the boat on the far shore he knew he had been badly sunburned. And by morning, he could readily diagnose it as second degree burns of the arms, face, back and shoulders, all of which were covered by giant blisters. He stayed in bed in Tiberias for two days, semiconscious and with a raging fever, and then Stephens took him back to Damascus where the indifference of doctors sent them on to Jerusalem. Richard was conscious and his fever had abated, but the pain involved in even turning his head was excruciating. Stephens loaded him gingerly into the front cockpit of the Stearman and they took off for Gaza, the nearest landing field to Jerusalem. From Gaza, it was a jouncing 60-mile drive by car over a rutted road and Richard passed out from the pain two or three times. He was finally hospitalized in Jerusalem where doctors put him under sedation and applied soothing unguents to his blistered body. It was a week before the torture ended and, because he had eaten almost nothing, he was gaunt and weak, his peeling face covered by a stubble of dark blondish beard. But he was immensely proud of himself, for the seven-mile swim was his first since the Panama Canal.

Stephens flew on alone to Cairo to overhaul the plane's engine and Richard remained in the Holy City for a month, until early October, sightseeing, writing and frantically searching, as usual, for adventure. He prowled one night through the 3,400-year-old, quarter-mile-long tunnel which carries water beneath the old city of David. The tunnel, barely three feet wide and six feet high, was waist-deep in icy water and Richard's only light was a candle which kept going out. He scaled the vertical shaft in the center of the tunnel, the shaft discovered by Joab of David's Army in its first assault on Jerusalem. Emerging on the summit of the hill in the center of the city, Joab took Jerusalem by surprise and conquered it. Richard tried imagining himself to be Joab, but when he reached the top of the 60-foot shaft, he found it covered over with rubble and he could not emulate the great feat altogether. He climbed back down and waded out.

Richard had bought pontoons for the plane and they were waiting in Cairo. Stephens foresaw no need for them at least until Singapore and Richard shipped them there. His arrival in Cairo signaled another relentless social whirl among the consular and embassy worlds and when the Flying Carpet took off in early November, even the U.S. Ambassador was at the airport to wave good-bye. They flew along the Mediterranean coast to Gaza, inland to Jerusalem and over the Dead Sea to the big Royal Air Force Base at Amman where Richard thought of Lawrence again and where both he and Stephens got into trouble.

Their arrival touched off a number of spirited parties among the British pilots and officers whose life was hot, dusty and monotonous. At one of these parties, a flight lieutenant named Mickey Murphy drank more than he should have and behaved so badly that the ranking officer at the party brought him up for courts-martial on charges of being drunk and disorderly and conduct unbecoming an officer. Murphy was an engaging Irish-

man who, apart from being from Belfast, probably had no business in the Royal Air Force anyway and Richard and Stephens
were so touched by his plight that they decided to testify at his
trial. Both described Murphy as a model of military decorum
categorically and specifically refuted the charges against him.
Murphy was acquitted but the officer who had initiated the case
never forgave Richard and tried in vain to have the Flying Carpet banned from the airfield.

Richard's immediate objective was the dead city of Petra,
dating back to eternity, an architectural marvel cached in a box
canyon in the middle of the desert. It had been a Roman citadel, a Moslem capital, and, lastly, a fortress occupied by the
Crusaders in the 1300's. To reach it, Richard and Stephens flew
along the railroad from Amman to Maan and set down again at
a British outpost. Richard's musings over Lawrence were
brought to life by a spy—a British Army major who, apparently
inspired by Lawrence, had taken to living as an Arab and reporting the plots of various unruly tribes to the British.
Lacking Lawrence's love of the Arab people, the major was
something less than successful. A number of Bedouin chieftains
had discovered his real identity and they were looking forward
to killing him, a fact of which the major was not unaware.
Richard was fascinated and thrilled by a man who lived under
such a relentless threat of death and not a little envious of him.
He made several brief forays with the major into the desert,
uneventfully, and the two men became friends.

The major loaned Richard a truck and a squad of soldiers for
the trip of some 30 miles across the desert to Petra and as they
were returning late one night, bouncing over the rutted road, it
occurred to Richard that he might be mistaken easily for the
major and be killed in an ambush, an event the major had
already survived two or three times, or so he said. It gave Richard a thrill unlike any other to contemplate that behind the
dunes and low hills flanking the road any number of Arab rifles
might be aimed at him. The palms of his hands became moist,
his heart thumping with increasing rapidity, and his throat was
peculiarly dry. His apprehension must have communicated it-

self to the driver sitting next to him and to the soldiers in the rear of the truck who suddenly hoisted their rifles to the ready. The tension reached a level finally that was barely endurable and suddenly a sharp report cracked in the moonless night. Richard and the soldiers flung themselves to the floor of the truck while the driver ducked low and stepped on the gas, waiting for the hail of bullets to follow. The truck careened wildly, nearly spilling its occupants out into the sand, but no more shots followed. One by one the soldiers began peeping over the truck rim. Still no fire from the dark hills. And then in an instant the driver straightened up and began to laugh, easing back on the accelerator.

"It was a rock," he said, grinning broadly with unabashed relief, "the wheels throw them up against the fenders." And Richard laughed, too. He also brought out his notebook and scribbled a reminder that the imagined Arab attack might merit inclusion in his books and lectures. He could see them, now, the fluttering eyelids and the open-mouthed stares of his audiences, as he told them of riding through the dark desert night, Lawrence-like, the awareness of sudden death on every side—he would exaggerate his terror, because it was a nice lecture platform touch of humility—and build into a high-key dramatic narrative. He would end it with the false alarm, followed by some simple humor such as whenever afterward a rock hit his car fender, he instinctively ducked.

Stephens returned to Amman alone and Richard followed a few days later without offering any explanation for lingering in the desert. He was more restive than ever, Stephens noted, refusing to remain at the dinner table, for instance, for coffee and cigarettes. Instead, he would lurch to his feet and leave the room, often doing no more than pacing up and down in the street. He disappeared less and less with the mysterious friends to whom he did not introduce Stephens and he became tense and unpredictable. After announcing that he wanted to remain in Amman, he abruptly changed his mind and asked Stephens to ready the plane for the flight to Bagdad the next morning, an anxious two-stage hop across 600 miles of desert, landing

midway for gasoline at an oasis with the romantic name of Rut-
bar Wells.

The U.S. Consul in Bagdad was Princeton, class of 1907, and
Richard's entry into the local equivalent of cafe society pro-
gressed in a few days to a meeting with the Crown Prince of
Iraq, a smiling, shy sixteen-year-old boy whose greatest desire at
the moment was to be taken for a ride in the now-battered
Stearman, its scarlet and gold paint peeling badly. The prince's
father, King Feisal al Husain, had no more success dissuading
his son from the flight than most fathers would and he nervously sent two Royal Air Force planes aloft as an escort. They
flew seventy miles up the Tigris to Samarra and ate a picnic
lunch prepared by the royal kitchen on the steps of an ancient
mosque. Approaching Bagdad on their return, the Prince spotted his military school below. He asked Stephens to perform a
few gentle stunts, such as a slow roll, wingover and one loop,
and Stephens obliged. The roar of the engine brought the students out into the courtyard and the Prince knew that when he
went back to his classes he would be a private, as well as a
public, hero.

Stephens flew from Teheran alone to Bushire on the Persian
Gulf where he would meet Richard who was traveling overland. Richard could now trace his tension to his anxiety over
whether the flight would ever produce enough material for a
book, and setting off across Persia sounded so ripe with adventure that he began to relax. He bought a nightingale at a shop
in Teheran, he spent two days in a political prison and, before
Stephens left, he besought the Shah to permit his two daughters
to try an airplane ride and was doubly foiled. Not only would
the Shah not permit his precious giggling daughters in an aircraft, they were both so overweight Stephens doubted he could
get the plane off the ground. They settled for two slender
nieces and the wife of the recently-deposed Shah who still had
hopes of recovering the throne. It occurred to Richard that by
the time he got back to America, political developments might
well enable him to say he had been flying with the Queen of
Persia.

It took Richard and his nightingale, which he had named Gabriel, two weeks to cross Persia by auto, mail truck and an assortment of lesser vehicles, and although it was a journey singularly barren of breathtaking adventure, it produced one of Richard's more touching stories, a story about the nightingale Gabriel, a tiny mud-colored thing in a wooden cage. Persia was cold in December and the bird huddled quietly most of the time, but occasionally after it was fed and the hotel room was warm, it would sing in a tentative way, little fragments of simple notes and trills, and Richard liked to think the bird was dreaming of its freedom, that its heart was a prison choked with melody. It is remarkable, he thought, that Gabriel's spirit survives the shock of the cruel nightingale merchant's snare net, and the prospect of an eternity of suffocation in a cage for the capricious amusement of mere human beings. And he remembered that in the bazaar where he had bought his bird, there was not a sound of song. Or, if there was, it was a song of tears and despair. The nightingale is born to sing love songs to the rose, he thought, to celebrate in overflowing melody the passionate miracle of spring in Persia when gardens emerge in lushness and love is on everybody's mind. But it was still winter in Teheran and Gabriel in his cold confinement had nothing to celebrate. Richard wrapped his bird cage in an old blanket and set off by truck for his 800-mile overland journey south through Persia's bleak, cold, snow-bound interior. Once on the Persian Gulf he would set Gabriel free, provided the bird did not freeze to death in the meantime. He saw little of Persia, he was so busy keeping Gabriel warm and worrying about him, but he did have time to read Hafiz, the fourteenth-century Persian poet who wrote of nothing but freedom, love and drinking, and whose recurring symbol of happiness was the nightingale. ". . . drunk with joy is the nightingale," Hafiz wrote, and Richard fretted with anxiety and guilt. As the trip wore on, a sad and shivering Gabriel became a symbol of cruelty and betrayal to Richard who hovered over it as it struggled desperately to hang on to its perch while the truck rolled and bounced over the rutted roads. He cooed reassurances which amused the truck driver but otherwise served only to bolster Richard's morale.

The only portion of the trip even remotely free from worry was the first 280 miles—which took sixteen hours—from Teheran to Isfahan in a limousine owned by the Anglican Bishop of Persia, a pillar among missionaries and the headmaster of an English boys' school in Isfahan. Richard stayed three days in Isfahan, inspecting a giant turquoise mosque which he thought rivaled the Taj Mahal, and buying a hand-tooled silver cocktail shaker to send home to his father. Mail trucks took him the rest of the tortured way to Shiraz, passing through Persepolis which Alexander the Great once leveled in revenge, Richard remembered, for Xerxes' savage invasion of Greece.

It was in Shiraz, on the balmy Gulf, that Richard discovered the tomb of Hafiz set apart in an otherwise crowded graveyard and marked by one towering pine tree. Each year in Shiraz there is a festival to Hafiz, celebrating his religion of liberty and his morality of love, and poets and students emulate him and venerate him in wine and song and Richard arrived in the midst of it. He joined one party of men in the garden of a summerhouse and drank with them and tried to dance and sing with them, but Richard knew Hafiz only in translation so all he could do was revel in the spirit of a somewhat libertine evening. And when he groped his way back to his hotel moments before dawn, there was Gabriel, reproachfully silent.

"Oh Gabriel," cried Richard, exhilarated by the wine, "how I have abused you." And Gabriel's symbolism became even more profound. Gabriel was oppression everywhere and Richard would free them all. He grabbed the cage and stumbled out into the Persian dawn. By the time he found his way on foot to Hafiz' tomb, the grey sky was streaked with pink and gold and Richard set Gabriel's cage on the stone tomb itself. Fumbling, he opened the door and Gabriel shot through the opening, whirred his wings furiously and flew so rapidly Richard could not follow up into the pine tree where he was lost from sight. Richard recalled later that Gabriel sang, loudly, madly and unceasingly, and Richard sniffled with pride and happiness. Then he threw the bird cage to the ground, crushed it beneath his feet and left it there in shattered fragments, a token of his overflowing sentiment of the moment. And, still later, he found the suitable verse of Hafiz:

> In the clear dawn, before the east was red,
> Before the Rose had torn her veil in two,
> A nightingale through Hafiz garden flew,
> Stayed but to fill its song with joy . . . and fled.

⤐ 4 ⤑

Elly Beinhorn, the German aviatrix whose flying skill was exceeded, everyone said, only by her femininity, showed up in Bushire the same day Richard arrived there. She was then on her way, alone, from Berlin to Australia in a tiny single-seater Klemm which had crash-landed on an arid stretch of coast some sixty miles north of Bushire. She had hitchhiked into town and, trying to find someone to help her repair the plane's faulty engine, had encountered Stephens. He flew her back to her downed plane in the Stearman and the two of them overhauled the engine and got the Klemm in the air again. Miss Beinhorn had followed much the same route as the Carpet, and Richard decided the two ships might as well continue on together to India and, flying tandem, they made Delhi in three days by way of Jask and Karachi, and arrived on Christmas Eve. There was little of the Yuletide in the atmosphere, except privately in the homes of the British, for sedition and independence were in the air and there were rumors of assassination plots daily against the Viceroy.

Richard had one objective in India—to fly as far as he could up the slopes of Mount Everest and, if possible, to fly around it. Everest was still the unconquered giant of the Himalayas in 1931, for it had barely been seven years since Mallory and Irvine, the two British mountaineers, had vanished while groping toward the 29,141-foot summit in a blinding blizzard.

The fact that the Nepalese government had recently refused countless adventurers access to the forbidding slopes did not dim Richard's optimism. Even after his formal application for permission had been rejected, he was airily confident he would find a way. It came in the form of a telegraphed invitation from the Calcutta Flying Club to take part in an air show for the private enjoyment of the Maharajah of Nepal.

Richard finally soft-talked and pleaded the Maharajah into allowing the flight, but he very nearly died in the air show. Always impatient and forgetful, Richard had to be reminded constantly by Stephens to fasten his safety belt and to keep it fastened when in flight. As they took off down the Calcutta runway, Stephens issued his now routine reminder in a loud voice and Richard nodded, hooking the belt. Stephens banked the plane steeply at about 250 feet, turning about to make a pass over the field—and the admiring gaze of the Maharajah —upside down. As he flipped the plane on its back, Richard's safety belt—which had been looped beneath him creating nearly two feet of slack—pulled free and Richard plummeted out of the cockpit almost to his knees. Stephens flipped the ship back in a panic and Richard dropped back in, bruising his arms and legs severely on the side of the cockpit.

"You damned fool!" screamed Stephens, and Richard, mute with fright, cinched the belt as tight as he could.

Darjeeling, on the Nepal border, is about 325 air miles due north of Calcutta, and Everest is about 125 air miles north-west of Darjeeling. The Flying Carpet spent a night in Darjeeling and on the morning of January 9, 1932, Richard's thirty-second birthday, the husky plane was stripped of everything but its two occupants, one of them armed with a camera, and gasoline for five hours' flying time. Stephens took the plane up from 6,500 feet, the elevation of Darjeeling, to 15,000 feet and flew west along the Nepal frontier, turning due north toward Everest, 70 miles away. Stephens inched the throttle forward, the tachometer nearly red-lined, and the Stearman labored its way upward through the ever-thinning air. But its rate of climb did not exceed that of the land below and when Everest itself, the magnificent, loomed out of its eternal mists barely twenty miles ahead, the plane was a mere 500 feet above the stark ridges below and it was barely flying, in a nose-high altitude approaching a stall. There was no more power to be wrung from the engine. The flight up Everest had come to an end at slightly more than 18,000 feet, not enough to clear the passes on either side.

The plane was trembling violently and the freezing air pierced the heavy flying suits of Richard and Stephens as though they were made of cotton. Stephens' hands and feet were numb and he was losing his critical feeling of the response of the controls. An experienced pilot knows when a stall is coming from the sluggishness of the controls and Stephens knew that he was running out of time. In a matter of seconds the frozen slopes below would be too close for the plane to recover from a stall.

It was at this moment that Richard, wild with excitement— for no aircraft had ever been this close to Everest before—unbuckled his safety belt and stood up in the cockpit to photograph the soaring giant in front of them. The drag of his protruding body in the thin airstream stalled the ship and it dropped, nose first, like a rock. Richard clawed his way frantically back into the cockpit while Stephens rammed the stick forward and wondered if he had grossly overestimated the distance to the ground.

The ship was plummeting almost straight down, its air speed gaining furiously, but when Stephens began tugging back on the stick there was no response. Farther and farther back he pulled it, but there was no answering pressure. The slopes of Everest were dead ahead, bleak, barren, snow-whipped rocks and ridges and the stick was in the pit of Stephens' stomach before the Stearman's nose slowly began to rise and it pulled from its dive with a sickening mushing sensation, clearing the ridges by a few feet. Slowly, Stephens banked to the right and gently eased the ship around until it was headed nose low and downhill all the way to Darjeeling. Richard had gotten his snapshot of mighty Everest but he would find out later that the vibration of the plane had so fuzzed the outlines of that famous profile that it was barely recognizable. Yet, if nothing else, it was proof that he had been there and Richard was keenly sensitive to disbelief, especially after so many critics had challenged his claim to the Taj Mahal swim.

The Everest incident suggested to Stephens that Richard had

an affinity for disaster and a corresponding luck which spared him. He wondered when it would occur again and whether the luck was enough for them both. It happened in Pontianak, in Dutch East Borneo, a small coastal port strewn inland along a nameless river. The Flying Carpet stopped there on its way south after a months' delay in Singapore having pontoons installed. Few of the inhabitants of Pontianak had ever seen a plane before and most of the population may have been on the waterfront when the ship landed and anchored off a dock, and when it took off the next morning.

Stephens started the engine to hold the plane against the river current and sent Richard out on the pontoon to reel in the anchor. A vision of Richard stumbling obliviously into the spinning propeller shot through Stephens' mind but he tried not to think about it. Richard was supercautious but he nearly killed both of them anyway.

Coiling the anchor line around his arm and shoulder, Richard lost his balance as the plane bobbed with the motion of the water and, trying to regain it, he looped the rope into the propeller. Two things happened, instantaneously. The propeller whipped the rope from Richard's arm, and took great streaks of skin with it, and it snatched the 40-pound anchor from the water as though it were a top and flung it directly at Richard, grazing the side of his head. The line severed itself, or it would have jerked Richard into the propeller, but it bent one blade of the prop about ten degrees out of line. It took Stephens five hours to hammer the blade straight, while a local machine shop patched a hole in one pontoon gouged by the anchor as it whistled past.

They were still shaken by the incident late in the day when they landed at Kuching, the capital of Sarawak, the private country of the fabled White Rajah, James Brooke, to attend the annual Grand Prix Ball in the palace. Brooke was long since dead, his throne having been succeeded to by his nephew, Charles, and then by Charles' son, Vyner, whose wife, the Ranee Sylvia, was a young lady of British nobility. Times had changed since James Brooke not only had to win the confidence of the Dyak headhunters and force recognition of his miniscule nation by Great Britain, and the current Rajah ruled a relatively solvent and peaceable kingdom.

Richard and Stephens showed up at the ball in clean but tattered cottons, danced with the Ranee and the next day took her riding in the Carpet, an event which produced Sarawak's first civil strife in years. The wives of some of the government officials were jealous of the Ranee because they had not been invited to go flying too, and they persuaded their husbands to formally protest the Ranee putting her life in the hands of two unknown and untrusted Americans.

The Palace was in a turmoil all that morning, but the Ranee went flying anyway and the crisis subsided. And before Richard left Sarawak to go deeper into Borneo for an adventure, he hoped, with headhunters, he sent off a cable to his father in Memphis saying he was bound for Borneo to "hunt pythons and take chewing gum to the natives." His father, naturally, released this bit of flippant whimsy to the press. He also sent a letter to his father, and another to his publisher, that he was nearly out of money and would have to terminate the flight at Manila, instead of continuing on south to Australia and New Zealand as he had planned.

They were a month reaching Manila, a month in which Richard hoped for more than he found. In the Borneo interior, they learned to use a blowgun and poisoned darts, and they made an old Dyak chief almost a local deity by taking him flying. The chief, in return, gave Richard a dozen human heads, two of which turned out to be those of orangutans, and the remainder of which were later dumped in the Philippine Sea because their odor was overpowering and because Stephens was convinced they were bad luck. They made the plane overweight, anyway, for they weighed more than ten pounds each. They landed at Brunei, on the north Borneo coast, the legendary home of the legendary China Sea pirates, then flew on to Sulu in the southernmost part of the Philippines, which was savagely damaged by a typhoon the day after they departed. The fringe of the storm caught them at Zamboanga, but the plane rode out the weather at anchor behind a breakwater. At Lake Buluan in Mindanao, they hunted crocodiles and ducks for three days, and taking off from the Buluan River, the plane was nearly forced down by a 500-foot-deep cloud of locusts that enmeshed them. At Cebu, they visited Magellan's grave, and in Luzon, barely fifty miles from Manila, Richard was severely burned by the caustic-laden water in Lake Taal which occupies a volcanic crater.

They arrived in Manila the end of April, 1932, and were hailed as international heroes. The newspapers were filled for days with their exploits, they were constantly in demand as public speakers, and they were entertained royally and interminably by government officials and the U.S. Navy.

They crated up the Flying Carpet and sailed from Manila for San Francisco on May 9 aboard the American President liner *President McKinley* by way of Hong Kong and Shanghai, where they tried, in vain, to get close to the invading Japanese Marines. Yokohama was the next stop, and Richard went into Tokyo. He had first visited the city early in 1923, before the earthquake which devastated it, and he wanted to see how it had been reconstructed. In Honolulu, he lectured before 2,000 high school students and made arrangements, by cable, to begin lecturing the moment he landed in San Francisco because he was, in fact, flat broke.

It took four days to reassemble the Carpet at Alameda airport, across the Bay from San Francisco, and Richard used the time to make money lecturing.

When they landed at Burbank on June 4, after a four-hour flight from Alameda, Richard calculated that he had flown better than 40,000 miles, that the trip had cost him close to $50,-000 and according to frantic letters from his banker in New York, he was $2,000 overdrawn.

Three days later, he was sitting on the porch swing of his father's new house on Court Street in Memphis, chatting excitedly with friends and neighbors and reporters from the Memphis *Commercial-Appeal* and the *Press-Scimitar*. He was blabbing almost all of his new book away, but he talked so fast and erratically that the reporters took little of it down. The important thing they extracted from the gush of words was the fact that *New Worlds to Conquer,* published almost two years before, was still number one on the non-fiction best-seller lists and the impression that Richard didn't have a care in the world. But then Richard never displayed his anxieties to strangers. Probably no one but Stephens, for whom Richard now held a profound affection and admiration, knew the truth.

They had been nearly two years together, sharing the same anxieties and risks, and it was inevitable that sooner or later Richard would have to tell Stephens about the fear that never left him—that all that stood between him and an oblivion of total failure was the caprice of the public, that once he was unable to court the popular fancy, he would perish like a meteorite immersed in the sea, and with scarcely a ripple. There were times when he thought he understood the dynamics of his fame, but it more often bewildered him. All he knew, he said, was that his public did not want reality, at least not his reality.

"I want to write about the world as it is, and as I see it, instead of these adolescent romantic tales spun from a few bare facts, but I know my readers won't accept anything else. I can't write this stuff much longer; it gets harder and harder for me to do. Why can't I just write the truth?"

His exuberance, however, showed no signs of lessening. He was irrepressibly optimistic when he visited Chambers in Indianapolis, and full of enthusiastic promise when he conferred with his lecture agents in New York and agreed to begin a new tour the following October. This gave him only five months in which to finish his new book which he and Chambers had decided to title, simply, *The Flying Carpet.*

Richard left New York hurriedly for Alexandria, Virginia, just across the Potomac from Washington, where he took up residence with Paul Mooney, the young writer he had met two years before at a party in Pasadena. And it wasn't long before he let Chambers know that Mooney was collaborating with him on the new book. Not only that, said Richard, but if the book were of better quality than the others, it was all due to Mooney, which may not have been precisely true because the statement was embodied in a request that Bobbs-Merrill pay Mooney's travel expenses to New York for editorial conferences. Chambers agreed.

Richard's finances at this time were probably at their lowest ebb. For the entirety of 1931, he had earned—despite his best-selling status—only $9,468 in total royalties and he was reduced to begging advances of as little as $100 from Chambers whose firm was as hard hit by the depression as any other publisher. Book sales volume had dropped more than sixty percent since the crash of '29, and a good many publishers were not giving advances to anybody. The magazine market had withered away, too, for chapters of *The Flying Carpet*—which Richard shipped off to Indianapolis as soon as he wrote them—were being offered to the magazines as separate articles but there were no takers.

Richard struggled on through the summer, returning to New York in September. He stayed for a time at the Connecticut home of the Maxwell Aleys and then moved into the Standish Arms in Brooklyn Heights, directly across the East River from lower Manhattan, and Mooney came up from Alexandria to join him there. They gave the impression now of being inseparable and Mooney did, in fact, live with Richard for many of the few remaining years of Richard's life.

VII

Siberian Exclusive

A traveller has a right to relate and embellish his adventures as he pleases, and it is very unpolite to refuse that deference and applause they deserve.

—RUDOLF ERICH RASPE
(*Travels of
Baron Munchausen*)

◄§ I §►

MONEY problems plagued Richard until mid-October when he began his lecture tour. Not only had his bank debts in New York mounted, but the Internal Revenue Service was after him for two years' worth of unpaid income taxes. Richard's personal accounts were in such fuzzy shape, for he had no accountant and he kept no records, that neither he nor the IRS had any precise idea of how much he owed. He was subsisting on what amounted to handouts from Bobbs-Merrill, while he worked day and night to finish the book. He wasted several days vainly auditioning for proposed radio travel shows but his voice, which was still strident and scrawny, repelled every sponsor who heard it: not a friendly voice, they said.

He sent off the last chapter of *The Flying Carpet*, telling Chambers to disregard his father's criticisms of the manuscript, and spent his last few days in New York selecting 64 photographs to illustrate it from a mountain of his own snapshots and stock photos, and helped design the map of the Carpet's journey for the end papers.

Radio may have rejected him, but the movies now wanted him. He had barely begun his tour—which augured as one of his most successful, for crowds were bigger than ever—than he had an offer of $10,000 for six weeks of acting in a motion picture, *India Speaks*, being produced by Walter Futter, a young independent, for United Artists, and the cameras were to roll on November 2.

Richard terminated his lecture contract after a talk one night in Durant, Oklahoma, and caught a plane the next day from Tulsa for Hollywood. His seatmate on the flight was actress

Bebe Daniels but both she and Richard were too airsick to bother with introductions.

India Speaks turned out to be a collection of film clips on India, Tibet and the Himalayas, which Futter hoped to link together successfully with a thin romantic plot involving Richard and a young dark-haired actress named Rosie Brown who played the part of a Kashmiri maiden. They had one love scene —in a rose garden—but the script called for it to be aborted by a sudden rainstorm simulated by a fire hose. Both Richard and Rosie were drenched, and Richard came down two days later with a severe cold that blossomed into pneumonia and he was taken off to Cedars of Lebanon Hospital where for two days he was reported "critically" ill. His illness made all the papers, but Richard's parents failed to hear about it until Richard wrote them after he had recovered.

Most of this quasi-travelogue was filmed in the UA Studios, with three days of shooting on location in Yosemite Valley, 400 miles northeast of Hollywood, but the nearest thing to Tibet in California.

The Flying Carpet was published in late November to more general critical praise than his other books had received, but to the leanest market the book industry had ever seen. Chambers was more than disappointed that Richard was unavailable for personal appearance promotions, for a few autograph parties might have spelled the difference, but he understood, he wrote Richard, that his young author's need for money was the most important thing.

Richard's earlier fears that his writing had lost its gaiety and wonder were groundless; the reviews, if anything, lauded his new maturity.

"Halliburton seems to have grown up . . . [from] the hunger for applause . . . the sophomoric hee-haw humor," said the venerable critic Joseph Henry Jackson in the San Francisco *Chronicle.* "If he keeps on like this, people who had been wishing he would make enough royalties to retire will wish instead that he would lose it all so he would have to keep on writing about faraway places."

The San Francisco *Examiner* also cited his "growth," adding that *The Flying Carpet* "is a big step forward for him, artistically. One wonders what he will be doing next."

The New York Times described the book as a "fresh, unhackneyed, happy performance that gives to the reader something of the sensation of magic implied in its title."

Richard spent Christmas in a rented bungalow on Pinehurst Road in Hollywood, but resumed lecturing in early January.

He had also committed himself, in his scraping for money, to a 20-lecture tour on the Pacific Coast through a Los Angeles agency. Unfortunately, the tour was to begin March 1, the same day *India Speaks* would have its premier in New York and he had promised to be there too.

The anxiety of this conflict, which he never did figure out how to resolve, stayed with him until mid-February when Futter postponed the film's opening until April. In the meantime, Richard swept the East, South and Midwest, giving 76 lectures in 101 days. In addition, he appeared at more than a dozen bookstore autographing parties; it availed nothing but Chambers' everlasting gratitude. At Wanamaker's in Philadelphia, for example, a mob of 400 people showed up but only 12 of them bought books.

Finally, Chambers suggested Richard suspend all autographing parties until after the slump. Herbert Hoover had lost the presidency to Franklin Delano Roosevelt to whom not a few Americans were already attributing messianic powers; perhaps prosperity was now, as Hoover had said, just around the corner.

Richard appeared to have reached a plateau of professional skill in his lecturing for he found them easier than ever to give and his audiences more responsive. In Kansas City, 12,000 schoolteachers attending a convention there stunned him with a thundering ovation and in Chattanooga, although the death of former President Calvin Coolidge was announced to his audience just before he spoke, he was roundly cheered. There were other signs of his growing popularity on the rostrum. Students at the University of Chattanooga presented him with a model they had made of the Flying Carpet, and at Florida State College, he was the object of a massive petition delivered to the dean by a student delegation demanding "more speakers like Richard Halliburton and fewer musicians" in the college's annual lecture series.

There was some concern in Richard's mind over whether his appearance in *India Speaks* might in some way infringe on the purchase of the film rights to *The Royal Road* by Fox, but he was alone in his worry. Fox executives had repeatedly postponed production of their movie, and they regarded *India Speaks* as a possible index of Richard's appeal at the box office. If *India Speaks* was a hit—even a modest hit—they would feel more confident about *The Royal Road.*

It was also alarming to Richard, because of his continuing financial squeeze, to realize that the sales of all his books, despite the flagging sales of *The Flying Carpet,* had passed the half-million mark. Where had all the money gone?

He wound up his eastern circuit in Washington where he had a brief audience with the outgoing President Hoover, and lunch with U.S. Senator and ex-governor Huey Long, still at the zenith of his demagogic reign over Louisiana and who, less than two years later, would be assassinated.

He landed in California to start his 20-city western tour, saw a sneak preview of *India Speaks* at a theater in San Diego and came away feeling that the movie was good but that his voice "sounded funny."

He had driven himself almost compulsively since returning from the Flying Carpet trip eleven months before, and it came as both a relief and a source of new anxiety to find that half his Pacific Coast lectures had been canceled, apparently the result of a rumor that he would not show up because the opening of *India Speaks* had already been announced for early March. He desperately needed a rest, for he was underweight and chronically tense, but he needed money more. He received an unexpected royalty check of $1,100 from the sales of the dollar editions of his earlier books but he sent it to his mother as a payment toward completion of his parents' new home. The margin of cash that he should have had he had given to Mooney for his help on the book.

He rented a beach house in Laguna Beach for the few days he would be able to use it and was in a grocery store in town on March 11, 1933, when the disastrous Long Beach earthquake hit, killing some 200 persons. Richard fled to the street as soon as he felt the ground shake and heard the plate glass windows of the store shatter and the bottles and canned goods cascade to the floor, and he reached the sidewalk just as the store roof caved in. He was spared again, but his rented beach house lost its chimney.

Richard was enchanted with Laguna Beach, and he thought of it as the place where he would someday come to roost, perhaps to build his own house on the beach near the thunder of the surf, or on a mountaintop nearby. He was riding horseback along the sand a mile south of the village one morning when he saw a trail twisting up the steep slopes at the mouth of Laguna Creek Canyon. Half an hour later, he was atop the narrow ridge, spellbound at the view—the foaming surf below, the serpentine coastline, the grassy canyon floor, purple mountains and not another house in sight. A month later, without telling anybody, he bought the summit of the ridge for $1,900. Someday he would build his home there, when the struggle was over.

He began to see the dream coming true later that year while attending a performance of *Salome* at the Barbizon-Plaza auditorium in New York. He met an architect named William Alexander, a young visionary who had studied a year at Taliesen with the great Frank Lloyd Wright. Richard described his property to Alexander and said, "You're going to build my house."

He filled the remainder of his California lecture dates, spent a few days in San Francisco with his art patron friend Noel Sullivan, and then visited Charles and Kathleen Norris on their Saratoga ranch. It was the nearest thing to a vacation that he could manage for as soon as he returned to Laguna, he was off to New York for the official premier of *India Speaks* at the New Roxy Theater where he had to appear briefly five times a day for a week, a grind for which Futter paid him $800. The film received a welter of mixed reviews, most of them suggesting that it was neither fish nor fowl.

Billboard magazine appraised it to be what it was: fragments of travelogue strung together by a pointless melodrama and "will the public believe any of it?" The public believed it for a time, but the box office dropped rapidly and *India Speaks* was a flop. Futter took the picture to England where it fared even worse because Richard's innocent flirtation with the "half-naked" olive-skinned Kashmiri girl was taken as a colossal threat to British prestige in India. Futter said later that his losses on the film were sizable.

The movie critic for the San Francisco *Examiner,* however, was dazzled.

> . . . through vales of beauty and down streets of horror, into temples of strange gods, into danger-infested jungles, across the snow-swept plains of Tibet, up the perpendicular heights of the Himalayas; it is India, vast and many-peopled, wierd, mysterious and unfathomable.

The summer of 1933 was an unending frustration to Richard. His need for money gave him no time to contemplate another book and he dissipated nearly three months trying to sell himself to radio, the movies and to magazines, and managed only to sell one article, a gushy piece titled "The World Is Still Wide," to *Cosmopolitan.* He even consulted several literary agents in the vain hope of stimulating the market for himself. He was suffering, too, from lack of attention. *Liberty* magazine finally published the Foreign Legion chapter from *The Flying Carpet* and Richard immediately proposed that Chambers suggest to the French Government that it award Richard a medal for the publicity he had given their great fighting force. Chambers ignored the proposal.

To help promote the dying *India Speaks,* Futter had persuaded Grosset and Dunlap to publish a $1 picture book of stills from the movie with the captions to be written by Richard. Futter would receive $1,000 advance, which he would split with Richard.

Chambers protested the idea on grounds it might eat into the Garden City reprints of Richard's own books and he offered to advance Richard $500 a month against unearned royalties if he would forget the picture book. But Chambers asked Richard not to mention the advance to other writers because, he said, "we aren't giving advances to anybody."

Richard begged Chambers' forgiveness, went ahead with the picture book which flopped badly, but Chambers paid Richard the $500 stipend anyway.

When President Roosevelt closed the nation's banks in March of 1933, to halt the growing run on deposits, Richard was unaffected. His primary involvement with banks was that he owed them money. Otherwise, he was living out of his pocket. Whatever came in he either spent or sent home to Memphis.

He spent the summer driving around the show places of the Deep South alone or with Mooney, and he went to the Chicago World's Fair with his parents who began admonishing him for his failure to marry and settle down.

They had no clear idea of his affairs, financial or personal, for he had never balked at sending money home, and his attentiveness to them had been something more than most parents have any reason to expect. And, with dutiful courtesy, he promised his father then he would sire some grandchildren for him soon.

This parental concern, Richard knew, was symptomatic of his father's painful realization that Richard no longer confided in him. "He's pulled away from us," his father told a friend in Memphis, "we don't really know what he's doing."

But he plunged like a talking dervish into lecturing in October, scheduling himself out of five speakers bureaus—Alber-Wickes in Boston, Alkahest in Atlanta, World Celebrities in Portland, Oregon, Emerson in Chicago, the Dixie Bureau in Dallas, and Allied in Los Angeles. Although ninety percent of all Richard's lectures were before schools, colleges, town halls

or civic groups, he was still popularly tabbed as the hero of the
women's club teas, an image he contested as endlessly, and with
as much futility, as he struggled to get out of debt.

Richard was so absorbed in his own monumental problems
that the struggles that seemed so important to everybody else in
the depression-torn thirties escaped him altogether. The economic landslides which had buried the hopes of millions of
Americans he appeared to regard as a mere personal inconvenience. He had no sense of politics anyway, so perhaps he could
never have become embroiled in the great moral decisions that
other writers of the time found so dynamically compelling; decisions rooted in the handy suspicion that the depression was
the inevitable outcome of a warping of the social order. If
Richard had money troubles, he blamed nothing beyond himself, for he had been taught—and had always believed—that
each man is the master of his own fate. It wasn't a social theory
that one could challenge intellectually; it was an article of private faith. It was, in fact, something he would not talk about.

"Never have opinions," he said. "A really mature person
never has opinions. I'm glad I've reached that stage myself."

⊸§ 2 §⊷

Bobbs-Merrill continued to nag Richard to produce another book, and to his reply that he couldn't afford it unless he had some other source of income, Chambers stimulated a deal with the Bell Newspaper Syndicate that called for Richard to undertake a new trans-world peregrination and write a series of 50 weekly articles for newspapers.

Richard balked at the proposal. He was still hopeful something would come of his assorted negotiations with radio and the movies. All he wanted at this time, he said, was an income. A brewery offered him $500 a week to do a series of 25 weekly travel programs, and Fox Movietone News approached him with the idea of making travelogue shorts with on-the-spot narration. This would mean travel at its most hectic, and he would be operating in an unfamiliar medium. He turned down both projects, although he confessed that he really didn't know what he was looking for.

He accepted the Bell proposition, almost by default, stipulating only that they sign up enough newspapers to guarantee him at least $200 a week. And, as Chambers pointed out, the series could be easily converted into a book. After conferring for several days with Chambers and the Bell editors in New York, Richard settled on an approximate itinerary of adventures. He would begin with the Seri Indians in Baja California, move on to Fort Jefferson, the abandoned old Federal Civil War prison off the Florida Keys, then to Havana, Haiti, Martinique and Santo Domingo, the Caribbean island believed to have been the San Salvador of Christopher Columbus' momentous landfall in 1492. Columbus' bones, and those of his son, were interred in the cathedral there in 1540 in a leaden casket which was displayed every October 12 during Columbus Day ceremonies. Richard hoped to persuade church authorities to open the casket and permit him to examine the bones.

From the West Indies, he would go to France, Germany and Russia, the Middle East and Ethiopia, climaxing it all by borrowing—or buying—an elephant to ride over the Alps like Hannibal, a stunt he regarded as "gay, ridiculous and outrageous" and one bound to attract the instant attention of the world.

His only concern was meeting the Bell deadline of one 2,500-word article every week for almost a year. But the stimulation of the challenge pleased him and thrilled his restless nature and when he returned to California in the spring of 1934 he was eager and happy. He stayed a month in San Francisco, reading —as he always did—every book he could find on the places he would visit, lecturing spasmodically, and placing himself at the disposal of his private social world. He bought a used Ford roadster and in June drove to Hollywood where he lectured and otherwise enjoyed himself until early July when he went into Baja California and to Tiburon Island.

Speaking one night in the Greek Theater in Griffith Park to the honor classes from ten Los Angeles high schools, he was trapped afterward by a demented young woman who had written him one tortured love letter a week for the past five years and who sent him sausages on Christmas.

She hung on the fringes of the crowd of students which thronged around Richard after the lecture, and she remained doggedly until Richard had signed his last autograph and received his last gush of praise and given his final counsel to the last glassy-eyed young man who wanted to follow in his footsteps. He saw her hovering there, a wispy blonde in a neat cotton dress, a plain-looking girl in a zealot's cast. He knew instinctively that she embodied trouble, but he found himself more intrigued than apprehensive, and instead of fleeing when he might have been able to, he waited to see what would happen.

The girl walked slowly toward him, clutching a black patent

leather handbag in both hands before her and staring into Richard's eyes. He smiled in his boyish way and the girl, who may have courted other celebrities and was conditioned to seeing them in full retreat, was taken aback and she stopped, a good ten feet from Richard, but said nothing. Richard still did not know who she was, beyond a moon-struck fan, until finally she stammered out her name and he recognized it, for the bale of love letters had become an office joke back in Indianapolis.

There were still a dozen boys and girls clustered about, forming a sort of funnel emptying toward Richard and they stared at her in puzzlement, a few of the girls giggling at her trance-like posture. Then the giggles subsided abruptly, leaving a fumbling silence.

Richard suspected that if he ignored the girl, he might galvanize her into action, for he had never answered her letters or otherwise acknowledged her existence, and yet she had not given up writing them. It also occurred to him that her adulation might have been a kind of fantasy that she, having her chance, could not convert into reality. But that was a tenuous theory and he could not be sure. He continued to smile at her in an impersonal way, slowly resuming his chatting with the cluster of students who, one by one, began drifting off. The girl had still not moved, nor spoken, nor had she taken her eyes off Richard. He began moving obliquely away from her toward the stage exit, and as he came abreast of her he stopped, insulated from her by a boy at his side.

"Would you like my autograph, too?" he asked her in an offhand voice, but there was no response. She was only staring, frozen into immobility by the conflict between her emotions and her mind.

"Give me a piece of paper," he said to the boy, who clumsily tore a sheet from the notebook which Richard had autographed for him. Richard scrawled his name and, stepping up to the girl —now genuinely fearful that he would trigger some awkward scene—he slid the paper under her fingers on the handbag, glanced quickly at her face and hurried out the door.

She made no move to follow him, nor did she ever write him

another letter. Yet the encounter haunted him for days for he had seen that her eyes were full of tears.

His lectures then were salted with expectations of adventures he would find on his forthcoming trip and, as usual, he was advocating shoestring vagabondage.

"Travel is rewarding in inverse proportion to the amount of money and property you take with you. I have only one suit. Travel with as much imagination and as little baggage as possible."

The Baja California expedition was held up by a bad reaction to typhoid inoculations which put him in bed for three days, and by a commission from United Artists, then producing a film on Benvenuto Cellini, to write a newspaper promotional puff on Cellini's love affairs, and he had to read two books to do it.

Early in July, he chartered a plane to Hermosillo, hired a guide and an auto and struck out across the 100 miles of desert for a spot on the Gulf of California opposite Tiburon Island, home of the Seri Indians. He spent a depressing week with these dying, primitive peoples, who had given up warfare for marginal survival since there were less than 200 of them left alive. Richard slept on the beach in a blanket, hunted sea turtles and pelicans with the Indians, and grew somewhat accustomed to their almost total diet of raw fish. The Seri had stopped building houses, or planting crops. They simply roamed like gypsies and lived as they could off a barren land and a dangerous sea.

Richard hurried back to Hollywood, finished his first Bell piece and caught the plane for Memphis. His seatmate this time was novelist William Faulkner, who had been in Hollywood writing screenplays, and was on his way home to Oxford, Mississippi, which is just 60 miles south of Memphis. He and Richard glanced shyly at each other during the long flight, but neither spoke. Richard was met at the plane by his parents, and Faulkner by his wife and infant son. As they parted at the foot of the plane ramp, the two men gave each other a farewell glance. In the terminal building, a reporter from the *Commer-*

cial-Appeal hopped back and forth between Richard and Faulkner.

"Who is that?" his mother asked, and Richard told her.

"Why didn't you introduce us?" she said.

"I don't know him," Richard replied, sulkily, for he had been afraid to speak to the great and somber novelist.

His Tiburon adventure brightened the pages of several Sunday newspaper supplements that month, competing successfully with lurid accounts of the melodramatic killing of the gunman's idol, John Dillinger, by FBI agents in front of a Chicago movie theater.

Richard bristled slightly when he saw his story juxtaposed with that of such seamy violence. "Who ever heard of John Dillinger?" he asked his mother.

When Richard saw his parents' new home, and his mother reported on the profitable investment she had made with all the royalty checks he had sent her, he marveled at what he assumed was her frugality.

If he had sent his mother more money, he wrote Chambers, he would be rich now instead of broke. And he asked for another advance so he could get under way to the Caribbean.

If he ever got out of debt, he added, he would go far away from all the ruthless demands of his success.

And when the $750 check arrived, Richard acknowledged it gratefully, as he acknowledged almost every letter or courteous gesture he ever received—the volume of words he put in letters to friends and acquaintances might well have exceeded those of his books—by saying that it arrived at a critical time—but then, they all did.

He also instructed Chambers to send all royalty checks to his mother for the year that he would be gone.

Richard linked his journey to Fort Jefferson in the Dry Tortugas off Key West with the harrowing saga of Dr. Samuel Mudd, the Maryland physician who had set the broken leg of John Wilkes Booth—without knowing who he was—after the assassination of President Lincoln and who had been sentenced to this grim American Devil's Island as an accomplice. Dr. Mudd became the hero of the place, however, and was ultimately pardoned, after a yellow fever epidemic swept the prison and killed, in addition to scores of prisoners and almost all the guards, the prison physician.

Richard reached the now abandoned Fort, a gigantic brick monolith, after a 10-hour trip by fishing boat from Key West. He prowled the ruins, tried to imagine the suffering of the heroic Dr. Mudd, petted the thousands of sea terns and noddies that had taken over the place, and returned to Key West the same day.

Abandoned after Dr. Mudd's pardon, Fort Jefferson had been occupied briefly during the Spanish-American War because of its proximity to Cuba. Its original purpose had been to protect American shipping in the straits of Florida, and it had proven—with its battery of 400 cannon—to be one of the all-time U.S. white elephants.

In Havana on August 9, Richard typed out his Fort Jefferson story and shipped it off to Bell. Already, the pressure of the weekly deadline was beginning to harass him, especially since he was as much a celebrity in Havana as in Kansas City, and he was besieged with interviewers, autograph hunters and dinner invitations. He had no time to enjoy himself and, resentfully, he moved on to Santiago to inspect the wreckage of Spanish ships sunk in the war, and to dash—like Teddy Roosevelt—up San Juan Hill.

He focused his Cuban story, however, on Richmond Pearson Hobson's heroic—and unsuccessful—scuttling of the converted coal collier, the *Merrimac,* named after the famed Civil War vessel, in the channel entrance to Santiago harbor to bottle up the Spanish fleet. Hobson, consequently promoted to Rear Admiral and awarded the Congressional Medal of Honor for his feat, sank the *Merrimac* all right, but in the wrong place, and he and his crew of six volunteer Navy enlisted men were captured by the Spaniards.

Hobson had lashed six torpedoes to the hull of the *Merrimac,* but the fire from the Spanish fort at Morro Castle overlooking the channel had destroyed the torpedo firing mechanisms, swept away the rudder and both the bow and stern anchors and Hobson could not scuttle the ship where he had intended.

Richard was a week in Haiti, exploring the mountain citadel of Henri Christophe, the illiterate one-time slave who was Toussaint L'Ouverture's chief aide in the liberation of Haiti in 1800 and who became its king in 1811. In Santo Domingo he did, indeed, fondle the bones of Columbus, and on September 1 he was at the New Weston Hotel in New York on his way to France to cross the Alps on an elephant.

He had now completed six articles for Bell, but the series was to begin in just a week which meant he would have less than a two-month margin to meet deadlines if anything went wrong. He was beginning to regret he had gotten involved in such a pressure-ridden project and he began to count not the stories he had done, but the forty-four he had yet to write.

✑ 3 ✐

Richard finished one more Bell story on the boat, and another in a hotel in Le Havre, which gave him a sufficient backlog to ease his deadline anxiety. He arrived in Paris at the end of September and, remembering that Hannibal had crossed the Alps in October, decided to see if he could find a suitable elephant in a week, ship it to Montreux and start over the Great St. Bernard Pass to Turin or, if he was lucky, Rome. En route he would visit the St. Bernard Monastery, home of the dogs of the Alpine rescue legend, which would give him an additional story.

The French press gave daily play to the Hannibal stunt and when Richard went searching among the zoos and circuses of Paris for a gentle elephant, he was accompanied by a gaggle of reporters, French and American. At the Cirque d'Hiver he found a pleasant female named Lulu, but she was pregnant. The circus management, amused as anybody else at the stunt— and the publicity—offered him Yvonne, another docile female, for 1000 francs a day rental. Richard insured Yvonne against all forms of disaster with Lloyds of London and was all set to sign the agreement when the circus manager remembered that his year's supply of advertising posters boasted that his circus featured sixteen performing elephants. If Yvonne went into the Alps, he would only have fifteen. He would have to have all his posters reprinted because Frenchmen, he explained to Richard, will demand their money back if they go to a circus advertising sixteen elephants and find only fifteen. The manager was sorry, but unless Richard wanted to pay for the new posters, too, he would have to withdraw from the arrangement.

At the zoo in the Bois de Bologne, Richard found Elysabethe

224

Dalrymple, an elephant so gentle children were permitted to ride her. Further, she was smaller than the average elephant which meant he would have less trouble finding a stable for her on the journey.

Richard entered into the same 1000-francs-per-day agreement with the zoo, insured Dally, as he called her, and hired her Parisian mahout and on October 15, 1934, set out from the Bois de Bologne for the railroad station. They made it across the Porte Maillot through a jam of traffic, although Richard, following in a car, noticed that Dally skittered badly and seemed frightened, switching her head nervously from side to side. She had just entered the Avenue de la Grand Armée, with the Arc de Triomphe in the distance, when a taxi cut in front of Richard's car, pulled up behind Dally and blew his horn, apparently to amuse his passengers. Dally bolted. She dashed straight down the boulevard for almost half a mile before the mahout could stop her. A truck took her back to the zoo.

Snow would come any day to the Great St. Bernard Pass and Richard had no time to get Dally accustomed to the outside world. She was a park elephant, he concluded, and would always remain one. The zoo officials suggested an elephant at a zoo in Hanover, Germany, but by the time Richard got there, she had been leased to a circus. He hurried on to Berlin and might have found his elephant but blizzards had hit the Great St. Bernard Pass and it was now closed to all traffic. He would have to wait until spring.

Berlin was much the same as Richard remembered it from his last visit in 1921, except that Hitler was now chancellor and the streets were bristling with youth in uniform.

"The older people seem very cool about Hitler," he wrote to his father, "but the kids are all maniacs on the subject—and they will be in command in a few years."

Richard had arrived in Berlin with $1,500 in German marks to rent his elephant and when he went to board the plane for Leningrad, he was forbidden by German customs to take the money with him. It took the U.S. Embassy two days to obtain a release for the marks and when Richard landed in Leningrad on October 26 he had the money, irritatingly still in marks. He took the train to Moscow where he remained for two months, off and on, of what he described as continual "amazement, infuriation and frustration."

For all its inconvenience and discomfort—the bitter cold of a Russian December, the bad food, the poor hotel service, the dirty toilets, the relentless spying by the GPU agents and their informers—Moscow yielded one of Richard's better stories, and one that hardly anybody he knew believed.

Richard took a room at the Hotel Metropole, then the gathering place for foreign correspondents, and they told Richard how impossible it was for a western journalist to operate in Russia and, also, how he could manage. The cardinal rule was to zealously avoid displaying any friendship for a Russian, no matter how nice or helpful he might have been, and under no circumstances to mention either his name or his identity in dispatches or articles; it could only get the Russian in trouble. He would at least be questioned and if he had indeed been a friend to an American, he could well join the three million Soviet citizens reportedly held then in Siberian labor prisons.

The only exception to this rule was the interpreters who worked for the newsmen and for the news agencies. Many of them were friendly and helpful, but they couldn't be trusted; perhaps all of them were spies.

From Robin Kinkead of *Reuters* (later with *The New York Times* and, still later, a public relations counsel for Pan American Airways), Richard learned how to negotiate the frozen streets of Moscow in the absence of taxi cabs and public transport: flag down one of the many trucks that rumbled constantly through the city and offer the driver a few rubles for a ride.

But from William Stoneman of the Chicago *Daily News* Richard got the tip to his big story. Stoneman and several other correspondents had been scouting Siberia for stories on the reported slave labor camps, and they had also been searching— unsuccessfully—for the man in charge of the mass murder of Czar Nicholas II, his wife, his son and his four daughters on the night of July 16, 1918. There were persistent rumors that he lived in Ekaterinburg, a city whose name had since been changed to Sverdlovsk, where the executions had taken place. But nobody had been able to find him.

Richard hired Stoneman's interpreter, a personable young man who was the American-born son of a Bolshevik hero killed by the White Russians in 1918. The interpreter, whose name was Walter, wanted to return to the United States where he had been reared, but because his father was a hero he was not permitted to leave. At least, that was his story. Richard said afterwards that Walter was a GPU agent.

The two of them left Moscow for Sverdlovsk, forty-eight hours on the Trans-Siberian Railway. It was a miserable trip, for the jammed coaches were without light or heat, and Richard sat sleepless on his suitcase for the two days. The only real lead he had, apart from Stoneman's tip, was the published report of the White Russian investigation of the assassinations made a week afterward when the Whites captured Ekaterinburg briefly from the otherwise thundering Bolsheviks. In the report, the man in charge of the killings had been identified as Peter Ermakov, an ex-convict and wild-eyed revolutionary terrorist. He had, at one time, been made warden of the prison where the Czar and his family had spent their final days, a building later converted into a revolutionary museum. There was no trace of the Czar there now, apart from a newspaper headline applauding his annihilation; even the bullet holes in the floor and walls from the assassins' guns had been concealed.

Richard went first to the museum and learned that Ermakov was still warden, a patronage reward for his role in the revolution, but that he had not been at his desk for many weeks. He was home, dying of cancer of the throat.

Naively, Richard went to Ermakov's home, a tiny two-room apartment in a somewhat squalid apartment house where he lived with his wife, a haggard, once attractive, grey-haired woman much younger than Ermakov who was then nearing sixty. Richard and Walter knocked and were admitted. Mrs. Ermakov was tense but cordial and seemed reluctant to refuse Richard his interview.

"I'm sorry," she said, "but my husband is very ill. He can see no one."

Ermakov, lying in the next room, had overheard Richard's inquiries, however, and called out to him.

"You come in here. I'll tell you what happened. Don't ask my wife. She doesn't know anything about it."

Ermakov lay on a low bed, under a pile of red cotton quilts. He was a heavy man, unshaven, with labored breathing, and his eyes, with their black pupils, were violently bloodshot. At intervals he spat a mouthful of bloody mucus into a bedside pan. He was clearly dying.

Richard sat down gingerly on the edge of the bed and Walter eased into a chair by the door. Mrs. Ermakov stood behind him.

"What do you want to know about the Czar?" Ermakov asked.

"Everything," Richard replied.

It took Ermakov three and a half hours to tell of the slaughter of Nicholas, his German-born Czarina, Alexandria, their invalid hemophiliac son, Alexis, who was fourteen, and their four beautiful daughters, Olga, twenty-two; Tatiana, twenty-one; Maria, nineteen; and Anastasia, seventeen.

Nicholas had abdicated in March of 1917 when Alexander Kerensky and the provisional Revolutionary government seized control of the country. They were placed under house arrest in their own palace at Tsarskoe Selo near Petrograd and for five months lived much as they always had, while their nation burned and raged about them. Lenin and the Bolsheviks were growing stronger daily, and crying for the blood of the Czar, so Kerensky shipped the royal family off to the Siberian city of Tobolsk where, geographically, at least, they were safer. Further, the town was full of White Russian and royalist sympathizers who were plotting to rescue the Czar and his family and smuggle them to England to await better days.

But Kerensky and his moderates were suddenly gone, banished by Lenin and his immoderate Bolsheviks, and the Czar's safety was their peril so they moved the royal family again, this time to Ekaterinburg, 300 miles nearer Moscow, and right in the middle of several thousand Bolshevik irregular troops whose mere presence appeared to render any rescue impossible. These ragged irregulars, however, were busy much of the time fighting elements of the White Russian army which included the Czar's military staff and a regiment or two of Czech troops, and the Whites, by July, were within theoretical reach of Ekaterinburg. The Central Committee in Moscow ordered the Czar, his family and retainers executed, and their remains destroyed so that no bone or shred of garment could be recovered and enshrined and deified by the Whites.

The executions were to be carried out by Yourovsky, the commandant of the local Cheka, the counter-revolutionary terrorist unit. And at midnight on July 17, Yourovsky awoke the Czar and his family and informed them they were being moved —along with the Czar's physician, a maid, a cook and a valet— to another part of the city to spare them from a possible White assault into Ekaterinburg itself.

While Yourovsky herded the family and the staff—eleven persons in all—into a basement room adjoining a corridor with a street exit, Ermakov rounded up a truck, a dozen motley soldiers, several tins of gasoline and sulfuric acid, and parked the truck and its contents by the basement door.

Accompanied only by Ermakov and a sailor named Vaganov —armed with Mauser rifles—Yourovsky stepped into the room and slammed the door behind him. He pulled from his pocket a sheet of paper upon which the Central Committee had drafted the death sentence—"for crimes against the Russian people." He held the paper with one hand and with the other he unslung a Nagan repeating rifle from his shoulder. At the same moment that Yourovsky began to read, the driver of the truck raced the engine filling the room with a deafening, sputtering roar to muffle the sound of the shots, but Yourovsky's voice carried above it.

Yourovsky had chosen to kill the Czar, and his sick son himself. Ermakov was to shoot the Czarina, the doctor, the cook and the valet. Vaganov was to execute the four daughters and the maid.

The Czar, his son and the Czarina had been seated in the only chairs in the bare room when Yourovsky entered. As he began to read, Nicholas and Alexandria stood up. The little boy put on his cap. Yourovsky shouted the death sentence and the Czar cried out, "What! You mean we're not leaving . . ." and Yourovsky's bullet crashed into his brain. Ermakov shot the Czarina in the mouth, killing her instantly, and his next bullet went into the physician's neck. He crumpled to the floor.

Yourovsky's second shot knocked the little Czarevitch out of his chair and he lay on the floor, moaning. Vaganov shot the four daughters in quick succession and after they fell he kept pumping more bullets into them.

The maid, miraculously, was not hit at all. She was later bayoneted to death by soldiers waiting in the corridor outside.

Some of the others weren't killed immediately, either. Alexis was still groaning and writhing and Yourovsky fired two bullets into the boy's head.

Anastasia, too, was groaning, and Yourovsky called in the soldiers to finish the job. They clubbed her to death with rifle butts.

The soldiers stripped the eleven bodies and heaved them into the truck, and Ermakov directed it to an abandoned mining pit about twelve miles out of the city. Ermakov and his crew piled the bodies onto a funeral pyre of logs at the bottom of a shallow pit, and left them there with a guard of soldiers until the next night when Ermakov dumped gasoline and the acid over the bodies and set them afire.

Ermakov tended the blaze as he would a bonfire, poking and turning the remains of everything—bodies and logs—until there was nothing left but ashes. He and the soldiers shoveled the ashes into buckets and loaded them into the truck. The site of the fire was watered down and raked so that no sign of it remained. As the truck rumbled back into town, Ermakov scattered the ashes overboard with a shovel.

There was no truth, he said, to the rumor that Anastasia had escaped death, and had been smuggled away from the place of cremation during the day. He had heard the rumor—that

Anastasia was alive, in New York—but he had seen her body burn. He had seen them all burn; he had watched closely, because he hated them so.

At least that was the story with which Richard taunted the correspondents in the Hotel Metropole when he got back to Moscow. If it were true, it was a singular scoop, but they knew better.

"Halliburton," said Stoneman grinning, "you're a story teller posing as a journalist. The next thing you'll tell me is that Ermakov died in your arms."

"No," said Richard, "he didn't. As far as I know, he's still alive. Why don't you go to Sverdlovsk and talk to him yourself?"

≈§ 4 §≈

Nobody believed the Ermakov yarn—except most of Richard's readers. He made no attempt to file the story with Bell while he was still in Russia and, in fact, did not write it until a month later and Bell distributed it in four hair-raising installments. By the time it appeared in print, and the Moscow press corps was compelled to check it out, the Soviets had declared Sverdlovsk off-limits to correspondents and Richard had been kicked out of Russia.

Walter, the interpreter, was questioned extensively by Stoneman and the other newsmen but all Walter would do was smile.

"I think the smile means it's a fake," said Stoneman, "but on the other hand, he may be smiling AT us."

Richard's story, for all its high melodrama, did not settle the Anastasia dispute. There were those who still believed she died, and there were those who still believed she survived.

Richard interviewed the widow of Vladimir Lenin, the father of the Soviets, a hunched, white-haired, dynamic woman of seventy-two, who was serving as Commissar of Education under Joseph Stalin who had been ruling Russia since Lenin's death in 1924. She and Richard chatted for an hour amiably, mostly about her then grandiose plans to liberate Soviet womanhood from the yoke of domestic subservience, to educate them into full equality with men in leadership of all occupations and professions. Richard was somewhat appalled, but did not protest. Women everywhere resented their natural role in life, he knew, and wondered if the Soviet plan would ever reach America to make wives and mothers even more domineering than they were already.

The correspondents at the Metropole missed Richard, for he

had been a refreshing personality in the drabness of everything, and they had been flattered by his quiet charm and his keen interest in what they did and what they thought. Richard, of course, was simply getting information.

They had enjoyed chiding him for what they regarded as his tall stories, and for being a dandy, for even in Moscow—perhaps because of the oppressive atmosphere of Communism—Richard wore his spats and cane and rings and stickpins.

Vagabondage was no mere lark, he told them, it was just damned hard and unpleasant work, but it was the only occupation he knew. His adventures were ordeals which he did not want to repeat, and he romanticized it all "because that's what people want."

He had, however, conveyed his shock over the tyranny of the Soviet in letters to his father, which the police had opened and read, and in his articles to Bell he had expressed incredulity that a country which sustained social order by terror could also produce the greatest ballet and theater he had ever seen; that a nation which executed for trifling nonconformity could also have a school which teaches children to be circus performers, a phenomenon which gave him an article he titled "The Hundred Happiest Children in the World"; that a nation which had all but abolished illiteracy would also produce nothing in the way of literature and motion pictures except the most blatant, sermonizing, half-truth, arrogant propaganda; that a nation which destroyed religion as a spiritual opiate would create its own religion "in which Karl Marx is God and Lenin is Christ."

The GPU read all this and did not like it. They also did not like Richard gallivanting around the countryside seeing whatever he pleased, and in mid-December two surly police agents called on him in his hotel room and told him he had ten days in which to leave the country.

He still wanted to visit Caucasia, on the Black Sea, and the mountains around Tiflis where the descendants of the Crusaders still wore the chain armor handed down to them since the twelfth century, and he could barely do it in ten days. But his departure from Moscow was delayed by the assassination of Sergei Kirov, a chief aide of Stalin who accused counter-revolutionaries of the murder and set off the infamous purges of the thirties. Moscow was shut down for three days of "mechanical grief," as Richard called it, and then it took him two more days to get his money out of the bank. And when he finally left on the train for Abkhazia, on the Black Sea, 108 "enemies of the people" were executed by a firing squad to avenge Kirov's death.

Yet despite the terror and the bloodshed, Richard said later, Russia is a land of miracles, a proud and purposeful nation which will one day restore its history, its heritage and its culture, and perhaps even lead the world with a truly civilized society. In the meantime, he couldn't wait to leave.

In Abkhazia, Richard interviewed an old sheepherder named Zapara Kiut whom Soviet scientists claimed was one hundred and fifty-three years old and, therefore, the world's oldest living human. A short and scrawny man with a brief grey beard, he admitted he had been drinking heavily since 1803, but he could still hear fairly well and had almost half his own teeth.

"You don't look a day over one hundred," Richard told him, and the old man smiled.

In the mountains of Georgia, near Tiflis, there is a race of people called Kheysoors who came east from France in the mid-1100's to wrest the Holy Sepulcher from the Moslem infidel and who, for reasons lost in antiquity, took refuge in the farthest reaches of the Caucasus Mountains, a perch from which they never moved. Richard found them after a day's grueling hike out of Tiflis. They still wore the garments of Crusaders—with the initials AMD (Ave Mater Dei) embroidered on them, but there were actually few suits of twelfth-century armor surviving, and they were quite rusty and torn and seldom used, but every man in the village carried a broadsword and a shield. Although the Kheysoors still practiced Christianity, they had superimposed on it a number of primitive tribal customs, including banishing pregnant women to goatsheds to bear their young alone. The Kheysoors were self-sufficient, living completely off the land, and had neither need nor desire for money since they never left their mountains. It was ancient history encapsulated, Richard felt, until he came to the one-room school recently established by the Soviets to teach Marxist doctrine to the Kheysoors. Across one wall of the school was an immense banner, in Russian (which the Kheysoors could not read, having their own language and being illiterate anyway) with the words: "Workers of the World—Unite."

Back in Tiflis, Richard found the GPU waiting for him. He was escorted to Batum, the nearest port, and locked in a dirty hotel room for two days to wait for a ship to Istanbul. He immediately came down with the flu and when the ship did arrive the captain refused to take Richard aboard for fear he was infected with some communicable disease. The police took Richard back to the hotel and confined him there three more days. The hotel was so filthy, Richard reported later, that it suggested a primary Soviet defect. "Communism might have more appeal," he wrote, "if the hammer and sickle were replaced by the mop and broom."

Desperately ill when the next boat docked, Richard forced himself to walk aboard, proclaiming good health, until the ship sailed and he collapsed in his bunk. He lay there, alone and unaided, for the three-day voyage to Istanbul where he was hospitalized for a week.

His recovery, he believed, was hastened by his re-entry into the world of freedom and never again, he vowed, would he be indifferent to politics and social problems for now he knew what it meant to be free. He could talk about anything he pleased, buy any book, see any movie, even one with a sophomoric love story, and he could write whatever he chose; it would never be read by police agents.

In Istanbul, Richard dug up a story about Aimee Dubuc de Riviry, cousin of Napoleon's Josephine, who became Empress of Turkey and caused, indirectly, Napoleon's defeat in Moscow.

From Istanbul, he hopped by boat to Athens, writing frantically all the way, visited the monasteries on Mount Athos where no woman has ever been, and then he skipped to Missolonghi to write a piece about the death of Lord Byron, his ancient hero.

He was two months in Athens, cranking out his Bell series, interrupted by a request from *Cosmopolitan* for a 600-word article on his favorite place (Kashmir), and a request from his English publisher, Geoffrey Bles, to write an introduction to a book by the German aviatrix of his Flying Carpet expedition, Elly Beinhorn. When he mailed off the 32nd article to Bell, he moved on to Cyprus, then Jerusalem (for a moonlight night in the Garden of Gethsemane), to Cairo for a story on a colony of eunuchs (which Bell refused to distribute), to Jedda for an interview with Ibn Saud, the King of Arabia, and to Addis Ababa to chat with Emperor Haile Selassie, the Conquering Lion of Judah, whose proud little country would be invaded in just four months by the Italian Army to fulfill Mussolini's promise that Ethiopia, independent for 3,000 years, would become a colony of Rome.

Richard now had only five articles remaining to complete his Bell contract, but he had run out of ideas and he was bone-tired from the pace of the deadlines. All he could think of was his elephant ride over the Alps, and he hoped the zoo in the Jardin d'Acclimatation in Paris had made some progress in acquainting Elysabethe Dalrymple with the outside world. He cabled a reminder to her trainer from Cairo where there was eight weeks of mail waiting for him, most of it good news. *Liberty* magazine had taken the series on the execution of the Czar, the *Reader's Digest* had reprinted another piece, and his Russian reports had attracted considerable attention, especially from the *Daily Worker* which denounced him viciously in a long front-page editorial titled, simply, "Liar!" Richard was delighted. There were also checks from his publisher and from Bell, and not a moment too soon for he was dead broke again.

Richard hurried on to Paris, by way of Athens, Ankara (he wanted to climb Mount Ararat, the site of Noah's Ark, but was refused permission), and Vienna. He managed to stretch Ethiopia into a second article, a violent anti-Italian tirade. It did not occur to him until later that if it appeared in print before he and Dally crossed the Alps, he might be halted at the Italian border. Fortunately, it did not.

Dally's trainer had done little more to broaden the elephant's experience beyond teaching her to follow a truck. But Paris police would not allow Dally on the streets again, after her harrowing bolt in October, and she would have to be trucked to the train, thus eliminating the ballyhoo of Richard astride an elephant in the boulevards of Paris. There was no lack of publicity anyway, for the stunt triggered the whimsy of newspaper editors around the world and Halliburton-Hannibal became a kind of international joke. In the news columns, it was as much a running story as Lindbergh's flight across the Atlantic, reported in full—with pictures—daily. Newspaper cartoonists exhausted their imaginations on it, too, and a favorite in France showed a French peasant meeting Richard and Dally on a narrow mountain trail. "Mon Dieu!" exclaimed the Frenchman, "Hannibal!" In the U.S., the Washington *Post* ran a front page cartoon of Richard, hat in hand, beseeching monks of the St. Bernard Monastery to give Dally shelter from an Alpine blizzard—"I hope you don't mind, but I've got an elephant out here"—while Dally shivered in the background, knee-deep in snow.

Richard spent the entire month of July traveling between Paris, Lausanne and Rome, obtaining permissions, health clearances, insurance policies, and a variety of other official sanctions for the three-country trek. In Lausanne, he bought a used truck for $100 and drove it over the St. Bernard Pass, acquainting himself with the terrain, finding lodging for Dally en route, and alerting the St. Bernard monks of his impending arrival. They had never given succor to an elephant, they said, because Hannibal and his herd of thirty-seven elephants had made their crossing in 218 B.C. and they looked forward to meeting Dally. Richard, the elephant and her trainer, Louis Harel, had their rendezvous in the freight yards at Martigny where the highway starts up through the Great St. Bernard Pass.

Historians at the time argued that Richard had chosen the wrong pass if he wished to emulate Hannibal precisely. There

was no point, they said, in the Great Carthaginian going so far
out of his way on his march from southern France into Italy.
The Little St. Bernard Pass and the Mt. Cenis Pass to the south
were directly in front of him and they were less steep and more
than 1,000 feet lower in elevation.

But Richard, the relentless and fastidious researcher, had an
argument. The Great St. Bernard at that time was so generally
impassable that the Romans left it unguarded. Hannibal, anticipating them, had therefore chosen it as his invasion route. Further, said Richard, the pass was identified by the Roman his-
torian Livy, just two hundred years after Hannibal and his
Punic War, as the "Poenine Pass," meaning Phoenecian, or
Carthaginian. But it was not the Romans who balked Hannibal, as much as it was the Alps. He lost half his troops to the
weather and the cliffs and chasms, and when he finally descended onto the plain of Italy he was in poor condition to
fight.

And so it was with Richard, for Dally barely made it to Turin. She started off briskly from Martigny, preceded by the
truck and followed by all the children of Martigny, not to mention a swarm of reporters and photographers. Richard rode
Dally's back for a time, while Harel the trainer walked alongside, guiding Dally's steps. The truck was driven by a young
Swiss. Richard avoided paying him by promising to give him
the truck.

Even if Hannibal did not come this route, Richard said, it
was rich in ancient glory anyway. Caesar had passed by, and so
had Charlemagne. Napoleon had invaded Italy through the
Great St. Bernard with 40,000 men, and before him, an endless
procession of popes, kings and lesser conquerors. Then, too,
Dally was an East Indian elephant, unlike Hannibal's mounts
which came from Africa, and she weighed a mere 6,000 pounds,
while Hannibal's weighed nearer 10,000.

Further, Dally was no beast of war and had probably never
even heard a harsh word in her twelve years of life. She enjoyed
children, she liked to lumber along the bridle paths of the Bois
de Bologne, and recently Harel had taught her to play the har-

monica by gripping it in the end of her trunk and blowing. True, she had no sense of melody, but how many elephants can play the harmonica at all?

It was late in the day when the bizarre little procession left town, for the chief of police had persuaded Richard to show off Dally in the courtyard of the children's hospital. Dally stood on her hind legs and blew her harmonica while the children shrieked with laughter. They made eighteen kilometers the first day, to Orsieres, and the entire population of the village turned out for the occasion, scores of them standing all night outside the stable where Dally slumbered.

The next day they covered fifteen kilometers to St. Pierre, and while the passing trucks and buses and autos did not upset Dally, she encountered several horses which were terrified by her, a condition that prevailed in Hannibal's day and gave him a slight advantage over Roman horsemen. There were 500 astonished people in the village square when Dally and her entourage arrived, and they watched in growing amazement as she dipped her trunk in the village fountain and gave herself a bath.

Word of Dally's march had spread clear across the pass, and by the third day the road was choked with cars of sightseers looking for this incredible elephant. Glancing over his shoulder at the wake of skipping and running children, Richard began to feel like the Pied Piper and he frequently hoisted three or four youngsters up beside him to ride briefly. As always, the adulation of children thrilled Richard more than anything.

It was in St. Pierre in 1800, Richard noted, that Napoleon and his 40,000 men had stopped for lunch. And the moment he left, the hotel there changed its name to Dejeuner de Napoleon (the Hotel of Napoleon's Lunch).

They reached the summit of the pass, 15 kilometers out of St. Pierre, on the third day, and the 8,000-foot altitude began to trouble Dally. She had never been above sea level, and in the thin air her breathing was labored and her heart beat at what seemed like a furious rate. Richard now wanted to hurry Dally to lower elevations, but was afraid any strain might kill her.

Hannibal, he remembered, had lost several elephants on the summit, but perhaps from falling boulders.

Dally set her own pace now, and Richard climbed down from her back to lighten her load. Every few hundred feet, she would stop and sit down in the road, blocking it completely, and nothing could budge her until she had rested and eaten a tub of moist meal and two pounds of sugar. In spite of her discomfort, she never lost her mellow disposition. Harel would caress her trunk, call her "my little cabbage" and she would struggle doggedly to her feet and continue on.

At the gates of the St. Bernard Monastery, they were greeted by a mob of 2,000 men, women and children, fifteen monks and as many giant St. Bernard dogs all barking furiously and a score of photographers and newsreel cameramen. Harel got Dally to kneel once and to loose a single blast on her harmonica, but that was all; she was too tired. The crowd cheered her anyway.

The monks moved their supply truck out of its garage, covered the floor with a layer of sweet hay three feet deep and Dally heaved herself into it, luxuriated briefly and, after Richard covered her with canvas blankets, she slept for thirty-six hours. The crowd lingered until midnight, celebrating Dally in the cafe across the road from the monastery, toasting her in wine and beer, and dance and song.

"It has not been like this," the Prior told Richard, "since we entertained Napoleon."

The St. Bernard Monastery was built in the year 950 by a French monk named Bernard to shelter wayfarers in the impossible pass and to convert the local heathen to Christianity. The big dogs, bred since the sixteenth century by the Augustinian monks who maintain the hospice, have become a symbol of heroism and fidelity throughout the world, hardly anybody remembering that the St. Bernard is a cross of bulldog and sheep dog.

The monastery has always existed on donations from travelers, although most of them had nothing to give. Queen Victoria and the Kaiser both stopped there for a night (at different times) and left behind large donations. The monks saved fewer lives in Richard's day, for the Simplon Tunnel and the age of the auto had taken the hazard out of Alpine crossings. Most of the guests at the monastery now, the Prior told Richard, were tourists, few of whom ever got lost in the snow and needed rescuing by a dog with a brandy keg hung from its collar.

The Prior shared Richard's belief that Hannibal had crossed by the Great St. Bernard, and may have camped on the very site of the monastery before starting down to the River Po, to Turin, Genoa, Florence and, finally Rome, and when he got there all his elephants were dead, and most of his troops, too.

Richard shuddered briefly at the recollection as he and Dally and Harel and the truck started downhill. But Dally grew increasingly vigorous as the altitude lessened and there was hope they would all reach Rome. But the next day they came upon an Italian regiment on maneuvers and Dally bolted again as a battery of howitzers went off, the blasts reverberating through the mountains. She dumped Richard on the ground, broke from Harel and charged into a column of infantry, scattering it. She ran for almost a mile before she exhausted herself in the rare air and Harel and Richard caught her in a creek. It was the beginning of the end. Harel and the truck driver rode ahead into Turin to explore the road and they were both injured, and the truck demolished, in a collision with a speeding roadster. And when Harel, his cuts and bruises bandaged, returned to Dally, he found that her feet, softened by life in a zoo, were dangerously cracked and blistered. She could go no farther.

They all rested several days in the village of Aosta, then limped the ten miles into Turin where they were met by a mob of five thousand and a brass band provided by the Fiat Motor Company. Dally enjoyed the attention, or appeared to, before she was put in a box car cushioned with a ton of hay and sent back to Paris and her stall in the Jardin d'Acclimatation where Richard, three days later, went to bid her goodbye and to give her a new harmonica and two pounds of sugar. And when he walked away to catch the train for Le Havre and the ship home, he confessed to a curious lump in his throat. He had often become attached to animals, like the ocelot in Panama, but it was more than that with Dally. He felt remorseful, he admitted later, because he had tricked her; she never knew it was all an outrageous stunt, she thought it was very important.

VIII

The End of the Road

'The voyage which I was born to make in the end, and to which my desire has driven me, is towards a place in which everything we have known is forgotten, except those things which, as we knew them, reminded us of an original joy.
—HILAIRE BELLOC
(*The Harbour in the North*)

❧ I ❧

RICHARD did not come directly home. Instead, he stayed in Paris for two weeks, sleeping late, overeating and otherwise indulging himself in everything except alcohol which he still shunned. It took a worried letter from his publisher, anxious to launch another book, and several clamoring cables from his various lecture agents to budge him onto a ship.

The newspaper series which appeared in some forty papers had stirred his popularity to new heights, and the lecture bureaus could book him into three stands a day for the next year.

His stay in Paris had been simple procrastination for he was physically and mentally weary, and he knew the Bell series would take an immense amount of rewriting to make a book. But he did think of a title. He would call it *Seven League Boots* since its material spanned so much of the globe.

And again, when all else failed to make him work, there was the interminable need for money. His parents met him at the New York dock on August 9, and Richard went home for a month and heroically pulled his fifty syndicated articles into a book.

He was back in New York in early September, besieged with demands for personal appearances and for magazine articles, some of which he accepted, and in October he was on the lecture circuit, with higher than ever fees and record crowds. Then, in Birmingham on November 1, his voice vanished with laryngitis so severe he could scarcely whisper. He canceled five engagements and rested for five days but it wasn't enough. He gave nine gravel-throated talks and lost his voice again in Oklahoma City where his lectures were not only mobbed, but his

245

hotel room, too, and he could get no rest until he hired a detective to keep visitors away.

He got through a huge book autographing party at Scruggs, Vandervoort and Varney store in St. Louis, and caught a train for Indianapolis to see the doctor who had cured his sinusitis in 1928. He was put to bed for three days, but he couldn't bear the inactivity and he set out again on the lecture trail, hoarse-voiced but game, and ricocheted around the country until Christmas when he went home to Memphis.

His father gave a black tie stag dinner for him in the gilded Louis XVI Room at the Peabody Hotel, and precipitated a fresh round of local acclamation as the original home town hero. School children made pilgrimages to the house, the Cossitt Library gave away his books (autographed) as prizes in a school essay contest, and his parents were called on repeatedly, in person and in print, to praise their son.

"There were times when I worried about his escapades," said Mrs. Halliburton, "but all in all he has been a perfect son to his mother."

He even gave a lecture in the home town, "with special seats for Negroes," and he tossed off some of his adventures of Russia, Ethiopia and Dally, occasionally prophetic.

> "Italy's invasion of Ethiopia is meaningless. The more victorious Italy is now, the better chance the cruelty of the country will have . . . especially the mosquitoes."

> "I tell the story of the Czar's assassination because I want to put an end to the fable that the Princess Anastasia escaped and is still alive. . . ."

> "If Russia has gone to extremes in the repudiation of religion, remember that religion brought it about. The revolution was the reaction to the spirit of religious bigotry which flowered into cruelty and greed. It is in the name of religion that the thumbscrew, the rack and the stake have been called into service."

And then he was off again, to Chicago, Kansas City, back to Chicago, Indianapolis, Lansing, New York, Atlantic City,

Reading and Allentown, Pennsylvania, Cleveland and Dayton, and to New York where the Bell Syndicate wanted him to be both the author and the hero of a comic strip; but in Indianapolis, Chambers opposed the comic strip and proposed instead more books, beginning with a sort of *Royal Road to Romance in the U.S.A.*, an idea which finally jelled in Richard's mind.

Seven League Boots was selling badly despite his still rising popularity and despite generally enthusiastic reviews; at least, they were emphatic.

"The world continues to be Mr. Halliburton's oyster, and the oyster continues to yield its pearls to this indefatigable epicure. True enough, the gems are cultivated, but they are none the less spectacular for that. . . ." said *The New York Times*.

"It is all extremely readable, utterly superficial and frequently unbelievable," assayed the *Saturday Review of Literature*.

"Some of the material . . . would be good reading . . . if its readers had any reason to believe the author was interested in it as anything but a stunt," said *Books* magazine.

The Chicago *Tribune* sarcastically suggested that, for his next book, Richard "take a thousand wives like Solomon, cross the Delaware in a rowboat, or perform some Hindu stunt, such as sitting on nails."

Richard's voice remained hoarse all that season, compelling him to cancel occasional lectures, but he carried on otherwise and finished the season in San Francisco in June. He bounced back and forth between there and Los Angeles for a week, unable to make up his mind where he wanted to stay, until a friend found him an apartment on Telegraph Hill, at 1407 Montgomery Street, with a stirring view of the harbor. San Francisco, he said, "is the most wonderful and beautiful city in the world."

In one appearance in the author's series at Paul Elder's bookstore, Richard became unwittingly prophetic again when somebody asked him about the Japanese invasion of Manchuria. Japan, said Richard, is socially and materially impoverished.

"It is incredible that a nation so backward as Japan, in comparison to the nations of the west, would risk her national existence by going to war. It is madness. If she continues to hurl her defiance at the world, she will find herself engaged in a death struggle against an unbeatable combination of powerful foes."

His other indecision—over what kind of book to attempt next—was resolved by Bobbs-Merrill which cannily suggested a book especially for children, a blend of adventure and geographic fact. Their reasoning was purely commercial, and it struck Richard as sound. A substantial portion of his audience was adolescent and even younger, and every high school library had a stock of his four works. He could automatically appeal to the younger audience by writing what was really a geography text in the first person. It might even be adopted as a textbook by elementary schools. It would be easy to write, since it would be largely photographs and long captions, and it was bound to be profitable.

Richard and Chambers decided, after a flurry of correspondence, to do it in two volumes, one on the occidental world, the other on the orient. They would both be called *Richard Halliburton's Book of Marvels.* He could write it at his leisure and the material for it was obtainable without making another trip. He settled down to spend the summer on it, and resume lecturing in the fall. He didn't really want to make another trip, at least for a year.

The book loomed easy, since it amounted to no more than 50,000 words, and he imagined himself dashing it off over a few spare hours daily. He wanted to begin it with a chapter on the Golden Gate and the San Francisco-Oakland Bay bridges, whose great towers of concrete and steel were then rising, miraculously it seemed, out of the bright blue waters of San Francisco Bay. He could see the Bay Bridge from the terrace of his apartment and it fascinated him as much as the Matterhorn.

He telephoned the California Toll Bridge Authority, the governmental agency responsible for the two bridges, and was handed over to Walter Gaines Swanson, the public relations representative.

"How would you like to walk across the bridge?" asked Swanson, happily anticipating the play the city's four newspapers, not to mention the Oakland *Tribune*, would give to such an event.

"I'd love to," said Richard, breezily, and agreed to meet Swanson the next morning. Swanson hurriedly phoned the newspapers and there were ten reporters and photographers waiting with Swanson when Richard arrived.

The towers of the bridge were up, and the immense cables strung, with catwalks erected in a crosshatch fashion. The deck itself was only partly installed.

"It's scarey," Swanson said, "but it's safe enough."

Richard shrugged.

It was a long hike from where the bridge ramp joined the land to where the bridge began its magnificent arc out over the water some 250 feet below and when they got there the wind was blowing a gale.

All the workmen, crawling like ants over the steel and cable webbing, had been alerted to Halliburton's arrival and they could not resist showing up a man they assumed was a daredevil. They shouted down to him from perches obviously precarious, but Richard did not answer them. He was clinging grimly to the catwalk railings, stanchions and cables—anything substantial—while he stared apprehensively at the ships passing beneath him so far below as the wind whipped mercilessly at his hair and clothing.

Now, the shouts of greeting from the workmen above had changed to hoots of derision, but Richard ignored them. Many of the cables and girders that Richard grasped for support had been freshly doused with anti-corrosion paint and when he came off the bridge at last, after holding still for several ignoble photographs and uttering a number of flippancies he did not feel, his face, hands and clothing were smeared with streaks of drab orange.

He was annoyed at the wind for harassing him, and annoyed at himself for not being more debonair about the whole thing, and when Swanson informed him that nobody had yet walked across the Golden Gate Bridge, Richard volunteered to do it the next day.

He was accompanied this time only by Swanson and by Barney Peterson, a photographer with the *Chronicle*, who thought Richard could recover his fearless image, sullied somewhat the day before. They were halfway out on the girders of the span, deckless like the Bay Bridge, when Peterson suggested Richard grab one of the many cables dangling from the main cable above and swing out over the water, for photo purposes. Richard stopped as though he had been slapped.

"You must be crazy," he said, "that water is 300 feet down."

"You won't fall," said Peterson, unlimbering his camera and popping a flashbulb into the reflector, "I thought you would do anything."

"I don't know where you got that idea," Richard replied.

"From your books," said Peterson, grinning. "I'm one of your more faithful readers."

Richard grinned, too, at the suggestion he wrote tall stories, but he still refused to perform any acrobatics. Swanson was relieved, for the vision of Halliburton falling to his death from his clients' bridge had made him shudder.

But Peterson was determined and proceeded to shame Richard into it by doing what he wanted Richard to do with one hand, the other holding the camera. Richard gasped.

"If I can do it with one hand," said Peterson, "you can do it with two," and Richard did. He glanced down briefly at the sparkling blue water and found the whole experience exhilarating. Emboldened, he climbed to the top of the bridge's south tower, 500 feet above the water, and Peterson photographed him there, too.

There was no wind this day, but the tower seemed to be swaying slightly, and the longer he sat there, the more excited he became. It was the same sensation he had experiencd atop the Matterhorn, and in the Flying Carpet, the sensation of being suspended above the world, in time as well as in place, and it triggered the recurring wish that he could remain that way, surrounded forever by beauty and stillness. There was no sound except that heaving hush of the movement of great disembodied masses of air, a sound that is felt rather than heard by those who sit on mountain peaks and marvel at the privilege.

A freighter glided seaward beneath his feet, but it had no more reality than the rest of the picture book panorama upon whose summit he was perched. The bay was full of ships, seemingly motionless in water that was speckled with shimmering iridescence by the late morning sun. Behind him, the city was scrubbed and silent, its soft white buildings artfully stepped on the slopes of dark green hills, like something done in miniature. He could see the pine trees, too, on the Berkeley skyline to the east, and before him the sculptured granite-streaked cliffs plunging down from the moss brown hills that folded back from each other, in ever higher layers, to the northern horizon.

Some insignificant terror, like the whistle of a boat or the rasp of an auto horn, plucked him back from his euphoria of secret rapture, and his first thought was that he could not write the book. It will be like sawing boards, he thought, or less; like digging a hole in the ground and then filling it up again, and he had the further feeling that the world was laughing at him because he could not do what he wanted to do, or because he did not know what he wanted to do.

The world is not as wonderful as I thought it was, he decided, it is only my world that is wonderful and I have used up my world. I have exhausted its resources and I have become the dreary drudge that I said I would never be. And he could think of no place to go, nor anything to do, to restore his dying fancy. Then, brightly, he thought of death, with the same catch of expectation as when he had first seen Timbuctoo on a map and had known that he would go there.

He thought, too, of the beautiful Rupert Brooke, mercifully cut down at the apogee of his youth and fame, before his genius spent itself, or had been extinguished by the terrible caprice of the public. Later that day, he wrote his father to ship to him the trunk full of Brooke research material that he had so laboriously assembled in England so many years before. Perhaps now he would write Rupert's biography, perhaps now he understood what it meant to be driven by a genius that knew no course but its own.

❦ 2 ❧

Richard and Swanson met again several times; Richard because he needed a fresh and outrageous idea for a new book, and Swanson because he wanted to lure Richard into the World's Fair opening in San Francisco in 1939, just three years away. They both got what they wanted.

Swanson proposed that Richard go to the Far East, Shanghai or Hong Kong, buy a junk and sail it across the Pacific to the Fair, arriving on opening day if possible. The notion of a sea voyage had never occurred before to Richard and he grasped at it with a desperate enthusiasm, as though there might never be another idea.

Swanson gave Richard a few days to assemble the project in his mind and then presented him one night to the members of the Chinese Six Companies, the social, moral, spiritual and economic leaders of the Chinatown community which was investing heavily in the Fair. Richard gave them one of his more fevered talks, although his reputation needed no embellishing, even in Chinatown, and he guaranteed them maximum publicity, through newspaper and magazine articles and books, and maximum return on their investment by taking fairgoers cruising on San Francisco Bay for a suitable fee. He asked them to invest $35,000 in the project, to buy the junk, hire the crew and otherwise pay for the voyage.

His canny audience applauded him generously and then asked him to leave the room so that they could discuss it without embarrassment to him, although Swanson could remain. Richard paced the hallway outside the Six Companies meeting room for nearly an hour before Swanson emerged, smiling profoundly. He was sure they would accept his proposal, he said.

The meeting had been held in July, 1936—the same month the Spanish Civil War broke out—and it was October before he heard a word from his erstwhile backers, despite weekly demands that Swanson press them for an answer.

"They turned you down," Swanson reported, finally. "They loved the idea but, being practical, they want to back something that will assure them a greater return on their investment."

What they wanted, Richard learned later, was a promoter to open an opulent Oriental restaurant with gambling facilities. Nothing, they knew, is more profitable than gambling. Richard was disgusted, but he was also determined to go through with the junk idea and get financing somewhere else, even if he had to invest his own money—assuming he could get some.

He plodded away at the book, indifferently, and with constant interruptions from friends such as Noel Sullivan, the wealthy bachelor art patron, who took Richard off to a number of idyllic diversions, including the Carmel Bach Festival, in which Sullivan sang, and the Bohemian Grove, an exclusive private club on the Russian River north of San Francisco.

He rented a beach house in Laguna and sent to Alexandria for Paul Mooney. He not only wanted permanent companionship, and whatever security it could give him, he wanted help on his *Book of Marvels* which he still loathed but which he now had to complete because he would need the money. With Mooney's arrival, his life took on a comfortable kind of regularity and progress. All it lacks now, he believed, was his own home on his own Laguna clifftop where he would be above and away from a predatory and unpredictable world, suspended in what he visioned as his private world of beauty and serenity. And he also sent to New York for William Alexander, his young architect acquaintance, and told him to design and build the house.

"I don't know where I will get the money," he admitted, "but I'll get it. You just build the house."

Alexander was less interested in money than he was in creating an architectural wonder and persuading Richard to accept it. He had already drawn some preliminary plans out of sheer enthusiasm and hope months before and he now expanded them and gave Richard a full-scale presentation. Richard was even more excited than Alexander and his misgivings about being able to raise the money vanished.

Alexander's concept was a revolutionary one, apart from its adherence to the Frank Lloyd Wright principle of indigenous architecture. It shocked even Laguna Beach, a fairly Bohemian place in those days; it brought oglers and sightseers by the hundreds, and it was something no building contractor wanted to have anything to do with. Alexander and Richard interviewed several, and most of them said, "It can't be built." One termed it a "crackpot house." Alexander finally decided he would have to be his own contractor.

The site itself was difficult enough, since it occupied the peak and the point of a mountain ridge that fell away to a sheer drop of 400 feet on two sides, and an only slightly less precipitous descent on the third side up which a hairpin road would have to be gouged. The lot itself was 600 feet square, but most of the area was perpendicular.

Essentially, Alexander's house was a rectangular block, straddling the ridge on retaining walls. The rooms were arranged in a single row linked by a corridor which ran the length of the house. There was a kitchen and a dining area, a massive living room and three bedrooms. The entire house, including the roof, would be of pre-stressed poured concrete. There was a garage beneath and on the roof a partly-enclosed terrace which could be converted later into a second floor.

Richard decided he would name his new home "Hangover House," because of its perch, but the name came to take on another meaning in the village of Laguna Beach because, although Richard never drank, some of his guests did and only the fact that the property was just outside the city limits prevented the police department from disbanding occasional weekend parties.

Alexander estimated he could build the whole thing for less than $10,000 but, as the contractors had predicted, the project

was plagued from the outset by material problems, labor problems, construction problems and by the time Richard moved in
fifteen months later, he had spent $36,000 on the place.

But there was no denying the majestic beauty of the setting.
One side of the house would be faced with glass giving him a
view of the Pacific Ocean, 600 feet below and an infinity before
him, and from a narrow terrace on the other side he could look
down into a lush green canyon directly below, or up at the
rugged grandeur of the Saddleback Mountains to the east.

With all these idyllic expectations, Richard wrote his parents
and told them about the house. They were shocked and
horrified. They didn't like Alexander, they didn't like Mooney
and, for that matter, they didn't like any of Richard's friends
with their sophisticated airs and their brittle manners. "Richard's following," his father called them, and he used the term
to convey all the derision he knew. Richard, his father said, had
become cynical and morose because of his friends.

Richard replied with an anguished letter, vainly trying to
explain that he was "different" from other people, that social
conformity was the most abhorrent thing in the world to him.
He tried to persuade them that, in his heart, he was more sensitive than the mass of humanity, and he begged them not to
frustrate his one consuming need to create his own island of
serenity.

Somewhat dispirited by all this, he set out in late October for
another transcontinental lecture circuit, leaving Mooney to
finish the *Book of Marvels* and Alexander to finish the dream
house. And between then and the following April, when he was
able to return to Laguna for the first time, he sent his two
friends almost every cent he made enclosed in long letters
trying to patch up quarrels between them. Mooney said Alexander was incompetent, and Alexander said Mooney was offi-
cious and domineering.

During one mid-construction visit to the site, Richard found
a local physician there, listening to the walls with his stetho-
scope while a workman on the roof made rattling noises.

"The electrical conduits got buried in the concrete," Alexander explained. "We're trying to find them so we can install the electrical outlets." The workman was jiggling wire in the conduit from above, the doctor pinpointing the sound. It worked.

"How much do we owe you?" Alexander asked the doctor, when they were through.

"Nothing," he said. "It was fun."

Somehow, the house got built.

He stopped in Memphis occasionally during his 1936-37 tour, and each time there was a fresh confrontation over his house, his friends and, finally, the entire conduct of his life.

"You're throwing your money away," his father said, "and you don't even know where it goes."

And after he had gone, his mother articulated what was perhaps the tragic essence of it all.

"His money doesn't matter," she said. "The way he lives, Richard will be killed and his money won't matter at all."

ᨋ 3 ᨐ

Mooney completed editing the *Book of Marvels* in March, and Richard started right in on the second volume. But he had no sooner started, than he saw the galley proofs of the first volume and realized that it bore Mooney's mark, and not his own, and he began rewriting it in type, a process that cost him several hundred dollars in printing charges. He didn't mind Mooney's help, in fact he wanted it, for Mooney had a professional competence he admired, but he was still the master of his own works.

Richard returned to San Francisco in the summer of 1937 to revive his junk project. He was totally committed to it now, in his own mind, for he saw it as the exciting prelude to a new book of adventure within the U.S. He would relive such momentous events as Custer's Last Stand, John Wilkes Booth's horseback flight from the assassination of President Lincoln and the construction of Boulder Dam.

He was unable to solicit private financing for the venture, so he appealed to the management of the Fair, now known as the Golden Gate International Exposition. Through Swanson, he was introduced to two of the key publicity men for the Fair, Dean Jennings, later a prominent journalist, and Art Linkletter, who was soon to reach a new zenith of fame and success as a radio and television personality. Both men were keenly interested in allying Richard with the Fair because, as Richard knew full well, when it came to drawing crowds, there was hardly anybody who could do it more effectively than Richard Halliburton.

And in courting their enthusiasm, Richard was at his most flamboyant, appearing at meetings and conferences decked out in his spats, homburg and cane, with a lace handkerchief stuffed up his coat sleeve. He did not impress Jennings and Linkletter, but he did amuse them. And in the end, it all came to nothing. The Fair wanted Richard to be a part of it, but not enough to justify an investment of $35,000.

Richard did some extensive promotions for both himself and the Fair, giving luncheon talks and radio and newspaper interviews, and he generated so much ballyhoo about himself and his junk voyage that the San Francisco *Examiner* said, "Richard Halliburton does make Marco Polo seem like a mumbling porch sitter."

Richard even went out to Fleishhacker Zoo and posed astride Marge, their prize elephant, as he told once again of his bizarre Alpine crossing, and he was asked repeatedly if he minded being known as the darling of the women's clubs.

"No, I don't mind," he said. "As long as my books sell, the cartoonists can have their fun."

Well, the books weren't selling as well as they once had, and, if the truth were known, there had been a perceptible drop in the size of his lecture audiences in the past year. Richard was aware of this, but he tried not to think about it; and when he did, there was only one explanation—he had not lost either his talent or his appeal, but an increasingly cynical world was losing its appreciation.

If Richard thought the world had reason to be cynical, he did not say, but he was as aware as anybody that he lived at a time when ideals one day became folly the next. A cruel and bloody war was raging in Spain, and in Ethiopia brave warriors defending their homeland with spears were being annihilated by the hundreds by bombs and machine guns from Italian aircraft; Emperor Haile Selassie, the Conquering Lion of Judah, had escaped the bombs by fleeing to Palestine aboard a British warship. And in England, King Edward VIII had stepped down from the throne to marry the woman he loved, handsome Wallis Warfield Simpson, the divorced wife of a Baltimore insurance agent.

Back in Laguna Beach again, Richard reveled in his new

home, attracting the attention of the village with seemingly lavish parties and his outward affluence. He was as broke as ever, but it never showed. He was so broke, in fact, that he failed to pay a $150 pledge to the Princeton Alumni Association and when the association asked him to write a magazine article about the Class of '21, his class, he refused. It wasn't a salable article, he told them, for apart from his own antics and a couple of scandalous divorces, the Class of '21 was notable chiefly for its lack of achievement.

Princeton was proud of him anyway, and the alumni bulletin reported the building of his new house in a way that irritated him.

"Dick Halliburton is getting to be like any other mortal. He's built a home. Next thing we'll hear that he's married and bragging about his youngsters, just like everybody else."

He was still corresponding amiably, however, with his old classmates, and whenever he lectured in the cities where they lived, he always invited them to attend and frequently stayed as a guest in their homes. Richard was "the different one," and they were perversely proud of him.

He had sent photographs of his house to his parents, but all his father could say was that the structure had a "harsh exterior." To this, Richard insisted that he had never seen a house "so far away from man and so close to God." He waxed lyrical, all over again, about how it simultaneously gave the impression of "floating in space" and of having "sprung from the ground," two not-incompatible qualities that attracted the attention of architectural journals which cited it as among the more visionary structures of its time.

To soften his parents' resentment of the house, Richard implied that he might, after all, sell it, if he could do so at a profit. The gesture was unnecessary for his father was reconciled that Richard would never leave it.

He left it in October of 1937 and took to the road again to lecture, to dwindling audiences, and to trumpet the publication of his *Book of Marvels* which loomed immediately as his most successful book. The reviews were almost uniformly raves, and substantial orders began to come in from schools whose librarians said that Richard had succeeded where all others had failed —he had brought life to arid geography textbooks. He had already started the second volume, on the Orient, and Bobbs-Merrill scheduled it for publication the following fall.

The *Book of Marvels'* special merit, said *The New York Times,* is that "It will lead to further reading and it will also appeal to the less bookish child."

Despite this, there were other signs that times were changing for Richard. He gave a lecture at Baylor University in Waco, Texas, to a half-empty house. To avoid straining his voice to reach the upper balcony, where most of the audience was concentrated, he invited them down into the expensive orchestra seats, most of which were unoccupied. This so infuriated the management of the hall that a reception later that night for Richard at the home of Baylor's president was canceled and he spent the late evening instead chatting in a Waco restaurant with the editor of the high school newspaper from the nearby town of McGregor.

He ended his lecture tour in March and went to Indianapolis to complete the second volume so that he would be free to organize his junk trip. His financial affairs were in their customary mess, including a staggering overdraft at his New York bank, and driven by economic desperation he turned in the last chapter and headed west in June. Both *Marvels* books had been much harder than he ever imagined, for in writing for children he had been forced to limit his vocabulary and his figures of speech, to write in brief sentences and to avoid all innuendo, a device he frequently employed, and still retain what he believed was his inimitable style and literary identity.

His father, meanwhile, was trying to dissuade him from making the junk trip which he regarded as a foolhardy risk considering the small amount of material it would yield. He was thinking, too, of the famed aviatrix, Amelia Earhart Putnam, who had been lost now in mid-Pacific for ten months on her round-the-world flight, and he weighed the infinity and magnitude of the vast sea against the mere struggles of his son.

But Richard had too much momentum to stop, and he could already visualize the book the voyage would preface; a pre-Columbian discovery of America and a chronological exploration of her historic wonders. And when it came time to tell his newspaper readers about it, some weeks later, his romantic rationale for this willy-nilly voyage was complete:

> It was seeing a schooner—years ago—with its great wings spread, sailing out through the Golden Gate at San Francisco, that first made me want to go to sea. My heart went straight aboard her and, until this day, it's never come back—for long.
>
> I spent several years in wandering by sea and land, visiting all the nice warm countries on the map. These travels at last brought me to China. And in the harbor of Foochow I found my first true love again—ships with sails . . .
>
> The ships, this time, were not schooners—something far more wonderful and exciting than that. Nor were they yachts or yawls, sloops or luggers, barks or brigantines. They were *junks* . . .
>
> The moment I set eyes on a Foochow junk I forgot all about my chaste and clean-lined schooners with the white wings, and cast covetous glances at the bedizened, painted galleons from the Orient. . . .

His reappearance in San Francisco triggered a new burst of ballyhoo in the press about the junk and brought forth dozens of half-baked offers from people who wanted to take part in it, and none of them had any money. In the midst of all this, he met Wilfred Crowell, an executive with the Schwabacher brokerage and paper firm, who thought Richard might be able to raise the funds for the trip by forming a corporation and selling shares in it to the public for as little as $10 each. He might well get far more than he needed, but several hundred solicitations, by mail, telephone and in person, produced not a cent. Money was still too precious to most people to risk it in what amounted to a publicity stunt.

Richard had no trouble, however, selling the idea to the Bell Syndicate, and to the San Francisco *News* under whose auspices he would later lecture to school children in northern California, and the junk itself might be used as a *News* circulation booster, Richard suggested; a free ride on the Bay with every new subscription.

Well, he couldn't finance a junk trip with fees from newspaper articles, so he took the train to Los Angeles to see his millionaire cousin, Erle Halliburton. He refused to invest, but Mrs. Halliburton promised to buy—and did—$2,500 worth of shares in the venture, and so did her daughter, Vida. The other daughter, Zola, did even more; she put Richard in touch with an old college beau, twenty-four-year-old John R. Potter of Southeast Harbor, Maine. Potter had considerable small boat sailing experience along the Atlantic Coast and, naturally, was eager to make a trans-Pacific cruise. And in the way that one thing leads to another, Potter interested a friend in the voyage and by August of 1938, Richard had $16,000 committed to him by the families of Potter and three other young men; and of them all, only Potter and his friend, Gordon Torrey, also twenty-four and a fellow yachtsman, heeded the intuitive warnings and left the junk before it sailed from Hong Kong.

Richard spent a few final days at Hangover House in Laguna, swimming, sunbathing and riding horseback along the beach, and then he and Mooney left it forever and moved to the Chancellor Hotel in San Francisco to complete the complex preparations for the trip. The corporation had to be formed, legally, a captain and an engineer hired, insurance policies obtained, berthing accommodations at the Fair arranged, promotions planned, and contracts with the *News* and the Bell Syndicate negotiated.

Distrustful of Richard's glib assurances about everything, the parents of one of the youths, Robert Chase, insisted the forming of the corporation be overseen by someone in whom they had confidence. This turned out to be San Francisco attorney J. Richard Townsend who, like Chase, was a Dartmouth man. Between the four young men and his cousin's family, Richard had raised $21,000, which he was afraid was not enough, but he pretended that it was ample. To reduce the chances of financial disaster, Richard mortgaged his home for $4,000. He had expected that book royalties due might swell this somewhat, but at the last minute he sent slightly more than $1,500 in checks from Bobbs-Merrill to Memphis so his mother and father could spend the summer in Europe. War was obviously on its way and this might be the last chance to see Europe for many years. He also brought his mother to San Francisco for a week in September so she could see how well-organized and how safe this newest venture of his would be. Things weren't nearly as sketchy as she had imagined and she was reassured.

Mrs. Halliburton was as impressed as Richard had been with Captain John Welch whose charm and good looks concealed his potential for becoming, as he did, a short-tempered tyrant. And when Richard put her on the train to return to Memphis, all she thought was, "well, there he goes again," and she later urged him to reduce the amount of life insurance he carried, to save money.

For all his preoccupations and harassments, Richard took time to send a present to Chambers' daughter on the occasion of her wedding. He had no sooner mailed the gift than he wrote a long letter to Chambers himself complaining bitterly that Bobbs-Merrill had never offered him a contract with increased royalties even though they had sold a million copies of his books. That off his mind, he plunged ahead merrily with his junk project, acting much like a Boy Scout about to embark on an overnight hike.

He was trying to force from his mind the fear that he was approaching the end of his professional life. He could see by the decline in his lecture box office that something was happening to the world and its people in which he might have no place. Perhaps it was the wars now rumbling on every horizon, perhaps the niche that he had so painfully carved for himself in the façade of his times was being obliterated by the new age now grinding down.

Perhaps, too, he was trying to find a reason that he should be driven to a stunt so complex and unfamiliar that it involved forming corporations and hiring employees just to sail a junk across the Pacific. Perhaps it was that his well had run dry. He wanted to think that this would be his last contrived adventure, that it would enable him to give it all up, to settle down and write that important book and quiet the longing in his soul, but he feared otherwise. He had had his chance and he had botched it. He dared not look too far ahead.

As boyishly enthusiastic as he had been the first time he set foot on a ship's deck nineteen years before when he had run away from home, Richard climbed the gangplank of the *President Coolidge* on September 23, 1938. With him were Mooney and Welch. The other young men would meet him in Hong Kong later in the fall. Six months later, almost to the day, all of them except Potter and Torrey were fighting for their lives aboard the *Sea Dragon,* caught in a storm of typhoon proportions somewhere west of Midway Island.

❦ 4 ❧

On March 23, 1939, the liner *President Coolidge,* about 1,800 miles out of Honolulu on her way to Yokohama, intercepted the *Sea Dragon*'s radio and sent a greeting. Dale Collins, chief officer aboard the *Coolidge* and an acquaintance of Welch's, suggested the two ships rendezvous, weather permitting, and he offered to supply the junk with fresh fruits and vegetables.

The *Sea Dragon* was now running at better than five knots directly before a 40-mile-an-hour wind and a 30-foot sea, under nothing but a double-reefed foresail. Welch sent this whimsical message to Collins on the *Coolidge* at midmorning of March 23:

SOUTHERLY GALES RAIN SQUALLS LEE RAIL UNDER WATER WET BUNKS HARDTACK BULLY BEEF HAVING WONDERFUL TIME WISH YOU WERE HERE INSTEAD OF ME.

By this time, the *Coolidge* had hit head-on the same steadily worsening weather that was hounding the wake of the *Sea Dragon,* and her captain, K. A. Ahlin, slowed the giant liner to less than six knots as she was shipping green water over her bow and pitching and shuddering violently in waves Ahlin estimated at well over 40 feet from trough to horizon. More than half the passengers were seasick, several of them were injured from being flung across their staterooms or down companionway steps, and everything movable aboard the liner had been lashed down.

Shortly after noon, Welch sent another message to the *Coolidge:*

SOUTHERLY GALE HEAVY RAIN SQUALLS HIGH SEA BAROMETER 29.46 RISING TRUE COURSE 100 SPEED 5.5 KNOTS POSITION

266

1200 GCT 31.10 NORTH 155.00 EAST ALL WELL WHEN CLOSER
MAY WE AVAIL OURSELVES OF YOUR DIRECTION FINDER RE-
GARDS WELCH.

Unable to take a fix on either the sun or the stars for the last
two days, Welch had figured his position by dead reckoning and
was somewhat uncertain of it. But by both his and Ahlin's cal-
culations, the two ships would pass within a few miles of each
other in the next two days. The position given by Welch was
about 900 miles southeast of Yokohama, some 1,500 miles due
west of Midway. The *Coolidge* acknowledged Welch's message
and periodically attempted to contact the *Sea Dragon* throughout the remainder of the day and night without result. On the
morning of March 24, still unable to raise the junk by radio,
Captain Ahlin doubled the bridge and fo'c'sle lookouts, altered
his course slightly to the northeast and offered a reward of a
bottle of champagne to any officer whose watch sighted the
junk. He assumed that the wind had ripped out the junk's
aerial or that sea water had damaged her radio. Although the
sea and wind moderated on March 24, there was no sign of the
junk and the *Coolidge* continued on to Yokohama still trying,
in vain, to raise the *Sea Dragon* on the radio. Another ship, the
American freighter *Jefferson Davis*, bound for San Francisco,
apparently passed within a few miles of the junk but neither
saw the little ship nor heard any radio signals. Richard Halliburton and his gallant, foolhardy little band had vanished from
the face of the earth.

Richard's parents heard about it on the evening of March 25
when Crowell telephoned them from San Francisco to report
only that radio contact with the junk had been lost, but that
there was probably nothing to worry about. Mr. and Mrs. Halliburton were sitting in the living room of their new home on
Court Street in Memphis when the call came. They both knew
what it was and they let the phone ring several times before
Mrs. Halliburton rose from her chair, crossed the room into the
hallway and picked up the receiver. She thanked Crowell for
calling and then she returned to the living room and stood before her husband.

"Well," she said, softly, "that's it. It's all over. It's the end."

But neither Richard's father, nor the families of the other young men aboard the little ship were quite so resigned. They waited four days, praying that the *Sea Dragon's* radio would come to life again, and it was only on March 29 that most of their hopes expired. The liner *President Coolidge,* to which the junk's final radio messages had been directed, docked in Yokohama and her captain, K. A. Ahlin, said it was his private opinion that the *Sea Dragon* had gone down.

"If she hit the same weather we did," added the *Coolidge's* Chief Officer Dale Collins, "there is little likelihood that she survived."

The U.S. Coast Guard in Honolulu, however, refused to conduct a search; radio failure did not mean disaster, it explained, and while the *Sea Dragon* had indeed encountered a monumental storm, junks were phenomenally seaworthy vessels and there was every chance she was still on her way to Midway Island. She was in an area of unpredictable winds known as "the horse latitudes" and, if her engine were out, might drift for weeks without incident as the ship had a 90-day food and water supply. It was also noted that a Los Angeles physician, Dr. E. A. Peterson, his wife and two Russian sailors had sailed a 36-foot junk from Yokohama to San Francisco over virtually the same route a year earlier.

Pan American Airways, however, instructed the crews of its Hong Kong–to–San Francisco flights to be on the lookout for the junk, and all trans-Pacific steamships were likewise alerted.

On April 4, eleven days after the *Sea Dragon's* last radio message, Richard's parents formally petitioned the Secretary of the Navy to order a search. A month later, after considerable pressure had been brought to bear on the Navy Department by Congressmen through the families of all the Americans aboard the junk, the heavy cruiser USS *Astoria,* en route home from Yokohama after delivering the ashes of the late Japanese Ambassador Saito who had died in America, turned back from Guam and combed 108,000 square miles of the Pacific with four seaplanes. It found nothing. The Japanese Navy was also requested, through the U.S. Embassy in Tokyo, to make a similar search but it refused, without explanation. It was obvious, however, that the Japanese had no desire to come to the aid of a man who had persistently insulted them from the lecture platform over the years.

On June 8, the U.S. Navy came to share the view that Halliburton and his band of amateur sailors were at the bottom of the Pacific and it held an official inquiry to formally dispose of the matter.

The hesitancy with which the Navy and the Coast Guard had responded to Halliburton's possible disappearance was born not of indifference but of suspicion. To vanish in mid-Pacific was a typical Halliburton stunt.

Halliburton had even told friends, before leaving the U.S. for Hong Kong, that he might well pull a disappearing act to dramatize the voyage. When he was presumed dead, he said, he would sail triumphantly into San Francisco Bay, bearded, bronzed, weather-beaten and seething with tall stories.

Millions of Halliburton's fans were confident, according to the thousands of letters they sent to their local newspapers, and to Halliburton's publisher and family, that Daring Dick had drifted onto some unknown Pacific atoll from which he would eventually be rescued to tell them amazing tales of adventure. There was even some responsible speculation that he had been hurled onto the reef of the same island where aviatrix Amelia Earhart Putnam had doubtless crash-landed when she vanished during her famous trans-Pacific flight two years before. That the last known whereabouts of both were at least 5,000 miles apart failed to discredit this theory altogether.

To Captain Charles Jokstad, master of the line *President Pierce,* who had inspected the junk before it sailed and who had warned Richard against the voyage, there was no reason for suspicion or uncertainty.

"I had the awful feeling, the day I inspected the junk, that I would never see that young man again," he said, "and I urged him not to attempt the voyage. It is my guess that the rudder snapped off in a heavy following sea, the ship broached-to in the trough, the masts went out and she broke up—probably in minutes."

Richard's parents, of course, knew their son was dead, and in mid-July, they asked a Chancery Court in Memphis to declare him legally so.

The nation's newspapers remained suspicious to the last for it was often said that Halliburton was the world's best press agent and his only client was himself. The story of his alleged disappearance was reported briefly and with great diffidence, mostly on the inside pages. By the time editors came to believe that Halliburton might, in fact, be gone, it was too late to move the story onto page one. The New York *Herald-Tribune* tried to give a tone of immediacy to an event six months old but, in so doing, it revealed that it, too, was still skeptical.

"Even in death," the paper said, "Richard Halliburton's formula for success did not fail him."

⁓§ 5 §⁓

The Chancery Court in Memphis declared Richard Halliburton officially dead on October 5, 1939, seven months after his disappearance, but the event rated little attention in the press. Richard had never been a part of worldly reality in the sense that statesmen and corporations, or even movie stars, exist in a space of time and have an impact on the tangibles of life. Richard was the embodiment of day dreams, the public manifestation of private fancies. He could have frolicked across the tapestry of history at any point, and mankind would have recognized him. He was what any of us like to believe we might have been.

The court's decree served two functions; it permitted the payment of life insurance benefits to Richard's now hard-pressed parents, and it punctuated all the eulogies by people who had known him intimately and slightly, and who were trying to define the loss.

"Few persons of any age have made a greater contribution to their fellow man," said Memphis *Commercial-Appeal* columnist George Morris. "He sent persons in quest of the secrets of the world which, when they are known, will add infinitely to its wealth of understanding and widen the horizon of those who might otherwise have lived narrowly."

Well, no; that wasn't quite it.

Richard's mother said that her son often remarked that when he died he would be remembered for two things, and both of them wrong; that he was a tea party lecturer and that he once dived into the Taj Mahal pool which is only three inches deep.

Richard's father said: "The world is not as beautiful now as when Richard wandered over it. The destruction of the old

271

world, in this coming war, the world he loved most, would have made him desperately unhappy."

Letters from thousands of fans and readers all over the world were dragged by the sackful into the Halliburton home on Court Street, or into the Bobbs-Merrill offices in Indianapolis.

Rear Admiral Richard E. Byrd, the antarctic explorer, sent a letter of sympathy and admiration, adding that he understood full well the urge that drove Richard. And Richard's father sent Byrd the flying suit Richard had worn on his Flying Carpet trip.

Overwrought sentiments appeared by the hundreds in the letters-to-the-editor columns of newspapers all over the world, not a few of them quoting Richard's own fervent and reckless wish, first uttered at the age of nineteen, that he be spared "a stupid, common death in bed."

Fellow adventurer, author and lecturer Lowell Thomas presided over a memorial service in the Second Congregational Church of Waterbury, Connecticut, a church where Richard had frequently lectured. The modest auditorium was jammed at the expense of breathing space while more than 1,500 men, women and children milled about outside, unable to get in.

Hundreds of other men, women and children wrote plaintive letters to Richard's parents, begging for some genuine memento of their son, a pencil, a button, a shred of garment, a fragment of handwriting, anything.

Richard was the subject of uncountable thousands of high school term papers, the authors of nearly all of which wrote Richard's father asking "if you could please tell me something about your son as I have been assigned to write a paper. . . ." It was fifteen years before this flow of letters ceased.

While this multitude waded in the wake of Richard's death, there was an even more vast audience whose seeming legions never knew where, or whether, Richard's life had ended and his death begun. Twenty-six years after the *Sea Dragon* vanished in a howling rage of sea, this other audience still writes, four or five letters a week, earnest adoring little handwritten missives from a school girl in Denver, in Oklahoma City or Miami or

Los Angeles, or a young serviceman on some remote U.S. Army base where there is nothing to do but read.

> Dear Mr. Halliburton:
> I have just read your wonderful book and I was wondering if the next time you go adventuring if you would please take me with you. I am eleven years old and in the sixth grade. I am strong and would be no trouble, even though my father says I am. . . .

Or:

> Dear Mr. Halliburton:
> I have just finished reading the Royal Road to Romance and I enjoyed it very much. I have been thinking of making such a trip myself when I get out of the Army and I wonder if you could give me any suggestions about getting articles or books published. . . .

In 1955, film producer Louis de Rochemont paid $22,500 for the film rights to *The Flying Carpet* and *Seven League Boots,* announcing that he planned to merge them into one huge Cinerama spectacle. Unfortunately, he never did.

The late Burton Holmes, surely the dean and perhaps the founder of the entire genre of travel lecturing, gave half his 1941 season's lectures on the subject of Richard whom he had both preceded and survived.

"A remarkable man," said Holmes. "It was one of my best lectures," a tribute on a tribute since Holmes had spent nearly fifty years on the lecture platform.

Poet Don Blanding, who was regarded as the master of dewy-eyed doggerel, wrote a six-line verse in eulogy to Richard, but he sent it privately to Richard's father.

Tom King, an Adelaide, Australia, concert pianist, composed "Nine Themes for Piano Based on The Royal Road to Romance," and mailed Richard's father a recording of a performance of the work.

The U.S. Maritime Commission gave the name *The Richard Halliburton* to a 10,000-ton Liberty ship built in 1944 by the J. A. Jones Construction Co. of Panama City, Florida, and later assigned to the Normandy Invasion during the Second World War.

Although Richard vanished without a trace, reports that the wreckage of the *Sea Dragon* had been found brought his name onto the front pages, briefly, over the years. It was none other than Captain Charles Jokstad who issued the first report. Jokstad was bringing the liner *President Pierce* from Yokohama to Honolulu in July, 1940, and was about 2,000 miles out when he spotted a mass of wreckage, looped with seaweed and speckled with a year's growth of barnacles. The sea was too rough for him to stop and hoist the wreckage aboard, he said, but he was confident it was the splintered remains of the *Sea Dragon*'s rudder. Its position, he added, was approximately where the current would have taken it in twelve or thirteen months.

In 1945, a section of a wooden keel with several ribs attached floated ashore at Pacific Beach, California, a point to which the junk's remains could have drifted, but no authoritative decision was ever made. Richard's mother, vacationing at the time in Tucson, Arizona, could not be persuaded that the wreckage might be that of her son's ship.

In death, Richard's affairs were far neater than in life. His will left everything in trust to his parents, with the residue, after their deaths, to go to Princeton University Library for the establishment, if possible, of a memorial room devoted to geography.

His estate, at the time he drowned, consisted of four modest life insurance policies and about $9,000 in royalties due him from Bobbs-Merrill. This, as it turned out, was a mere beginning. Richard's books sold just short of a million copies after his death in English language editions alone over a period of twenty-five years. In 1963, two of his books still in print—the *Book of Marvels,* the two volumes now combined into one, and *The Romantic World of Richard Halliburton,* an anthology— were selling better than 10,000 copies annually.

The Royal Road to Romance, the book which had launched him and whose title had come to be his middle name, proved the leader of them all for it sold 800,000 copies in its long life in print. The *Book of Marvels,* as predicted, sold more than half a million copies up to 1963 and was still going strong.

His great unfinished work, which he had never really begun, his biography of Rupert Brooke, was finally completed years later by somebody else. Richard's father shipped off the trunkful of Brooke material to novelist Arthur Springer and Bobbs-Merrill published the book in 1952 under the title, *The Red Wine of Youth.* It was a glowing tribute to Brooke, and to Richard in that it credited him with the concept, and Richard doubtless would have approved of it.

All of Richard's other private archives, his notebooks, correspondence, photographs, his manuscripts, published and unpublished, were given by his father to Princeton University Library; altogether, they filled twelve large cardboard boxes. The thousands of letters Richard wrote to his parents over a span of some twenty-six years were condensed by his father and published by Bobbs-Merrill in book form in 1940. Its sales were indifferent, only slightly more than 22,000 copies, as though the literature of Richard Halliburton had run its course.

Richard's estate also included Hangover House and his father went out to Laguna Beach to dispose of it in the summer of 1939 but was unable to find a buyer. The house was rented for a time to a succession of tenants, some of whom said it was haunted. This story gained such credence among the neighbors on the lower slopes of the mountain that the Los Angeles *Times* interviewed them at length on the strange noises and eerie lights emanating from the concrete structure on the clifftop.

Richard's father so detested the place, for it reminded him of those aspects of his son's life that he did not admire, that he decided finally to allow the property to be sold at auction to satisfy the mortgage and back taxes. And Hangover House, for which Richard had spent $36,000 and which, twenty years later, it would have cost an estimated $100,000 to replace, went on the block at the Orange County Courthouse in Santa Ana, California, in 1941. There was only one bidder, Wallace T. Scott, a Marine Corps officer, and his offer of $7,500 was accepted. He and his wife and three children lived there happily for many years, only occasionally pestered by sightseers, architectural students and newspaper reporters looking for feature stories.

There were suggestions that Hangover House would have been an appropriate monument to Richard and perhaps should have been maintained as a library or museum of exploration, travel and adventure. The elder Halliburton had no objection to a monument, and in 1962 he erected one—of brick and concrete—at a cost of $450,000. It was a graceful Gothic bell tower, constructed on the campus of Southwestern at Memphis, and it was far more consistent with Richard's person and spirit, his father believed, than that rectangular eerieness on the California coast. The tower adjoins the college administration building and contains a dulcet, mellow chime which sounds the hours, and a room full of Richard's momentos—notebooks, ship models, first editions, and many of the numerous exotic treasures that he bought in far-off places and sent home to his parents. The upper floors of the tower are occupied by college offices and its spire-like eminence is visible for a considerable distance from the picturesque, tree-shaded campus it was created to enhance.

The structure was formally dedicated in 1962 by Richard's father, and three of Richard's Princeton roommates attended the ceremony. One of them, J. Penfield Seiberling, president of the giant rubber manufacturing firm which bears his name, delivered the tribute to Richard.

> "For him life was something more than breathing, eating, drinking and sleeping, over and over again. Rather, it was a great, exciting, ennobling, precious adventure of the mind and spirit, to be experienced to the full as the Creator intended."

At the base of the tower is a bronze plaque bearing the soaring figure of the mythical Icarus and the words:

> To Richard Halliburton
> Traveler-Author-Lecturer
> Born 1900—Lost At Sea 1939

This Tower is Dedicated to
Memorialize a Wonderful Life
Of Action, Romance and Courage
Erected by His Parents
Wesley and Nelle Nance Halliburton
1961-62
'a daring modern Icarus
He flew too near the sun'

The critics who had labeled him a bad writer and a poseur every time he flashed in life through the literary firmament, softened considerably after his death, as though they had always considered him too unreal to be mortal, although they might have voiced some incredulity over a memorial citadel of Gothic spires.

Even *Time* magazine, which had never regarded him as more than "a rather hard-to-take public figure," relented somewhat:

> He was an appealing, confused individual, a U.S. phenomenon, a U.S. symbol. The nice son of a nice U.S. environment, he never entirely either outgrew it or betrayed it. He was essentially, if mildly, an artist and a rebel, he achieved neither art nor rebellion. He was an innocent sort of Byron-of-his-time.

The hardest posthumous look at him appeared in *Esquire* magazine, in April of 1940, just a year after the *Sea Dragon* went down. It was written by George Weller under the title "The Passing of the Last Playboy." It described Richard's career as "a cartoon of his times," along with marathon dancing and eight-day bicycle racing, but defended him from harsher earlier judgments such as those of the periodical *Vanity Fair*, which, in its "We nominate for obscurity" column, accused Richard of the most ruthless commercial betrayal of the ideals of the adolescents who worshiped him. Whatever else Richard may have been, argued Weller, he was only doing what he wanted to do, to live in reality what other people live vicariously, yet he was no more a daredevil than author Ernest Hemingway was a bullfighter.

"It is hard to think of him dying," said Weller, "but to imag-

ine him accompanying the century into its forties is painful. . . ."

If Richard Halliburton is to have an epitaph, it will not be
found among the proud tributes, the sentimental eulogies, or
the rude dismissals of his fame and talent; it will be something
Richard himself said once after he was introduced at a lecture
in terms so extravagant and praise so lavish, that even he was
touched by the absurdity. When the applause had subsided, he
inclined his head forward slightly, and smiled that shy little
smile that twisted the heart strings of every woman who could
see him.

"I'm none of those things," he said, "I'm just a little boy
playing Indian."

Index

Addis Ababa, Ethiopia, 236
Adriatic, S.S., 52, 53
"Adventuring in Republican Germany," 71
Afghanistan, 86
Agra, India, 81-82
Ahlin, Captain K. A., 266, 267, 268
Ainesworth (Burma planter), 86-87
Aix-les-Thermes, France, 72
Alameda, California, 203
Alber-Wickes lecture agency, 158, 215
Aleppo, Syria, 189
Alexander, Grand Duke, 137
Alexander, William, 213, 254-55, 256-57
Alexander the Great, 109, 196
Alexandria, Czarina, 228
Alex the Mexican, 122
Aley, Maxwell, 178, 187, 205
Algeria, 182-84
Alkahest lecture agency, 215
Allenby, General Edmund Henry, 50
Allied lecture agency, 215
American Library Association, 177
American magazine, 118
Amman, Transjordan, 191-92, 193
Amsterdam, Holland, 66-67
Anastasia, Princess, 230-31, 232, 246
Anderson, Captain George, 50
Andorra, Spain, 73-74
Andrews, Roy Chapman, 117
Angkor Wat, Indo-China, 91
Ankara, Turkey, 236
Aosta, Italy, 241
Arequipa, Peru, 153
Argentina, 153-54
Ashemore, England, 51
Asheville, North Carolina, 40, 137
Asia Society, 102
Association Against the Prohibition Amendment, 158
Astoria, U.S.S., 268

Athens, Greece, 110, 111, 112, 235, 236
Atherton, Gertrude, 137, 158
Atlantic City, New Jersey, 43, 164
Atlas Mountains, 180, 183, 184
Azores, 50

Bagdad, Iraq, 194
Baja California, 218, 220
Balboa, Panama, 148
Balboa, Vasco Nuñez de, 150, 151-52
Bali, 92
Bangkok, Siam, 90-91
Barcelona, Spain, 73-74
Barnes, Florence, 172
Barnes, Rankin D., 172
Barstow III, George, 22, 31
Basel, Switzerland, 67
Battle Creek Sanitarium, 41, 103
Batum, Russia, 235
Baylor University, 261
Beinhorn, Elly, 198, 236
Belize, British Honduras, 144
Belloc, Hilaire, *quoted*, 243
Bell Newspaper Syndicate, 25, 31, 217, 218, 223, 224, 232, 233, 236, 245, 247, 262
Benares, India, 81
Benét, Stephen Vincent, 158
Benét, William Rose, 124
Berlin, Germany, 65-66, 225
Bermuda, 166
Bernhardt, Sarah, 78
Bias Bay, China, 20
Billboard magazine, 214
Bingham, Hiram, 153
Birmingham, Alabama, 159, 245
Blanding, Don, 137, 273
Bles, Geoffrey, 236
Bluefields, Nicaragua, 144
Bobbs-Merrill Company, 104, 105-06, 111, 117, 119, 121, 128, 135, 136,

138, 142-43, 147, 150, 156, 165, 169, 171, 173, 178, 188, 205, 209, 217, 248, 261, 264, 272, 274, 275
Boise (Idaho) *Statesman*, 158
Bolivia, 153
Bolsheviks, 228
Bonaparte, Napoleon, 238, 239
Bond, Carrie Jacobs, 42, 123
Boni & Liveright, 104
Books magazine, 247
Booth, John Wilkes, 221
Bordeaux, France, 72
Bori, Lucrezia, 165
Borneo, 201, 202
Bournazel, Captain de, 185
Boylan, Malcolm Stuart, 121, 122-23, 169
Boylan, Robert J., 120
Boy Scout Magazine, 100
British Guiana, 162
British Honduras, 144
Britton, Nan, 101
Bromfield, Louis, 172
Brooke, Charles, 201
Brooke, James, 201
Brooke, Mary Ruth Cotterill, 112-13, 129, 130, 138, 180
Brooke, Rupert, 70, 107, 108, 111-12, 129, 130, 158, 251, 252, 275
Brooke, Sylvia, 201-02
Brooke, Vyner, 201
Brown, Rosie, 210
Browning, Montana, 55
Browning, Robert, 59
Brownsville, Tennessee, 40, 46, 47
Brunei, Borneo, 202
Brussels, Belgium, 67
Buenos Aires, Argentina, 153-54
Buffalo Express, 117
Budapest, Hungary, 188
Burbank, California, 177, 203
Burma, 86-87
Bushire, Iran, 194
Butcher, Fanny, 115
Byrd, Rear Admiral Richard E., 272
Byron, George Lord, 70-71, 79, 107, 108, 109, 236

Cádiz, Spain, 74
Cairo, Egypt, 79, 191, 236
Calcutta, India, 81, 86, 199

Calcutta Flying Club, 199
Cannes, France, 78
Canton, China, 92
Carnarvon, Lord, 79
Carnegie, Dale, 98
Carpentier, Georges, 67
Carter, Howard, 79
Caruso, Enrico, 67
Casals, Pablo, 78
Cather, Willa, 155
Catholic Vigil, The, 127
Catlin, Mr., 84
Cayenne, French Guiana, 160-61
Century Magazine, 106
Chambers, David L., 104-05, 106, 111, 121, 142-43, 144, 150, 156, 169, 178, 188, 204-05, 209, 211, 214, 215, 217, 221, 247, 248, 264
Chaplin, Charlie, 50, 172
Charlotte, North Carolina, 137
Chartres, France, 72
Chase, Robert, 22, 263
Chase & Sanborn, 171
Château de Chillon, 70-71
Chattanooga, Tennessee, 211
Chattanooga University, 211
Chicago, Illinois, 115-16, 121, 134, 166, 175
Chicago Adventurers Club, 116
Chicago *Tribune*, 115, 157, 247
Chicago World's Fair, 215
Chichen-Itza, Mexico, 143-44
China, 15-23, 92-93, 203
Chinese Six Companies, 253-54
Chlurs, 184-85
Christophe, Henri, 223
Chumpon, Burma, 87
Cincinnati, Ohio, 166
Cleveland, Ohio, 128
Cleveland, U.S.S., 144, 146
Cobb, Irving S., 106, 158
Coblenz, Germany, 67
Cole, Fred, 147
Collins, Dale, 266, 268
Cologne, Germany, 67
Colomb Bechar, Algeria, 180, 181, 184
Colon, Panama, 144, 146
Columbia (N.Y.) *Spectator*, 114
Columbus, Christopher, 217, 223
Communism, 93, 235
Constantinople, Turkey, 108, 110, 189
Coolidge, Calvin, 101, 211

Coolidge, President, S.S., 24, 28, 33, 265, 266-67, 268
Cornford, Francis and Frances, 129-30
Conford, Helena, 129-30
Cortez, Hernan, 142, 143
Cortot, Alfred, 78
Cosmopolitan magazine, 214, 236
Counselman, William, 174
Coward, Thomas R. (Tim), 104-05
Cozumel, 144
Crane, Roderic, 107-08, 109, 110-11
Crouse, Cecil, 102
Crowell, Thomas, 122
Crowell, Wilfred, 22, 31, 32, 33, 34, 262, 267
Cuba, 222-23
Curtis, John, 174
Cuzco, Peru, 153
Cyprus, 236

Daily Princetonian, 44, 45
Dallas, Texas, 133
Dallas News, 113
Dalrymple, Elysabethe, 224, 236
Damascus, Syria, 190
Dana, Richard, 64
Daniels, Bebe, 210
Dardanelles, 109, 111
Davis, Jefferson, S.S., 267
Defoe, Daniel, 153, 164
De la Mare, Walter, 130
Delhi, India, 81, 83, 86
DeLong, Edmund, 94
Delphi, Greece, 110
De Mille, Cecil B., 134
Dempsey, Jack, 66
Denver, Colorado, 93-94, 126
Denver *Post,* 126
Depression of the 1930's, 171, 175, 183, 188, 205, 211, 216
Detroit *News,* 114
Devil's Island, French Guiana, 18, 160-64
Dhamtari, India, 81
Dillinger, John, 221
Dixie Bureau lecture agency, 215
Dos Passos, John, 119
Draper, Ruth, 158
Dreyfus, Alfred, 160
Dry Tortugas, 217, 221-22
Dunlap, Maurice, 91

Durant, Will, 155
Dutch Guiana, 162

East Orange, New Jersey, 122
Ecclesfield, England, 51
Edward VIII, King, 259
Egypt, 79-80
Einstein, Albert, 58
Ekaterinburg, Russia, 288-30
Elder, Paul, 123, 247
Ellis, Havelock, 56
Elman, Mischa, 172
Emerson lecture agency, 215
English Channel, 180
Ermakov, Peter, 227-31
Esquire magazine, 277
Ethiopia, 236, 246, 259

Fairbanks, Douglas, 137
Fat Kau, 20, 21
Faulkner, William, 220-21
Feakins, William B., 100
Feakins Agency, 100-01, 104, 117
Fehren, Henry von, 25
Feininger, Andreas, 65
Feisal al Husain, King, 194
Ferber, Edna, 178
Fez, French Morocco, 180, 182, 185
Field & Stream, 66
Fire Island, 120
Fitzgerald, F. Scott, 63, 91, 97, 123
Flint, Michigan, 97
Florida State College, 212
Flying Carpet, The, 204, 205, 209, 210-11, 212, 214, 273
Flying Carpet flight, 177-78, 180-86, 187-97, 198-205
Fontevrault, France, 72
Ford, Carey, 117, 157
Formosa, 29
Formosa Straits, 21, 29
Fort Jefferson, Dry Tortugas, 217, 221-22
Fort Smith, Arkansas, 177
Fort Wayne, Indiana, 121
Fox Film Corporation, 121, 122, 123, 169-70, 173-74, 212
Fox Movietone News, 217
Francis, Emily, 137
Franck, Harry, 57
French Air Force, 181
French Foreign Legion, 18-19, 182-86

French Guiana, 160-64
Frieder, Pauline, 78
Futter, Walter, 209, 210, 211, 214-15

Galilee, Sea of, 190
Galli-Curci, Amelita, 58
Galsworthy, John, *quoted*, 139
Gandhi, Mahatma, 81
Gao, French Sudan, 181
Garden, Mary, 58, 115
Garden City Publishing Company, 165
Gaul, George, 103, 107
Gaza, Palestine, 190
Geldert, Grace, 120-21
Geldert, Louis N., 120
Geneva, Switzerland, 71, 187
Gibbons, Floyd, 185-86
Gibraltar, 19, 74-76, 84
Glorious Adventure, The, 112, 120, 121,
    122, 127-28, 130, 137, 150, 155
Glyn, Elinor, 125
Goethe, Johann Wolfgang von, *quoted,*
    167
Golden Gate Bridge, 250-52
Golden Gate International Exposition,
    see San Francisco World's Fair
Gold Shell, oil tanker, 80-81
Great St. Bernard Pass, 224, 225, 237,
    238-41
Greece, 110, 112
Green, Wendell, 146
Grew, Anita, 156-57
Grew, Joseph C., 157
Grosset & Dunlap, 214

Haarlem, Holland, 67
Hafiz, 195, 196-97
Haile Selassie, Emperor, 236, 259
Haiti, 223
Hall, Radclyffe, 149
Halley, Harry, 172-73
Halliburton, Chandler, 39
Halliburton, Erle, 123, 175-76, 177,
    263
Halliburton, Nelle Nance (Richard's
    mother), 39, 40, 41, 47, 48, 49, 79,
    90, 101, 108, 120-21, 129, 154, 156,
    166, 171, 174, 178, 212, 215, 221,
    245, 246, 256, 257, 264, 267-68, 270,
    271-72, 274
Halliburton, Richard, actor in *India
    Speaks,* 209-10, 211, 212, 213-14; Bal-
boa's trail in Panama, 150-52; boyhood in Memphis, 39-41; Brooke
biography research, 129-30, 275; Caribbean trip, 221-23; critics and, 113-
14, 116-17, 127-28, 156, 210-11, 247,
260-61, 277; death of, 35, 266-70,
271; decision to be a writer, 44;
Devil's Island visited, 160-64; earnings of, 25, 32-33, 94, 106, 119,
135, 141, 155, 166, 171, 205, 212, 274-
75; education, 39, 40, 41-46, 54-60;
estate of, 274-75; *Flying Carpet, The,*
204, 205, 209, 210-11, 212, 214, 273;
Flying Carpet journey, 177-79, 180-86,
187-97, 198-205; Gibraltar arrest, 74-
76; *Glorious Adventure, The,* 112,
120, 121, 122, 127-28, 130, 137, 150,
155; Great St. Bernard Pass by elephant, 224-25, 236, 237-42; Greek
odyssey of, 107-13; Hellespont swum
by, 108, 109-10; illnesses of, 41, 103,
136, 190, 210, 235, 245; impersonator
and imitators of, 156-57; Laguna
Beach home of, 254-57, 259-60, 263,
275-76; Latin-American journey, 141-
48, 150-55; lawsuits, 31, 188; lecture
tours, 98-99, 100-01, 102, 103, 104,
105, 115-16, 117-18, 120, 121, 123,
125-28, 132-37, 141, 154-55, 166, 177,
209, 211-12, 215-16, 218-20, 245-46,
256, 260, 261; love affairs, 19, 44-45;
Matterhorn climbed by, 68-69; monument to, 276-77; Naval officer training, 43; *New Worlds to Conquer,*
138, 157, 165, 169, 188, 204; Nile
swum by, 79-80; parents of, *see* under name of parent; Panama Canal
swum by, 144-48; philosophy of life,
53; Pyrenees crossed by, 72-73;
*Richard Halliburton's Book of
Marvels,* 248, 254, 256, 258, 260-61,
274, 275; ridicule and parody of,
157-58; *Royal Road to Romance,*
98, 99, 101, 103-06, 112, 113-14, 115-
17, 119, 122, 123, 130, 131, 133, 134,
155, 165, 169, 173-74, 212, 274-75;
runaway aboard the *Octorara* to
Europe, 47-54; Russian and Siberian
tour, 225-31, 232-35; *Seven League
Boots,* 245, 247, 273; showmanship
of, 115; Taj Mahal experience of, 81-
82; translations and foreign editions,

131, 134, 189; trans-Pacific voyage of the *Sea Dragon*, 19-35, 253-54, 258-59, 261-65, 266-70; will of, 274; world tour of, 63-69, 70-76, 77-82, 83-89, 90-94

Halliburton, Vida, 22, 176, 263

Halliburton, Wesley (Richard's brother), 39, 40, 42

Halliburton, Wesley (Richard's father), 39, 40, 47-48, 52, 54, 57, 58-59, 64, 71, 77, 79, 90, 92, 104, 120, 130, 141-42, 156, 159, 166, 174, 202, 215, 221, 245, 246, 256, 257, 260, 261, 264, 267-68, 271-72, 275, 276

Halliburton, Zola, 176, 263

Halliburton Trans-Pacific Chinese Junk Expedition, Inc., 22

Hamburg, Germany, 64-65

Hannibal, 224, 237-38, 240, 241

Hanover, Germany, 66, 225

"Happy Hunting Grounds, The," 55

Harbin, Manchuria, 93

Harding, Warren G., 56, 101-02

Harel, Louis, 237

Harper's Ferry, West Virginia, 54

Havana, Cuba, 222

Healey, Fred, 141, 142, 144, 152, 153, 154

Hellespont, the, 18, 108, 109-10, 156-57

Hemingway, Ernest, 63, 277

Hergesheimer, Joseph, 90

Hermosillo, Baja California, 220

Hibben, John Grier, 118

Himalayas, 85, 198, 199-200

Hitler, Adolf, 17, 225

Hobson, Richmond Pearson, 222-23

Hockaday, Irvine O. (Mike), 42, 59, 63, 64, 65, 67, 68, 69, 70, 72, 94, 116

Hokinson, Helen, 158

Holbrook, Josiah, 98

Hollywood, California, 24, 121, 122-23, 166, 169-71, 173-74, 209-10, 211, 218, 220

Holmes, Burton, 118-19, 273

Homs, Syria, 190

Hong Kong, China, 15-17, 20, 29, 31, 92, 203

Hong Kong Foreign Correspondents Club, 15-16

Honolulu, Hawaii, 203, 268

Hoover, Herbert C., 150, 211, 212

Houghton, Alan, 103

Howard, Roy, 43

Howland, Hewitt Hanson, 105-06

Hull, England, 50

"Hundred Happiest Children in the World, The," 233

Hurst, Fanny, 157, 158, 178

Hutchinson, A. S. M., 90

Hutchison, Mary G., 39, 41, 78, 92

Hutchison School for Girls, Memphis, 39

Ibn Saud, King, 236

Ile Royale, French Guiana, 161-62

Iles de Salut, 162-63

India, 81-82, 83-86, 198-200

Indianapolis, Indiana, 106, 121, 136, 166, 204, 246, 261

Indian Ocean, 81

India Speaks (motion picture), 209-10, 211, 212, 213-14

Innsbruck, Austria, 108

Internal Revenue Service, 209

Ipswich, S.S., 63-64

Isfahan, Iran, 196

Isle of Skye, Scotland, 129

Istanbul, Turkey, 235

Jackson, Joseph Henry, 210

Jamshedpour, India, 81

Japan, 17, 20, 21, 34, 92, 203, 247-48

Java, 91-92

Jazz Age, 56, 91, 169

Jedda, Saudi Arabia, 236

Jehan Shah, 81

Jennings, Dean, 258, 259

Jerusalem, Palestine, 190-91, 236

Johnson, Nunnally, 158

Jokstad, Captain Charles, 26-28, 269-70, 274

Juan Fernandez Island, 153

Judge magazine, 157

Kansas City, Missouri, 94, 211

Kansas City Star, 94

Kashmir, 84-85

Keats, John, 151

Keelung, China, 29

Kellogg, Frank Billings, 145

Kerensky, Alexander, 228

Keyes, Edward L., 42

Keynes, Sir Geoffrey, 130

Kheysoors, 234-35

Khyber Pass, 84, 85-86
King, Tom, 273
Kinkead, Robin, 226
Kipling, Rudyard, 86; *quoted*, 37
Kirov, Serhei, 234
Kiut, Zapara, 234
Klee, Paul, 65
Kowloon, China, 20, 30
Kuching, Sarawak, 201-02
Kyoto, Japan, 93

Ladies' Home Journal, 138, 141, 143, 150, 154, 155, 160, 164, 169, 171, 178, 182, 183, 187, 188
Lafayette, Louisiana, 156
Laguna Beach, California, 21, 213, 254-57, 259-60, 263, 275-76
Lahore, India, 81, 86
Lancaster, Pennsylvania, 132
La Paz, Bolivia, 153
La Rocque, Rod, 125
Lausanne, Switzerland, 71, 237
Lawrence, T. E., 130, 190, 191, 192
Lawrenceville School, 41-42, 44, 57, 66
Leander, 108, 109
Leek, England, 51
Leguia, Augusto, 153
Leh, John Henry, 42
Leh, Kashmir, 85
Lenin, Vladimir, 228, 232
Leningrad, Russia, 225
Lens, France, 52
Lewis, Sinclair, 98, 131, 158
Liberty magazine, 214, 236
Lichfield, England, 50
Liebling, A. J., 99
"Life in Republican Germany," 65
Lima, Peru, 152-53
Lincoln, Nebraska, 126
Lindbergh, Anne Morrow, 142
Lindbergh, Charles A., 128, 142, 155, 237
Linkletter, Art, 258, 259
Little St. Bernard Pass, 238
Livy, 238
"Log of the Sea Dragon, The," 25
London, England, 51-52, 67, 129, 180
Long, Huey, 212
Long Beach earthquake (1933), 213
Longbridge, Allen, 49
Los Angeles, California, 124, 125, 218, 247, 263

Los Angeles *Times*, 113-14, 275
Lownes, Jimmy, 188
Luca, Giuseppe de, 165
Luckner, Count Felix Graf von, 126
Ludwig, Emil, 155
Lundi Kotal, India, 85
Luxor, Egypt, 79-80
Lyceum movement, 98-99
Lyons, France, 53

MacDonald, Jeanette, 172
Macon, Georgia, 141
Macao, China, 20, 92
Machu Picchu, Peru, 153
Madison, President, S.S., 93
Madrid, Spain, 74
Majestic, S.S., 132, 178
Malay Peninsula, 19, 86, 87-89
Malta, 112
Manchester, England, 51
Manchuria, 17, 247
Manila, Philippine Islands, 202, 203
Marathon, Greece, 112
Maritime Commission, U.S., 273
Maroni River, 160, 161
Marseilles, France, 53, 76, 77-78
Marsh, Sir Edward, 130
Martigny, Switzerland, 238
Masefield, John, 129
Matterhorn, 19, 67-69, 116, 187
Mauretania, R.M.S., 107, 108, 113
Maximilian, Emperor, 143
Mayence, France, 67
Mayo, Catherine, 134
Mayo, Dr. and Mrs. Charles, 126
McAdoo, Eleanor Wilson, 172
McAdoo, William Gibbs, 172
McCutcheon, George Barr, 105
McCutcheon, John T., 157
McGrath, Paul, 74, 75, 76
McGuire, John, 170
McIntyre, O. O., 178
McKinley, President, S.S., 203
McMurry, Cornelia, 40
Melita, S.S., 129
Memphis, Tennessee, 39-41, 42, 46, 47, 94, 102, 105, 113, 116, 164, 166, 178, 203, 246, 257, 276
Memphis *Commercial-Appeal*, 64, 71, 86, 91, 93, 111, 203, 271
Memphis *Press-Scimitar*, 203

Memphis University School for Boys, 40
Mencken, Henry L., 99, 157
Mergui, Burma, 86
Merida, Mexico, 143, 144
Metropolitan magazine, 71
Mexico, 141-44
Mexico City, Mexico, 141, 143
Midway Island, 21, 31, 268
Mirs Bay, China, 20
Missolonghi, Greece, 235
Mollendo, Peru, 153
Monte Carlo, 53, 78
Monterey, California, 19
Montgomery, Alabama, 47
Montreux, Switzerland, 224
Mont St. Michel, France, 72
Mooney, C. P. J., 64
Mooney, Paul, 25, 26, 29, 32-33, 172, 204-05, 215, 254, 256, 258, 263, 265
Moore, Grace, 172
Morley, Christopher, 134-35
Morocco, 180-86
Morris, George, 271
Morrow, Dwight, 142
Moscow, Russia, 226-27, 231, 233-34
Mosley, Colonel C. C., 173, 174
Mouhot, Henri, 91
Mount Athos, 235
Mount Cenis Pass, 238
Mount Everest, 19, 198, 199-200
Mount Fujiyama, 93
Mount Olympus, 110
Mount Parnassus, 110
Mount Piri, 150-51
Mudd, Dr. Samuel, 221-22
Murat, Princess, 118
Murphy, Mickey, 191-92
Mussolini, Benito, 63, 149, 236

Nantes, France, 72
Naples, Italy, 112
Natal Mercury (Durban, S. Africa), 149
National Geographic, 92, 97
National Geographic Society, 117, 126
Neilan, Marshal (Mickey), 123
Nenndorf, Germany, 66
Nepal, Maharajah of, 19
Nesbitt, Cathleen, 130
New Orleans, Louisiana, 48, 141
New Worlds to Conquer, 138, 157, 165, 169, 188, 204

New York City, 57-58, 63, 97, 104, 120, 127, 132, 154, 164, 178, 205, 209, 213, 223, 245
New Yorker magazine, 147, 166
New York *Herald-Tribune*, 113, 127-28, 156, 270
New York *Post*, 117, 127
New York Times, The, 72, 109, 110, 111, 211, 247, 261
New York *World*, 114
Nicaragua, 144
Nice, France, 78
Nicholas II, Czar, 226, 228-31
Nile River, 79-80
Niles, Blair, 160
Norfolk, Virginia, 49
Norris, Charles, 123-24, 213
Norris, Frank, 178
Norris, Kathleen, 123, 124-25, 178, 213
Notre Dame University, 158

O'Brien, George, 174
Octorara, S.S., 48, 49, 50, 63, 64
Okinawa, 34
Oklahoma City, Oklahoma, 245
O'Neill, Eugene, 157
Oran, Algeria, 184
O'Sullivan, Maureen, 174
Ouverture, Toussaint l', 223
Oxford University, England, 51, 58

Pacific Beach, California, 274
Palmyra, Syria, 190
Panama, 144-48, 150-52
Panama-American, 147
Panama Canal, 18
Panama City, Panama, 148, 152
Paraná River, 154
Paris, France, 52, 53, 71-72, 108, 180, 186, 224-25, 236, 245
Parsons, Louella, 174
Pasadena, California, 123
Pavlova, Anna, 53
Peking, China, 93
Perrone, Roman, 68
Persepolis, Persia, 196
Persia, 194-97
Peru, 152-53
Peshawar, India, 85
Peterson, E. A., 268
Petra, Transjordan, 192
Pheidippides, 108, 112

Phelan, James, 166
Philadelphia, Pennsylvania, 44, 138, 164, 178, 211
Philadelphia Forum, 117
Philippine Islands, 202-03
Physical Culture magazine, 118
Pickford, Mary, 178
Pierce, President, S. S., 26, 33, 269, 274
Pirates, Chinese, 20, 21, 34, 92
Pittsburgh, Pennsylvania, 121
Pizarro, Francisco, 152
Pocatello, Idaho, 126
Pollock, Channing, 158
Pontianak, Dutch East Borneo, 201
Popocatapetl, 143
Portland, Oregon, 93
Portland *Oregonian*, 93
Port Said, Egypt, 80
Posados, Argentina, 154
Potsdam, Germany, 66
Potter, John R., 22, 25, 29, 32, 263, 265
Princeton Club, New York City, 102, 104
Princeton *Pictorial*, 55-56, 57
Princeton University, 41, 42-46, 54-60, 63, 91, 97, 101, 118, 260, 274, 275
Progreso, Mexico, 142, 144
Putnam, Amelia Earhart, 261, 269
Putnam's Sons, G. P., 141, 142
Pyrenees, 72-73

Rabat, French Morocco, 180
Raspe, Rudolf Erich, *quoted*, 207
Rathbone, Basil, 172
Rawalpindi, India, 81, 85
Reader's Digest, 236
Rice, Arthur, 144
Rich, Algeria, 184-85
Richard Halliburton's Book of Marvels, 248, 254, 256, 258, 260-61, 274, 275
Riley, James Whitcomb, 105
Rinehart, Mary Roberts, 105
Rio de Janeiro, Brazil, 154
Riviry, Aimee Dubuc de, 235
Rochemont, Louis de, 273
Rockefeller, John D., 150
Rocky Mountain News, 93
Romantic World of Richard Halliburton, 274

Roosevelt, Franklin Delano, 172, 211, 215
Roosevelt, Theodore, 56
Rothstein, Arnold, 149
Rotterdam, Holland, 67
Rousseau, Jean Jacques, *quoted*, 95
Royal Road to Romance, 98, 99, 101, 103-06, 112, 113-14, 115-17, 119, 122, 123, 130, 131, 133, 134, 155, 165, 169, 173-74, 212, 274-75
Rugby, England, 112-13
Russell, David, 81, 82, 83, 84, 85, 86
Russia, 225-31, 232-35, 246
Ryukyu Islands, 34

Sahara Desert, 19, 180-81
Saigon, Indo-China, 91
St. Bernard Monastery, 237, 240-41
Saint Joseph Island, French Guiana, 162
Saint Laurent, French Guiana, 161
St. Louis, Missouri, 121, 246
St. Marie aux Mines, France, 67
St. Pierre, Switzerland, 239
Saito, Ambassador, 268
Salt Lake City, Utah, 125
Samarra, Iraq, 194
Sandburg, Carl, 119
San Diego, California, 212
Sanford, Mr., 35
San Francisco, California, 125, 203, 213, 218, 247, 248-52, 253-54, 258, 262, 263
San Francisco *Chronicle*, 210
San Francisco *Examiner*, 125, 211, 214, 259
San Francisco *News*, 25, 263
San Francisco-Oakland Bay Bridge, 248-50
San Francisco World's Fair, 17, 19, 22, 31, 253, 258
San Marino, California, 123
San Miguel, Panama, 150, 151
Santiago, Cuba, 222
São Paulo, Brazil, 154
Saratoga, California, 124, 213
Sarawak, 201-02
Saturday Review of Literature, 113, 127, 247
Savoie, S.S., 53
Schaller, Adolph, 68
Schiller, Friedrich von, *quoted*, 61

Schuler, Loring, 138, 143, 150, 155, 164, 169, 171, 178, 186, 187, 188
Scotland, 129
Scott, Wallace T., 275
Sea Dragon, 22-23, 26-30, 31, 33-35, 265, 266-70, 274, 277
Seattle, Washington, 93, 125-26, 158
Seiberling, James Penfield, 42, 276
Selkirk, Alexander, 153
Seri Indians, 217, 220
Seven League Boots, 245, 247, 273
Seville, Spain, 74
Shanghai, China, 93, 203
Shattuck, Albert, 135, 155
Sheehan, Winfield, 122, 174
Shell Oil Company, 177
Ship-King, Mr. and Mrs., 66
Shiraz, Iran, 196
Siam, 88, 90-91
Siasconset, Nantucket Island, 103
Siberia, 92
Sicily, 112
Sidi-bel-Abbes, Algeria, 182-84
Simla, India, 82, 83-84
Simon, Lee, 130
Simplon Pass, 187
Simplon Tunnel, 241
Simpson, Wallis Warfield, 259
Singapore, Malaya, 91, 92, 201
Skyros, 111
Sligh, James, 32
Soldeau, Spain, 73
South China Sea, 34
Southwestern University, 276
Spain, 72-74
Spanish Civil War, 254, 259
Springer, Arthur, 275
Springfield *Republican*, 128
Srinigar, Kashmir, 84
Stalin, Joseph, 232
Stamford, Connecticut, 121
Stephens, Moye W., 174-76, 177-78, 180-87, 188-94, 198, 199-201, 202, 204
Stock market decline and crash of 1929, 165, 166
Stoneman, William, 226, 231, 232
Stowe, Leland, 156
Strachey, Lytton, 56
Strassburg, France, 67
Stratford, England, 51
Stratton-Porter, Gene, 105
Studley, Eleanor, 156

Sui An, S.S., 92
Sullivan, Noel, 166, 213, 254
Sunset magazine, 114
Surabaya, Java, 91, 92
Sverdlovsk, Russia, 227-31, 232
Swanson, Walter Gaines, 249, 250, 253, 254, 258
Sweet, Channing, 93
Sweet, Lenning, 93
Sweet, William E., 94

Taj Mahal, 81-82, 116-17
Taplee, Malaya, 86, 87
Tarkington, Booth, 105
Tate Springs, Tennessee, 40, 49
Taylor, Thorne & Company, 134
Teapot Dome scandal, 101
Teheran, Iran, 194, 196
Thibaud, Jacques, 78
Thiers, Alex, 118
Thomas, Atha, 47
Thomas, Lowell, 126, 272
Tibbett, Lawrence, 172
Tiberias, Palestine, 190
Tibet, 85
Tiburon Island, 218, 220
Tiflis, Russia, 234, 235
Timbuctoo, 18, 181-82
Time magazine, 127, 277
Titanic, S.S., 56
Titicaca, Lake, 153
Tobago, 153, 163-64
Tokyo *Advertiser*, 93
Torrey, Gordon, 22, 25, 32, 263, 265
Toulouse, France, 72
Tours, France, 72
Townsend, J. Richard, 22, 263
Trans-Pacific voyage, Halliburton's, 19, 28-30, 33-35, 253-54, 258-59, 261-65, 266-70
Trans-Siberian Railway, 227
Travel magazine, 74, 76, 84, 94
Treasure Island, San Francisco, 19
Trenton, New Jersey, 44
Trinidad, 160, 163
Tulsa, Oklahoma, 209
Tulsa *World*, 177
Turin, Italy, 238
Turkey, 109-10, 189, 235
Tutankhamen, King, 79
Tutweiler family, 81

Ulysses, 108, 112
United Artists, 209, 220
United Fruit Company, 24
Uttoxeter, England, 51

Vagabond Journey Around the World
(Franck), 57
Valencia, Spain, 74
Vale of Kashmir, 84
Van Druten, John, 118, 129
Van Dyke, Henry, 104
Vanity Fair, 117, 277
Van Overstraten, S.S., 92
Vassar College, 166
Venice, Italy, 187-88
Vera Cruz, Mexico, 141
Versailles, France, 52, 72
Victoria, Queen, 240
Vienna, Austria, 108, 236
Villers-sur-Mer, France, 186
Vladivostok, Siberia, 93
Vosges Mountains, 67

Walker, General M. L., 144-46
Ward, Dudley, 130
Washington, D. C., 54
Washington *Post*, 237
Waterbury, Connecticut, 272
Waterloo, Iowa, 133
Welch, John Wenlock, 24-25, 26, 27, 29,
30, 32, 34, 35, 264, 265, 266-67

Weller, George, 277-78
Wertzel, Saul, 122
Wescott, Glenway, 137
Wilde, Oscar, 99
Wilder, Thornton, 152, 155
Wilhelm II, Kaiser, 240
Williams, Mr., 91
Wilson, Marian, 165
Wilson, Richard T., 165
Wilson, Woodrow, 103
Wise, Stephen S., 103
World Celebrities lecture agency, 215
"World Is Still Wide, The," 214
World War I, 41, 43, 56, 73
Wren, Sir Christopher, 51
Wren, Percival Christopher, 183
Wright, Frank Lloyd, 213, 255
Wright, Sergeant Thomas, 146, 148
Wylie, Eleanor, 124

Xerxes, 196
Xpit, sailing vessel, 144

Yokahama, Japan, 203
Young, Waldemar, 123
Youngstown, Ohio, 135
Yourovsky, Commandant, 229-30

Zamboanga, Philippine Islands, 202
Zermatt, Switzerland, 67-69